IMAGINED ROMES

IMAGINED ROMES

The Ancient City and Its Stories
in Middle English Poetry

C. DAVID BENSON

THE PENNSYLVANIA STATE UNIVERSITY PRESS
UNIVERSITY PARK, PENNSYLVANIA

Library of Congress Cataloging-in-Publication Data

Names: Benson, C. David, author.
Title: Imagined Romes : the ancient city and its stories in Middle English poetry / C. David Benson.
Description: University Park, Pennsylvania : The Pennsylvania State University Press, [2019] | Includes bibliographical references and index.
Summary: "A study of ancient Rome as a prominent topic in the works of Middle English poets. Discusses how each of these poets conceives of ancient Rome and Romans, both pagan and Christian, and why it matters to their work. Includes the works of Gower, Chaucer, Langland, and Lydgate"—Provided by publisher.
Identifiers: LCCN 2018053163 | ISBN 9780271083209 (cloth : alk. paper)
Subjects: LCSH: English poetry—Middle English, 1100–1500—History and criticism. Rome (Italy)—In literature.
Classification: LCC PR317.R66 2019
LC record available at https://lccn.loc.gov/2018053163

Copyright © 2019 C. David Benson
All rights reserved
Printed in the United States of America
Published by
The Pennsylvania State University Press,
University Park, PA 16802–1003

The Pennsylvania State University Press is a member of the Association of University Presses.

It is the policy of The Pennsylvania State University Press to use acid-free paper. Publications on uncoated stock satisfy the minimum requirements of American National Standard for Information Sciences—Permanence of Paper for Printed Library Material, ANSI Z39.48–1992.

For Corynn, Hilary, and (of course)
Sophie Lee

CONTENTS

Acknowledgments | ix
Note on Spelling | xi

Introduction | 1

PART I Ancient Rome and Its Objects

1 The Relics of Rome: Christian Mercy and the *Stacions of Rome* | 13

2 The Ruins of Rome: Pagan Marvels and the *Metrical Mirabilia* | 33

PART II Narratives of Ancient Romans

3 Civic Romans in Gower's *Confessio Amantis* | 59

4 Heroic (Women) Romans in Chaucer's *Canterbury Tales* and the *Legend of Good Women* | 79

5 Virtuous Romans in *Piers Plowman* | 100

6 Tragic Romans in Lydgate's *Fall of Princes* | 121

Notes | 147
Bibliography | 178
Index | 192

ACKNOWLEDGMENTS

Inevitably, this book has taken longer to write than I imagined it would, but my compensation over the last decade has been much happy time spent in Rome and in thinking about Rome. For this enjoyment, I am deeply indebted to a host of friends and colleagues, those named below and those others, who, like so many of the martyrs of Rome, must go unnamed.

For research support, I thank Ross McKinnon, former dean of the College of Arts and Sciences at the University of Connecticut, and the University of Connecticut Research Foundation.

For walks in Rome and for talks about it, I thank Piero Boitani, Dora Faraci and Raffaele Morabito, Michael Maas, Anthony Bale, Julia Boffey, Tony Edwards, and Sarah Stanbury.

I thank the graduate students in the English Department and the Medieval Studies Program at the University of Connecticut for their ideas and interest as I was working on this book. For their hospitality and suggestions, I thank audiences that I have been lucky enough to address at Queen Mary College, London, at Cambridge University, at Glasgow University, at Harvard University, and at the University of California, Berkeley.

I am especially grateful to those friends who took the time to read drafts of my chapters over the years, sometimes all my chapters, and who helped me see where I was going wrong and tried to guide me onto a better path. I thank James Simpson for his unfailing encouragement, wit, and generosity; Ryan Perry and Spencer Strub for their learning and editorial shrewdness; Maura Nolan for her inspiration and advice; Rebecca Krug for her rigor and laughter; Christine Cooper-Rompato for being a better reader for me than I ever was for her; Beth Robertson for this, the most recent of many academic and personal kindnesses; and Jamie Fumo, Linda Georgianna, and Leah Schwebel for knowing so much and passing it on.

My greatest support in this, as in so much else, has been my learned, loving wife, Pam. Lucky the man who is married to a great editor, luckier still when her patience is as inexhaustible as her insight. We got to know Rome together and she has always believed in this book and in me when I doubted both.

It has been a pleasure to work again with Penn State University Press and I am grateful for all who have turned my manuscript into a book, especially Ellie Goodman, for her enthusiasm and advice, Laura Reed-Morrisson and Brian Beer, who shepherded the work through the process, and Suzanne Wolk, for her unfailing eye for error and awkwardness and her skill at remedying both.

I have dedicated this book to the three wonderful and wise women whom my sons have brought into my life.

NOTE ON SPELLING

Some Middle English quotations are slightly modified from the editions I have used. I use the modern forms of þ (th), 3 (gh or y), and the modern forms u/v when appropriate.

I refer to Roman churches, which are often dedicated to saints, by their Italian names except for St. Peter's. Saints themselves, however, are called by the English form of their names.

Introduction

The question this book asks may seem an odd one: how did Middle English poets imagine the city of ancient Rome? But odder still is that such a question has not really been asked before, let alone answered. Much has been written about the role of other, more legendary ancient cities in Middle English poetry, especially Troy (indeed, I once wrote such a book myself), but about Rome there is mostly silence, even though major poets such as Gower, Chaucer, and Lydgate tell a number of stories set in the city. Of course, articles and books about what Latin literature contributed to Middle English poetry are plentiful, especially those that trace the influence of Ovid on Chaucer. There are also many excellent readings of individual Roman narratives (though they do not give much attention to their Romanness), including the Trajan episode in *Piers Plowman* and the *Second Nun's Tale* of Saint Cecilia, but there is no systematic study of ancient Rome as a major theme in the works of late medieval English poets. No one has stopped to ask what it is about Rome and its stories that so attracts these poets—none of whom actually visited the city. How do these poets conceive of Rome and Romans, and why does that matter to their work? Do these poets share the same attitude about the city and its stories, or does each treat them differently? Rome and Romans have been hiding in plain sight in Middle English poetry, waiting to be recognized as an important topic for study.

The first part of *Imagined Romes* calls attention to two anonymous and little known poems, the *Stacions of Rome* and an interpolation on Rome in the *Metrical Version of Mandeville's Travels*. They are the only Middle English poems that describe the city itself and its antiquities, exemplifying a principle noted by Sarah Stanbury. She says that in the Middle Ages, Rome was always "linked imaginatively" to physical objects: "The Roman thing is a monument or a relic."[1] The *Stacions of Rome* surveys the enshrined bodies of Christian martyrs and other ancient relics in Rome's churches, along with the pardons from sin they offer, and the *Metrical* interpolation surveys the pagan city's monuments, including its palaces, temples, and statues, and names some of the ancient Romans associated with them. Both poems are based on Latin catalogues, but each, in its own way, enlivens its source to stimulate vernacular readers to envision the wonders of ancient Rome. Each creates its own fantasy city. Ignoring the realities of the actual medieval city, the *Stacions* creates a holy Rome whose ancient martyrs and popes make it a never-ending source of divine mercy for sinners, one unmatched elsewhere and perhaps as beneficial to devout readers of the poem as to actual visitors to the city. The *Metrical* interpolation derives from a Latin textual tradition that portrays pagan Rome, with its extraordinary marvels, as a worthy ancestor to the Christian city that follows it. The English poem describes an equally fabulous Rome, but its poet is more conflicted about the city: while its monuments are made even more ingenious and alluring, they present a greater danger to the triumph of Christianity precisely because of that allure.

The Middle English poems discussed in the second part of *Imagined Romes* are by four famous poets rather than two anonymous ones: John Gower, Geoffrey Chaucer, William Langland, and John Lydgate. Instead of surveying the city's material objects, they narrate Roman stories that are an integral, if unrecognized, topic in large, multiplex works. These narratives call attention to the Romanness of the people and events they describe and tell of men and women, both pagan and Christian, from the city's founding to late antiquity.[2] Through such stories, often the same stories, each poet creates his own individual portrait of the city and its culture. No other major Middle English poet deals with the idea of Rome as seriously as these four. Rome is named briefly at the very beginning of *Sir Gawain and the Green Knight* and then not again, and it is referred to only once more (perhaps) in the other three poems attributed to the author. The city exists primarily in anticipation in Gavin Douglas's translation of the *Aeneid*, and though Thomas Hoccleve does include a few Roman stories in his *Regiment of Princes*, they function as convenient examples to point a moral and reveal no more than a nominal interest in the city itself—other stories set elsewhere would do as well. The four poets I discuss stand out from their fellows because of their deep engagement with the city, yet, united as they are by an interest in Rome, they conceive of the city in radically different ways that contribute to their own distinctive thought and aesthetic. The topic of Rome provides a new perspective on each of these great poets.

Imagined Romes is not meant to be a comprehensive encyclopedia of Rome in all medieval English writing. It is a study of Middle English poetry that discusses the two Middle English poems that describe the material remains of the ancient city and the four major Middle English poets who tell its stories.³ To have included prose works as well would have diffused the focus of the book. Rome often appears in medieval chronicles, for example, but they do not treat the city in the same way. Chronicles narrate a sequence of successive events, whereas the poems I discuss include only isolated episodes from the city's history and make little attempt to distinguish between its different periods or to trace its other developments, such as the changes from monarchy to empire. Another kind of prose work, the *Gesta Romanorum*, despite its promising title and some classical names and allusions, is a collection of moralizing fables that often have nothing to do with the ancient city. Margery Kempe's long account of her visit to Rome in her *Book* is characteristically provocative, but her subject is not the ancient city but her own life, including serving an old, poor Roman woman (until she doesn't) and marrying God the Father in the Lateran, about whose history and relics she says virtually nothing. Two prose works by English clerics who actually went to Rome, Master Gregorius in the late twelfth or early thirteenth century and John Capgrave in the fifteenth, do contain information about the ancient as well as the medieval city, but, in addition to being in prose, their approach to the city is different again. Gregorius's work is more subjective than the works I discuss (animated by such emotions as his scorn of pilgrims and obsession with a naked statue of Venus), and Capgrave's work is more academic and homiletic (stuffed with a range of information and moral lessons). Interesting as they are for their contrasting responses to Rome, they belong in another book.

It is strange that the importance of the ancient city in Middle English poetry has been ignored, because the connection of England to Rome is often stressed in insular Latin and vernacular writing. Not only were city names, a highway system, two great walls, countless ruins, and even the Tower of London (begun, it was thought, by Julius Caesar) reminders of Britain's former status as a Roman province, but legendary histories told tales of other interactions between the island and the city. In his twelfth-century *Historia regum Britanniae*, Geoffrey of Monmouth invented an exciting and more equal relationship; he claimed that Britain, despite having once been subjected to Rome, also managed on more than one occasion to almost (but not quite) itself conquer the ancient city.⁴ Despite some contemporary scholars' disparagement of Geoffrey's accuracy, his work influenced England's popular sense of its past for centuries, primarily in romances, from Layamon's *Brut* to Malory's *Morte d'Arthur*, and in vernacular chronicles such as the popular Middle English prose *Brut*.⁵ Yet Rome is only a vague, if menacing, opponent in these works, for unlike the poems discussed in *Imagined Romes*, they are indifferent to the city's antiquities and its own stories.

Rome's special meaning for medieval English Christians derived from real rather than fictional exchanges with the city in late antiquity. In his influential eighth-century *Ecclesiastical History of the English People*, Bede argues that the island owed its very faith to missionaries sent from the city by Pope Gregory the Great. Indeed, as Francesca Tinti observes, the Anglo-Saxons "had a clear awareness of Rome as the source of their own Christianity, which further contributed to making it a place of special affection and devotion."⁶ Anglo-Saxon pilgrims, lay and clerical, sought the holy places of Rome, and some local kings, including Caedwalla of Wessex, even settled in the city with their retinues near St. Peter's "to spend the rest of their days near the shrine of the Apostle in prayer, fasting, almsgiving and other good works and at the end to be buried in the basilica."⁷ The area of the Vatican now known as the Borgo gets its name from *burgus Saxonum*, where a *schola Saxonum* (later *schola Anglorum*) was founded to aid visitors and survived into the twelfth century.⁸ English pilgrims and those on ecclesiastical business never stopped going to Rome, and in 1362 a new residence was established, the Hospital of Saint Thomas (now the English College), near the Campo de' Fiori, where Margery Kempe was housed, turned away, and eventually accepted back while in the city.⁹

The Rome that these medieval English visitors found was radically diminished from its former eminence as the teeming capital of an immense empire, when it earned such epithets as *caput mundi* (head of the world), *aurea* (golden), and *aeterna* (eternal).¹⁰ Although the Colosseum still existed, as did huge pilgrim churches built over the shrines of martyrs like Peter and Lawrence, the population of the city had shrunk from more than a million in classical times to no more than thirty-five thousand and perhaps as few as seventeen thousand; much of the area within the city walls had reverted to countryside, with cattle grazing in the unexcavated Forum.¹¹ Medieval Rome had also lost its reputation for Christian sanctity, for the age of the martyrs was long past. The pope and his court were absent at Avignon for much of the fourteenth century (1309–76), and the subsequent Schism (1378–1417), with rival claimants to the seat of Saint Peter, further damaged the prestige of the papacy. Even before these latest upheavals, the twelfth-century cleric and satirist Walter Map expressed a common medieval view when he wrote that ROMA is an anagram for *radix omnium malorum avaritia* (greed is the root of all evil), and the fourteenth-century English chronicler Adam Usk described the papal city he knew well as a place "where everything was for sale, and benefices were granted not according to merit but to the highest bidder."[12]

This sorry contrast between past and present Rome was a frequent theme in medieval European, especially Italian, writing. Indeed, the contemporary decline of the city may have caused memories of what had been there to become all the more golden. Poggio Bracciolini, in his fifteenth-century *De varietate fortunae*, quoted Virgil's celebration of the monuments on the Capitoline Hill in his own day when compared to the original scrub seen by Aeneas, "Golden now, once bristling with wild bushes" (*Aeneid* 8.348); Poggio, however, reverses the quotation to emphasize the city's present decay: "Golden once, now infested with thorn thickets and full of bramble-bushes."[13] With similar dismay, Adam Usk said that whereas Rome once teemed with princes and their palaces, "now it is abandoned and full of slums, thieves, wolves and vermin."[14]

Despite the brambles and vermin that overran medieval Rome, the glories of the ancient city could still be detected amid its ruins if a visitor used his imagination. Petrarch, in a letter to his friend Cardinal Colonna, recalled their walks in Rome, where "at each step there was present something which would excite our tongue and mind." Proceeding through the city, they would remind each other of ancient places and people (whether accurately identified or not)—both pagan ("this is the rock that Manlius defended and then fell from," "this was the temple of Jupiter, this was the home of all the triumphs," "here Caesar triumphed, here he perished") and Christian ("here Peter was crucified, there Paul was beheaded, here Lawrence was burned," "there Agnes after her death came back to life and forbade her kin to weep, here Sylvester hid, there Constantine got rid of his leprosy").[15] Two centuries earlier, Archbishop Hildebert of Lavardin wrote a pair of famous poems contrasting Rome's ancient magnificence with its current state. The first poem both laments the fall of the ancient city and praises its pagan glory:

> Par tibi, Roma, nihil cum sis prope tota ruina.
> Quam magni fueris integra, fracta doces.[16]
> (Nothing can equal you, Rome, although you are almost a total ruin.
> Broken into pieces, you teach how great you were when whole.)

If the surviving fragments of ancient Rome are nonpareil, the poet says, imagine what the city was like when it was intact. In a second poem, Hildebert has the Christian city reply, arguing that while it may be materially poorer than when it ruled the world, it is spiritually richer. To justify this claim, however, Hildebert looks not to the example of medieval Rome but again turns to the past, contrasting an ancient pagan champion to an ancient Christian one: "plus aquilis vexilla crucis, plus Cesare Petrus" (the standard of the cross is greater than that of the imperial eagle, and Peter greater than Caesar).[17]

Given the importance of the ancient city of Rome to the Middle Ages in general and to England in particular, and given the two detailed descriptions by anonymous English poets and the number of stories major poets set there, why have scholars not been more interested in the question I posed at the beginning of this introduction: how did Middle English poets imagine ancient Rome and Romans? Perhaps Rome is so pervasive in medieval literature that critics have not thought to isolate it as a separate topic in English poetry, though a more persuasive reason may be that even raising such a question requires that we consider the city from an unfamiliar perspective. *Imagined Romes* is not about ancient Rome and Romans as they were, or about the antiquities still present in the city today, but rather about how these long lost things and people were conceived in the living imaginations of Middle English poets.

The knowledge that these Middle English poets had about ancient Rome was, of course, doubly secondhand. They lived centuries after its decline and fall, and there is no evidence that any of them, in contrast to Usk, Hildebert, and Petrarch, ever visited the city and saw its pagan and Christian remains. What they knew of ancient Rome and Romans came from reading a limited number of medieval and classical texts, which did not always agree and whose information and stories they took and re-created in their poetry. Even today, when reading a well-illustrated, archaeologically informed book about the Colosseum or being present in the amphitheater itself, it is difficult to picture what it would have looked like when new and full of spectators and spectacles. Middle English poets, lacking our modern scholarly resources or personal experiences, were left to conjure up the irretrievably lost city and the inner lives of its inhabitants from witnesses whose reports were often fanciful, including claims that the Colosseum had been a temple of the sun, or that Constantine gave Pope Sylvester temporal power over the Roman Empire. From such material, and especially from their own imaginations, each of the poets I discuss constructed his own ancient Rome. As a creative invention, Rome in these Middle English poems is something like the American West in the movies. It exists in the realm of art rather than history: at their best, these works are more like John Ford's powerful film *The Searchers* than like S. C. Gwynne's deeply researched study of similar events in *Empire of the Summer Moon*.

Since the Middle Ages, we have come to know more about what ancient Rome looked like and what happened there, owing to increasingly sophisticated studies of sites that were once inaccessible or misidentified. Even medieval Rome, once so neglected by archaeologists and tourists, has recently become better understood thanks to the work of historians and art historians such as Richard Krautheimer, Robert Brentano, Peter Brown, Dale Kinney, and Chris Wickham, to mention a few. I have learned from their work, but my interests are different. *Imagined Romes* does not discuss what we now know (or think we know) about Rome and Romans but rather how they were represented by Middle English poets. Not only is my work not history; it is also not historicist in the sense that I do not see the poems I discuss as prompted by or making comments on specific contemporary events, though I do pay attention to late medieval English contexts when appropriate, including church practice and doctrine and literary and political history. *Imagined Romes* is a study of individual poems by individual poets, and I depend on close readings that pay attention to the stylistic elements and devices peculiar to poetry to understand how each poet makes use of the ancient city and its stories, reshaping and reimagining them for his own purposes.

Although each chapter of *Imagined Romes* looks at ancient Rome and Romans in the work of a single poet, many of these writers share some attitudes and emphases. All recognize the unique fame and past achievements of what Lydgate identifies as the "cite of cites" and Gower as "thilke cité chief of alle / Which men the noble Rome calle." The *Stacions of Rome* and the *Metrical* interpolation are dazzled by the city's countless relics or magnificent monuments; Gower, Chaucer, and Lydgate are attracted to the city's narratives and again and again turn to them; and Langland, who elsewhere in *Piers Plowman* shows no interest in antiquity, puts at the center of his poem two Romans who embody his most cherished virtues. Ancient Rome provides Middle English poets with a pattern book of human stories in its famous exemplary figures: conquerors like Julius Caesar, good rulers and churchmen like Trajan and Gregory, villains like Nero, heroic apostles like Peter and Paul, tragic wives like Lucretia, and holy women like Constance and Cecilia. Finally, each of these Middle English poets recognizes the fundamental bifurcation of ancient Rome into pagan and Christian cities. This dual heritage, the clash and continuity between these two systems of belief and their divergent views of human beings, is explored by each of these poets to varying degrees and with various results, all grappling with Rome's unparalleled heritage of pagan splendor and Christian sanctity.

Despite what they have in common, even more striking are the radically different ways in which these Middle English poets imagine ancient Rome. The *Metrical* interpolation on Rome describes the city's majestic, if sometimes disturbing, pagan marvels, while the *Stacions* says almost nothing about these secular monuments and instead celebrates the innumerable Christian shrines and other ancient relics in Rome's churches and the bountiful mercy obtainable there. Gower presents Rome as a model of good governance, while his contemporary Chaucer denounces it as a vicious oppressor of women; Langland sees it as a place beyond time where justice and mercy merge, while Lydgate finds only catastrophes there. Middle English poets are not alone in such disparate responses to this unique and irreducible city. As Catharine Edwards observes in her *Writing Rome*, just as "Rome's physical fabric has been appropriated and reappropriated over the centuries, ... so too has the idea of Rome, a city endlessly rewritten, symbol at once of eternity and of the fragility of all human achievement, of the triumph of Christianity and of the lasting authority of the pagan republic of letters."[18] The Middle English poets in *Imagined Romes* testify, as Edwards notes elsewhere, to "Rome's seemingly boundless capacity for multiple, indeed conflicting, signification."[19]

The multiple, conflicting signification of Rome for these poets can perhaps be seen most easily by briefly comparing how one of its famous tales (the brutal rape of the good wife Lucretia by the son of King Tarquin of Rome) is retold and reimagined by three of the major poets discussed in this study: Gower, Chaucer, and Lydgate. Gower's strong political interests are evident especially at the beginning and end of his story of Lucretia in the *Confessio Amantis*. He prefaces the violation of Lucretia with a long account of an equally deceitful and violent but more public attack on a nearby town by the king and his son, and he concludes it with a careful account added to his source of how the citizens of Rome came together to expose and then expel the vicious Tarquins and "taken betre governance." Even in this extreme example of misused power, as elsewhere in the *Confessio*, Gower presents ancient Rome as a model of civic governance—not because its leaders were always good, but because the wider community of Rome had the capacity to correct bad leaders and come together to repair the damage done to the city.

Chaucer was Gower's London contemporary and friendly rival, and the story he tells in the *Legend of Lucrece* shares basic facts with Gower's, but the effect is totally different. Much less political, Chaucer omits the Tarquins' other public crimes and the city's resolute response. His Tarquin is not a tyrannical exception to Rome's governance but is all too typical of Roman male leaders elsewhere in his work. Chaucer adds events and language to portray Tarquin as even worse than he appears in the sources and Lucretia as even better. She, like Chaucer's other Roman heroines, practices the virtues, such as courage and nobility, traditionally associated with the city's male heroes, but, as a Roman woman, she finds no consolation in the city except death, and as a pagan, no reward after death except a good name.

Lydgate's version of the Lucretia story in the *Fall of Princes* is more flamboyant in its presentation and more profound as tragedy than those of his Middle English predecessors Gower and Chaucer, whose work he knew well. Lydgate shows his artistic daring most obviously in telling Lucretia's story twice in successive books of the *Fall*, after saying that he will not tell it at all. Lydgate first offers a radically new approach, which says little about what happened during the rape and instead introduces a debate between Lucretia and her husband about whether she should take her own life, based on a sophisticated contemporary Latin work by the Italian humanist Coluccio Salutati. As if this were not daring enough, Lydgate deepens and further contrasts the characters of Salutati's two speakers, complicating their debate by adding a passage from Saint Augustine on Lucretia's possible sense of guilt. Lydgate's transformation of his source in this first tale of Lucretia and his different account of her state of mind in a second monologue combine to say more about Lucretia's psyche and mental anguish than either Chaucer or Gower does, and in this respect suggests, however faintly, the tragic figures to come in English drama. But even as Lydgate's Lucretia foreshadows some of the new directions that vernacular literature would take in the following century, his remarkable portrait reminds us again how much we miss by failing to appreciate the importance of Rome in Middle English poetry.

PART I

Ancient Rome and Its Objects

CHAPTER 1

The Relics of Rome
Christian Mercy and the *Stacions of Rome*

The medieval city of Rome was not a military or economic power but a religious one. Its reputation for holiness, however, derived less from the contemporary papacy, which was often absent and notorious for corruption, than from the many ancient saints buried and venerated there. John Capgrave, in his mid-fifteenth-century account of his visit to Rome, the *Solace of Pilgrimes*, gives several explanations for why the city became the seat of the church, concluding with a "grete reson": "the multitude of martires whech spilt her blood in confirmacioun of our feith in that same place."[1] Although some Middle English writers, including William Langland, questioned the wisdom of pilgrimage to the shrines of the saints of Rome and warned against relying on the indulgences offered there, the late Middle English poem the *Stacions of Rome*, the subject of this chapter, has no doubt whatsoever about the spiritual benefits of the city.[2] It proclaims that the abundance of Rome's sacred objects makes it an overflowing fountain of grace for sinners.

The *Stacions of Rome* was relatively popular in its own time, but it has received scant attention from modern scholars—and even less respect. Its first editor, Frederick J. Furnivall, calls it "simply (to me) a puff of the merits of the Papal City as a place for getting pardons and indulgences," and others have found little more to say on its behalf.[3] Eamon Duffy, usually so sympathetic to late medieval devotional practices, dismisses works like the *Stacions* as "essentially trainspotter's guides to the best and most powerful relics and indulgences."[4] The *Stacions of Rome* is certainly not a sophisticated work of literature or theology, but there are good reasons for its contemporary popularity, including its wealth of information about Christian Rome, the energy of its narration, and the ardor of its promises of divine mercy. Although fifteenth-century Rome could have used a "puff" after the long absence of the pope and his court at Avignon during most of the previous century and the subsequent papal civil war known as the Great Schism, the *Stacions* says almost nothing about the travails or activities of the contemporary church. Instead, it gives a detailed record, found nowhere else in Middle English verse, of Christian Rome's heritage of relics in churches and the pardons they offer from the punishment of sin. Although much of the substance of the *Stacions* derives from a Latin prose work, the *Indulgentiae ecclesiarum urbis Romae*, its style is distinctive. Employing four-stress rhymed couplets, like those in some native romances and other religious works, the *Stacions* translates austere and unemotional Latin prose into animated English verse that encourages its readers to imagine themselves to be present at the sacred places of Rome.

The contemporary popularity of the *Stacions* is shown by its survival in nine manuscripts that date from the late fourteenth to the late fifteenth century.[5] These manuscripts were produced in different locales and differ in form and content. Of the six extant long versions of the *Stacions*, two (Newberry and Bicester) were written on vellum rolls, two others (Cotton and Lambeth) appear in paper miscellanies along with secular as well as religious works, and a final pair (Vernon and Simeon) are part of massive vellum collections of Middle English religious writing apparently produced in the same workshop.[6] Several of these manuscripts have been linked with monasteries, while Cotton has been called a "household book," a collection usually associated with lay readers.[7] The extant versions of the English *Stacions* may well originate from a single act of translation, and they will be treated here as one work, given that they are generally similar in information, phrasing, and even rhyme, though each differs in its specific readings and length (Vernon and Simeon, for example, have original introductory material and Cotton is missing its conclusion).[8] There are modern editions of four versions of the *Stacions*: Vernon, Cotton, Lambeth, and Bicester.[9] I generally discuss the Vernon version because of the importance and early date of its manuscript, but, as the *Stacions* was not a fixed text, I note variant passages from other versions when relevant.

The *Stacions of Rome* is a survey of Rome's churches, relics, and pardons that argues for the city's importance as a source of divine mercy. This is made explicit in the "prologue" to the Vernon version, lines that are also found in

Simeon but not in the three other edited versions of the *Stacions*. This opening section identifies sin as the fundamental human problem and Rome as its solution. After a prayer imploring the Trinity to "seende us grace" in order that we may "hevene winne" (Vernon Prologue, 1–8), the first-person narrator addresses the reader who feels thwarted in his quest for salvation because "his soule [is] in synne bounde," informing the sinner where he "may medicyn fynde" to escape the horrors of the "fuir of helle" (Vernon Prologue, 9–16). He must "to grete Rome gon," for in that city is "the medicyn, crop and rote, / That men clepeth pardoun" (Vernon Prologue, 17–19). In a further image, suggesting baptism rather than healing, the narrative voice celebrates Rome as a "welle of grace" (Vernon Prologue, 21), declaring that "alle that visyteth that place" in "love and charite," while keeping themselves "clene," will achieve the bliss of heaven: "Withouten peyne lasse or more, / His soule to dwellen evere thore" (Vernon Prologue, 22–28). Unlike more famous late medieval English vernacular religious texts, such as the visions of Julian of Norwich, *Piers Plowman*, or Chaucer's *Parson's Tale*, the *Stacions of Rome* offers no theological argument to support such all-embracing forgiveness from God, nor does it indicate that any personal reformation or penance is needed to obtain it. All that is required is to be at Rome. As we shall see, even this may not be literally necessary, for the *Stacions* also suggests that the same rewards are possible to those who read its text and make a mental journey to the city. The *Stacions* announces that at the holy places of Rome, neither the quality nor the quantity of divine mercy is strained but instead is freely available to all who seek it.

Roman Relics

The ancient Roman objects at the center of the *Stacions of Rome* are the bodies of saints and other holy relics. As Peter Brown in particular has shown, the Christian cult of the saints was something new in religious history. Jews and pagans had long honored the burial places of those thought to be divinely favored, such as the patriarchs or Caesar Augustus, though it was presumed that their souls, as opposed to their bodies, were elsewhere. Christianity's radical innovation was that in addition to dwelling with God, "the saint in Heaven was believed to be 'present' at his tomb on earth."[10] As Patrick Geary puts it, most Christians, lay and clerical, thought that "relics *were* the saints, continuing to live among men" with all their supernatural power intact.[11] Early Christians of all classes and levels of education, according to Brown, sensed that this had "broken most of the imaginative boundaries which ancient men had placed between heaven and earth, the divine and the human, the living and the dead."[12] The holy saints in their shrines were regarded as a direct conduit between God and sinners, as made explicit in an early inscription at the tomb of Saint Martin of Tours: "Here lies interred bishop Martin of holy memory; his soul is in the hand of God but he is wholly present here, manifest in gracious miracles of every kind."[13] G. J. C. Snoek writes that whenever a supplicant "kissed the tomb and knelt before it, this expression of reverence signified ipso facto a visit to the saint in question, present in his relics. The visit was made so that the visitor could request the saint's intercession with God or ask the saint himself directly for a favour."[14]

It was the sheer multitude of Rome's martyrs, according to Capgrave in the *Solace of Pilgrimes*, that made the city especially holy and the West's prime pilgrimage destination. Shrines of saints were located elsewhere in Europe and beyond, of course, but Rome was exceptional because of the fame and number of those said to have died there for the new faith. The two most illustrious of these martyrs were Saint Peter, the chief of the apostles and believed to be the first bishop (and thus first pope) of Rome, and Saint Paul, the apostle to the Gentiles. The city boasted many other martyrs dating from the heroic first age of the church, such as the deacon Lawrence, the soldier Sebastian, the virgin Agnes, and thousands of others whose names went unrecorded.[15] Romulus and Remus are identified early in the *Stacions* as those by "whom Rome furst bigon" (10), but it is the second alliterative pair who won the city for Christianity: "Hethene hit was and cristned nought / Til Petur and Poul hit hedde i-bought" (11–12). The verb here is significant, for *bought* is the usual Middle English word to describe Christ's redemption of mankind by his bodily sacrifice on the cross, and it is used here to show that his chief apostles imitated their Lord by winning the city for the faith "with heore flesch and with heore blode" (14).

In accordance with pagan Roman burial customs, Peter and Paul and other Christian martyrs were interred in cemeteries outside the city walls.[16] Some of these extramural sites may have been venerated by the devout as early as the second century, when Christianity was still officially banned and subject to persecution.[17] After the emperor Constantine legalized Christianity in 313, he honored the bodies of Rome's most prominent martyrs by building large churches over their tombs to safeguard their remains and make them more accessible to pilgrims. The magnificent Constantinian Basilica of St. Peter, some of whose original foundations can still be seen despite its rebuilding in the Renaissance, was erected over the grave in a cemetery on the

Vatican Hill that had long been thought to house the apostle. The emperor built another great basilica over the supposed grave of Saint Paul, as well as two others over the tombs of native martyrs, Lawrence and Agnes, which also became major pilgrimage sites.

The bodies of Rome's most famous saints by no means exhaust the city's relics. In subsequent centuries, the remains of thousands of other bodies believed to be those of Roman martyrs (some, such as Cecilia, named, but most anonymous) were taken from their original burial places in the catacombs and enshrined, individually or collectively, in other churches throughout the city.[18] Rome also housed the supposed remains of saints who had died elsewhere. The body of the first martyr, Saint Stephen, was sent from the Holy Land to Constantinople and then to Rome, where it was placed in a tomb with Saint Lawrence within S. Lorenzo Fuori le Mura.[19] The bodies of the apostles James and Philip are also said by the *Stacions* to "lith in schrine" in the appropriately named SS. Apostoli (599), and the church of S. Bartolomeo on Tiber Island was the resting place of "that holi marter" (691). Saints from later periods were also venerated in Rome, including Saint Jerome, whose body was brought from "the cite of Damas [Damascus]" and put in a special chapel in S. Maria Maggiore (481–82), which also claimed to possess an arm of Thomas à Becket.

In addition to the bodies of martyrs and other saints, the *Stacions* also records Rome's vast collection of relics from the Holy Land.[20] The bodies of Christ and Mary were, of course, unavailable, both having been assumed into heaven, but the Lateran, according to the *Stacions*, possessed the blood and water that flowed from the Savior's side at the Crucifixion (335–36), as well as the Virgin's nursing milk (Cotton, 424).[21] What are called secondary, or contact, relics, that is, noncorporeal objects that had been in contact with living holy persons, especially Christ, or with their tombs, were also abundant in Rome.[22] The *Stacions* notes that St. Peter's possessed a famous cloth known as the Veronica on which Jesus, on the way to his death, imprinted an image of his face (59), which became the symbol of Rome on pilgrimage badges. Three of Rome's most important churches attracted pilgrims primarily because of their secondary relics. S. Maria Maggiore displayed the crib of the baby Jesus (the *presepe*), his swaddling clothes, and even the hay on which he lay (484–96), whereas S. Croce, as its name indicates, displayed pieces of the true cross, along with other instruments of the Passion (381–97). As befitted the pope's own church, the Lateran claimed to house the city's most extensive collection of secondary relics, including, in addition to those already named, leftovers from the loaves and fishes with which the disciples fed the five thousand (326–27), the table used at the Last Supper (305–7), and even a large assortment of Jewish relics taken by the Romans when they conquered Jerusalem in A.D. 70, such as the two tablets of the law given to Moses and the rod of Aaron (317–24).[23]

The Pardons of Rome

The relics of Rome, like the churches in which they are enshrined, are material objects possessing special spiritual power. Their great practical benefit for pilgrims, according to the *Stacions of Rome*, is generous indulgences, or pardons, from the punishment of sin. The pardons in the *Stacions*, unlike those offered by Chaucer's Pardoner, are not written documents (nor are they purchased), but are instead a kind of virtual (or, more accurately, divine) currency, tangible manifestations of God's mercy. The general availability of indulgences at Roman shrines is a development of the late Middle Ages. Early medieval accounts of the holy sites of Rome list churches and their relics but make no mention of pardons.[24] But indulgences are a central feature of the Latin source of the *Stacions of Rome*, the family of texts appropriately known as *Indulgentiae ecclesiarum urbis Romae*, which originated in the fourteenth century and quickly spread throughout Europe and England.[25] In addition to the traditional inventories of Roman churches and relics, the *Indulgentiae* tradition also records the exact amount of pardon available at each site.[26] These texts describe major basilicas at length but treat other churches more briefly, sometimes offering nothing more than the church's name and the pardons it offers, as in these three consecutive entries from a fourteenth-century Stuttgart manuscript: "Item in Sancto Alexio, ubi iacet corpus suum, sunt II M annorum. Item ad Sanctum Salvatorem de thermis sunt M anni et C anni et XL dies. Item in capella, que dicitur ad Tres Fontes, ubi fuit decapitatus sanctus Paulus apostolus, sunt M anni et tot XL" (Also in S. Alessio, where his body lies, there are 2,000 years. Also at S. Salvatore de Thermis there are 1,100 years and 40 days. Also in the chapel, which is called at Tre Fontane, where Saint Paul the Apostle was beheaded, there are 1,000 years and the same number of Lents).[27]

The abundant indulgences of Rome made its holy sites effective remedies for the burden of sin.[28] Church doctrine made a distinction between the guilt (*culpa*) of sin, which was forgiven by contrition and confession, and the penalty (*pena*) required by divine justice, which had to be satisfied by prayer, charity, or other penitential works.[29] It was assumed that most humans died without having made full restitution for their misdeeds and thus, before they were able to enter heaven, they had to pay their debt by penance in purgatory, which might be long and painful.[30] Indulgences, which could be granted only by the pope or other bishops, promised to significantly reduce or eliminate the time before the deceased was admitted to heaven. As early as the eleventh century, special dispensations from the debt of sin were promised to crusaders, and such pardons were gradually extended to those undertaking other arduous religious journeys, such as pilgrimages to the Holy Land, the shrine of Saint James at Compostela, or Rome.[31] Indulgences were subject to abuse as they became widespread during the late Middle Ages, as we see with Chaucer's Pardoner, but scholars have recently argued that the system as a whole was less corruptly intended and more spiritually effective than commonly assumed.[32] For example, R. N. Swanson concludes that even though indulgences were often monetized, even "the most inflationary spurious indulgences sought to stimulate devotional acts rather than charitable donations."[33] These scholars suggest that the driving force behind the expansion of indulgences in the late Middle Ages may not have been clerical greed so much as the hunger of the laity for such absolution.[34] The actual workings of the system of indulgences remain somewhat hazy in the texts that list them, however. Nothing is said about how sinners could calculate the precise amount of pardon needed to pay off their personal debts to God, for example, nor do the texts describe what system of bookkeeping kept track of it all.[35] Nevertheless, as IOUs redeemable after death, pardons were a form of wealth you could indeed take with you.

    The church based its right to grant indulgence on possession of a vast "Treasury of Merits" heaped up by the extraordinary virtues of Christ, the Virgin, and the saints, whose superabundance of spiritual capital (more than needed for their own salvation), could be drawn on to settle the debts of ordinary sinners in this life or the next.[36] The devout sufferings in Rome of so many and such famous martyrs meant that the city had contributed handsomely to this treasury, and so it was only appropriate that Rome should possess multiple locations where these sums could be withdrawn. Rome's pardons were ultimately the result of God's mercy and proclaimed by popes, but their dependence on the merits and intercession of the saints through their relics at particular sites is emphasized in the *Stacions of Rome*. An angel tells Pope Gregory the Great while he is celebrating Mass at S. Sebastiano that "bi Godes grace / Ther is of mony sunnes remissioun" at that place because of the "holy bones / That there weore buried" (149–64); likewise, a written notice at S. Pudenziana is said to declare that "thorw preyere of hem that ther be"—that is, the thousands of saints buried there—"this pardoun is graunted to the" (545–46).

The lavishness of the pardons of Rome benefited from the fact that the city was the seat of the church. All bishops had the authority to grant limited pardons, but the pope could offer much more, including plenary indulgences—the remission of all one's sins.[37] As Swanson puts it, the Roman pontiff was "the most important actor in the whole indulgence business."[38] The *Stacions of Rome* often draws attention to this papal role, attributing pardons at particular churches to the action of specific popes. It is revealing that most of the popes who can be securely identified in the poem are from late antiquity, such as Pope Sylvester, who is supposed to have converted Constantine, and Pope Gregory the Great.[39] Of course, the attribution of indulgences to long-ago popes is not historically accurate, as the widespread practice only developed much later, but it allows the *Stacions* to invoke the authority of heroic churchmen from the distant past instead of that of compromised, contemporary popes. In fact, the ecclesiastical institutions of medieval Rome are almost entirely ignored in the *Stacions*. Although the pardons of Rome were nominally proclaimed by a pope and obtained at individual churches, they are described in the *Stacions* as if they sprang from the desire of pilgrims themselves without clerical supervision, as in this brief entry: "At Seint Marie Rochel yif *thou wolt* crave / Two thousand yer [of pardon] ther may *thou have*" (697–98, emphasis added). Like manna in the desert, the pardons of Rome required neither purchase nor effort—they were there for the taking.

Animating Rome in the *Stacions of Rome*

Most of the information about Roman churches, relics, and pardons in the *Stacions of Rome* derives from the *Indulgentiae* tradition, but the energetic style of the English work is all its own. A conspicuous example is the easy intimacy with which the poet addresses his vernacular readers. The impersonal voice of the Latin prose work is replaced by a lively narrator similar to those in the native English romances that Chaucer burlesques in his tale *Sir Thopas* in the *Canterbury Tales*. *Thopas* begins, "Listeth, lordes, in good entent, / And I wol telle verrayment"; a similarly insistent, if more didactic, voice, is heard from the first lines of the Cotton *Stacions*: "He that wyll hys sowle leche, / Lysteneth to me, and I woll you teche" (Cotton, 1–2).[40] Vernon includes identical lines at this point, and its earlier "prologue" begins with equal enthusiasm: "Hose wot his soule in synne bounde, / I wol him techen in a stounde" (Vernon Prologue, 9–10). The first-person voice speaks to its audience throughout the *Stacions*, often in the familiar second-person singular: for example, "thi soule" (3), "thou schalt have" (23, cf. 91), "I telle the" (171, 314), "whon thou comest ther" (571), and "thi sinnes remission" (722). Addressing his readers as individuals, the poet assures them of the importance for each of what he has to say.

The *Stacions* also endeavors to involve its audience emotionally with Rome's objects, stories, and promises of mercy. As with contemporary works that are more consistent in their affective piety, such as Nicholas Love's *Mirror of the Blessed Life of Jesus Christ* or the *Book of Margery Kempe*, the *Stacions* contains passages designed to make readers identify with Christ's humanity and thus better understand the meaning of his sacrifice. Two significant relics at S. Croce, for example, the sponge offered to Christ on the cross and a nail with which he was crucified, are merely inventoried in the Latin *Indulgentiae*: "Item spongia qua Iudei porrexerunt Christo fel et acetum in cruce. . . . Item unus clavus cum quo fuit Christus affixus in cruce" (And also the sponge with gall and vinegar which the Jews extended to Christ on the cross. . . . And also the nail with which Christ was nailed to the cross).[41] The *Stacions* records the same items, though now they serve to re-create the terrible moment when they were first used:

> And a sponge of galle and eysel,
> Of that venym is ther gret del
> That Jewes profred him to drinke tho
> Whon he seide, "Ciscio."
> And a nayl whon Crist Ihesu was
> Don on Rode tre for ure trespas. (381–86)

The lines are not great poetry, but they vividly locate the relic of the sponge in the original drama of the cross by adding a single word from the Vulgate: "Ciscio," or "I thirst" (John 19:28). This brief cry reveals the human agony behind the object and helps the reader feel Christ's pain. Two short phrases that occur at the end of the second and last lines of this passage might be dismissed as simply empty fillers to complete the rhyme, but each further contributes to the emotion and religious significance of the scene. The first, "gret del," emphasizes the cruelty of Jesus's death by noting the amount of venom on the sponge with which he is taunted, and the second, "ure trespas," reminds the audience of their collective responsibility for this death and the gratitude they owe. In such brief narrative moments, the poem animates its catalogue of Roman relics by inviting readers to take part imaginatively in the original biblical event, while contemplating both the wickedness of human sin and our hope for its divine remission.

One of the most powerful of these brief affective scenes in the *Stacions* is the retelling of the creation of the relic of Christ's marble footprint in the chapel known as Domine Quo Vadis (211–12). The *Stacions* recounts that Saint Peter was fleeing Rome to avoid certain execution when he encountered Christ just outside the city's walls:

> And [Peter] seide, "Lord, whoder woltou?"
> Crist onswerde to Peter tho
> "Into Rome," he seide, "I go.
> Eft to dye on Rode for the,
> Thou dredest to dye, Peter, for me."
> "Lord," he seide, "Merci I crie.
> To take my deth I am redie." (204–10)

Some, but not all, versions of the Latin *Indulgentiae* give the opening exchange between master and disciple, but none that I have seen includes the crucial three lines that conclude the episode in the English poem.[42]

The effect of this expanded episode in the *Stacions* is to prompt the reader to relive an especially powerful Roman moment in Christian legend. The Savior expresses his unquenchable love for Peter (I will do for you again what you will not do for me once), as his all-too-human disciple is scurrying out of Rome to save his skin. For most medieval readers, it must have been easier to identify with Peter, in his weakness and disloyalty, than with the transcendent Christ, and in so doing come to recognize a central theme of the *Stacions*: the pervasiveness of human sin. How hard it is for an ordinary Christian to avoid sinning if even Peter, the chief of the apostles, betrays his heavenly Lord at Rome, as he has previously betrayed him after the arrest in the garden of Gethsemane. But if the brief scene asks readers to see Peter as a fallible fellow being, it also encourages them to share his hope of pardon and mercy. Christ does not abandon Peter, whom he calls by name, and his response to the disciple's cowardice is not punishment but the promise of more self-sacrifice. Suitably chastened, Peter is able to overcome his natural fear of death to become a hero for the faith. Reaffirming Christ as his Lord, in the passage's final lines, he passionately craves his mercy. With confidence in divine forgiveness, the apostle turns back to Rome and to the martyrdom that awaits him near the Vatican Hill.

Once again, the *Stacions of Rome* insists that the fundamental human problem is sin and that the remedy for it is to be found at Rome. The relic of Christ's footprint preserved in the church of Domine Quo Vadis affirms that even when we find ourselves most enveloped in shameful guilt, as Peter was, Christ will be there to aid us. Moreover, because Peter found the faith to return to certain death, his tomb and the church subsequently built over it became one of Christianity's holiest sites and one of the many Roman shrines to which pilgrims came to ask for God's mercy, as Peter did, in the expectation that they, too, would receive divine pardon and their souls be made fit for heaven.

The *Stacions* as Imagined Pilgrimage to Rome

When the *Stacions of Rome* goes beyond the *Indulgentiae* to engage readers emotionally with stories of individual relics, we might assume that its poet is drawing on his personal experiences in the city to prepare pilgrims for their own visits. It is more likely, however, that such passages are meant to be a textual substitute for Rome rather than a guide to it. For one thing, there is no reason to believe that any of the writers or readers of the *Stacions* (as opposed to those of the original *Indulgentiae*) ever made a pilgrimage to Rome.[43] Many manuscripts of the poem were clearly not designed to be taken on such journeys. While it is true that the Bicester and Newberry *Stacions* are written on portable rolls, it would have been exhausting to haul the enormous codices of Vernon and Simeon from England to Italy and back (they are hard enough to move across a room), just as it would have been awkward to locate an item in them when in a Roman church.[44] A few critics, among them Sarah Stanbury, have tentatively wondered whether the poem's "invitation to pilgrimage *may be* more virtual than literal" (emphasis added).[45] There is much in the *Stacions* to support such a possibility, as has been argued for that late medieval pan-European best seller *Mandeville's Travels*. Whoever originally compiled the *Travels*, he seems to have done more roaming in a well-stocked library than over land or sea, and though some, including Columbus, took the *Travels* with them on real voyages, most of Mandeville's readers in England and elsewhere were undoubtedly armchair explorers, experiencing exotic places and cultures only on the page and in their imaginations. In the late Middle Ages, a limited number of English men and women, primarily clerics on church business, were able and willing to undertake the arduous journey to Rome, but any number could do so in their mind's eye.[46]

Although the *Stacions of Rome* never explicitly presents itself as the script of an imagined pilgrimage, other such medieval texts did so. Citing Dutch manuscripts and printed books primarily from before the Reformation, Kathryn M. Rudy's *Virtual Pilgrimages in the Convent* demonstrates how nuns who were prevented from traveling to Rome and, especially, Jerusalem could, by undertaking specific devotions, make spiritual pilgrimages that satisfied their desire to draw closer to Christ and the saints and to obtain indulgences. Such virtual pilgrimages were also practiced outside the cloister by laypeople. Rudy discusses a lavishly illustrated manuscript owned by Margaret of York (1446–1503) that contains instructions on how to make such an imaginary pilgrimage to Rome, paying special attention to the city's seven principal churches.[47] In England, as elsewhere, the indulgences offered at Rome during a jubilee year could also be obtained from the papacy without the need to travel to the city, usually by paying a fee and undertaking certain religious acts.[48] Jonathan Sumption and others discuss such pardons granted both to royalty, such as Edward III, and to more humble citizens, such as the mayor of Berwick-upon-Tweed.[49]

The *Stacions of Rome* does not claim that it is clerically authorized or a substitute for a literal pilgrimage. Yet Rome is so described in the poem that individual readers are encouraged, should they choose, to imagine themselves at various holy sites in the city as they read the poem. The most obvious way in which the *Stacions* mimics in textual form an actual pilgrimage is in its organization. Most, though not all, versions of the Latin *Indulgentiae* known to me list the churches of Rome by their importance: typically, they first describe the city's seven principal churches and then lesser churches, sometimes sorted by category, such as all the churches dedicated to the Virgin Mary.[50] In contrast to this rational, hierarchal organization, the English *Stacions* presents its churches geographically, in the order that a pilgrim might encounter them while walking from one to the next. After beginning with the Basilica of St. Peter, the poem next mentions S. Paolo, also outside the old walls on the west side of the city (17–92). These basilicas are among the seven principal churches, but they are immediately followed in the *Stacions* by three lesser ones near St. Peter's (93–146), before it goes on to describe another principal church in the same general area, S. Sebastiano. The *Stacions* does not reach the Lateran, one of the two most important churches in Rome (along with St. Peter's but across the city from it and described first in some *Indulgentiae*), until almost a third of the way through the poem. The sense that the reader is taking an actual route through the city is reinforced by listing the distances between a few churches at the beginning of the poem: we are told that it is "foure myle" between St. Peter's and S. Paolo (72), for example, and "two myle" between S. Paolo and S. Anastasio (95). This information is roughly accurate, though not precise enough to guide an actual traveler (two or four miles in which direction?), and is soon abandoned, but it does contribute to the sense of moving through a real landscape, as do a few other details, such as the notation in one version that the church of S. Matteo is on "the right hande as thou shalt goone / To the chyrche of Seynt John" (Lambeth, 574–75). Whereas the impersonal *Indulgentiae* texts never address their audience directly, the *Stacions* is often quite solicitous about our journeying. One moment it tries to hurry us along—"Here mai we no lengore be / Into the popes halle moste we" (341–42)—while elsewhere it imagines the need for a break: "In the churche of Viti and Modesti, / Ther mowe ye sitte and resti" (465–66).

Despite these gestures of human sympathy, the *Stacions*, like the *Indulgentiae*, lacks the practical travel advice often found in genuine medieval pilgrimage guides: it does not describe the best routes to the city, explain how to deal with different currencies and languages, or advise where to stay and eat. An imaginary pilgrim would have no need for such details. Instead, the *Stacions* encourages its readers to visualize the holy objects it lists and to respond to them with the affective piety they inspire. In addition to recording the information that S. Croce contains the wooden *titulus* of the cross reading "Jesus of Nazareth, King of the Jews," the poem also asks us to imagine standing in the presence of the actual relic:

> And a titil of Sire Pilat
> Thei may hit rede that beo therat:
> This is Ihesu of Nazareth,
> Kyng of Iewes that tholede deth. (391–94)[51]

Likewise, whereas some versions of the *Indulgentiae* briefly explain how the chains of Saint Peter got to the church of S. Pietro in Vincoli, the *Stacions* enthuses about the act of viewing them:

> The cheynes there man may se,
> Sikerliche I telle the,

> Ther Peter was bounden sikerly,
> While he was in eorthe us by. (583–86)[52]

Such passages read less like tips on what not to miss when visiting the city than like vivid verbal re-creations of what the reader is never likely to see in person.

Other passages in the *Stacions* describe the physical sensation of being at specific sacred sites in Rome. In its account of the catacombs of Callisto at S. Sebastiano, the version of the *Indulgentiae* in Cotton Titus A.xix (which, as previously noted, has many similarities with the *Stacions*) mentions that anyone visiting this underground cemetery, where innumerable martyrs were thought to have been buried, needs to bring a light with him (*oportet deferre lumine secum*).[53] In the English poem, this bare statement becomes a dramatic scene addressed to the reader as active participant:

> But thou most take candel liht,
> Elles thou gost merk as niht,
> For under the eorthe most thou wende,
> Thow maight not seo bifore ne bihynde. (193–96)

The impersonal advice in the Latin is made both intimate (the second-person singular pronoun is used four times in four lines) and urgent ("most" and "maight"), while the eerie experience of the catacombs is evoked by the rhyme of "candel liht" and "merk as niht." The claustrophobia of being underground is stressed in the third line, and the experience of helpless blindness in the last line. The passage reads to me less like a warning than like a verbal substitute for the real thing.

The *Stacions* also stimulates the reader's imagination by appealing to senses other than sight. The fact that Saint Stephen and Saint Lawrence were buried in a single tomb at the latter's church is regularly recorded in the *Indulgentiae*, but several versions of the *Stacions* also encourage readers to imagine the very feel and smell of their tomb:

> An hole on this awter thou may fynde;
> Knele down ther with good mynde,
> Putte yn thy heed or thy honde,
> And thou shalt fele a swete gronde,
> A swete smelle of bodyes that ther be,
> Here sowles be with God in Trinite. (Cotton, 526–31)[54]

While this is hardly great poetry, it does strive to provide readers with the sense of truly being present at the shrine.

The Vision of Christian Rome in the *Stacions*

The Rome that the *Stacions* invites its readers to imagine is ahistorical, incomplete, and somewhat dreamlike. The poem ignores much of the city's pagan past and purifies its Christian present. There is no mention of Rome's political evolution from monarchy to republic to empire, for example, and the only non-Christian who receives more than a passing mention is the emperor Constantine, who soon converts. The classical remains of Rome, including its monumental statues and dominant structures, like the Colosseum, barely appear, and the Pantheon is included only because it was rededicated as a church. This carefully selective presentation of the city in the *Stacions* results in a more positive image of Christian Rome. Revered early popes like Sylvester and Gregory are named frequently, but the contemporary papacy and its reviled administrative arm, the Curia, are absent. The poem also has little to say about other aspects of medieval Rome: nothing about the contemporary city's shops and markets, housing, politics, sports, or even the elaborate papal processions that regularly wound their way through the city on feast days. Rome in the *Stacions* often seems uncannily empty. Other pilgrims are rarely glimpsed and ordinary Roman citizens not at all.[55]

The Rome of the *Stacions* is an idealized Christian city of heroic martyrs and noble popes from the distant past now represented by the sacred objects that the poem surveys: churches, relics, and pardons. Together, they justify the title "grete Rome," as the Vernon "prologue" and Cotton call the city (Vernon Prologue, 17; Cotton, 3), and all three kinds of objects are present in abundance. As for Rome's churches, only one version, Cotton, gives an exact number: 147 "kyrkes" and an astonishing 10,005 "chapelles" (Cotton, 17–20). Cotton does not name them all, but it and the other versions of the *Stacions* list so many major and minor churches that it is impossible to keep them straight, especially in the last part of the poem, where references to them become briefer, at times taking up no more than a couplet, or even a single line, with the emphasis less on the church itself than on its pardons:

> At Seint Marie Rochel yif thou wolt crave
> Two thousand yer ther may thou have.
> At Seint Petres prisoun

> Two thousand yer of pardoun.
> And an hundred yer at Seint Adrian.
> And as monye at Cosma and Damian.
> A thousand yer at Seint Marie the New verrement,
> And two thousand yer at Seint Clement. (697–704)

Despite the number of Roman churches in the *Stacions*, the relics they contain and the pardons they offer are even more bountiful. In discussing John Capgrave's *Solace of Pilgrimes* (1450), Sarah Stanbury notes Rome's "storehouses of important relics, unmatched for quantity and importance in any other single location."[56] The *Stacions* says that S. Prassede contained "a thousand bodies withouten mo / And threo hundred yit therto" (553–54) and elsewhere reports that Pope Simplicius amassed and placed in a single church "vij thousende holy bones" (415–19). The Vernon *Stacions* records no fewer than forty thousand martyrs entombed in the relatively small church of S. Pudenziana (542), though Lambeth puts the number at a more modest, though still impressive, three thousand (Lambeth, 666). That the lower figure is also found in versions of the Latin *Indulgentiae* suggests how easily figures could became corrupted in manuscripts, while suggesting that even an enormous body count did not surprise the copyist of Vernon.[57] The saints of Rome must have seemed beyond calculation.

Rome's pardons were similarly abundant. The *Stacions* quotes Pope Boniface's declaration that if men only knew the extent of "the pardoun that is at grete Rome," they would feel no need to go "over the see" to more distant pilgrimage destinations, such as Jerusalem or St. Catherine's shrine on Mount Sinai (285–93). The poem frequently treats Roman pardons as if they were limitless.[58] Denominations are sometimes quite precise (one church is said to grant 4,384 years [720–24]), but more often they come in multiples of a thousand. At the high altar of Saint Peter, the poem says the usual pardon is twenty-eight years, but from Holy Thursday to Lammas it shoots up to fourteen thousand (47–54). The difficulty of one's journey could also increase the total: when the Veronica (the cloth with the imprint of Christ's face) was displayed at St. Peter's, Roman residents were given three thousand years of pardon (four thousand in Cotton, 83), nonresidents nine thousand, and those who had made a sea voyage to the city twelve thousand years, plus the forgiveness of a third of their sins—amounts that were doubled during Lent (59–70).[59] And, of course, pilgrims could collect pardons at more than one church while in Rome. In the increasingly mercantile world of late medieval England, and in the face of those who accused Rome of greed and corruption, the *Stacions* asserted that the city operated another, benign economy of openhanded mercy.[60]

Some Roman indulgences, according to the *Stacions*, went beyond fixed sums to cancel the debt of *all* of one's sins. Such a plenary (full) indulgence was said to be available only on certain days at some sites: at S. Pietro in Vincoli on its feast day (578), and at S. Maria Rotundo (the Pantheon) on two feasts (616–18). But at a chapel in S. Sebastiano (186–87), at the Sancta Sanctorum in the Lateran complex (366), and at S. Pudenziana (537), complete absolution seems always to have been on offer.[61] Nor was death any bar to such generosity, according to the *Stacions*, despite theological debate about the validity of postmortem remission of sin.[62] The poem asserts unequivocally that attendance at the church of S. Lorenzo every Wednesday for a year would enable one to rescue another person from purgatorial suffering: "A soule to drawe from purgatori fer" (412). Such release was even more immediate at SS. Apostoli: each day, "whon thou comest thare," in addition to a pardon of two thousand years for yourself, "thou maight delivere a soule from care" (603–6).[63] Some versions of the *Stacions* appear to go beyond church doctrine on the subject. A passage in Cotton suggests that having a Mass celebrated at S. Maria Scala Coeli could save a soul already damned:

> Whoso syngeth masse yn that chappell
> For any frend, he loseth hym fro hell,
> He may hym brynge thorow purgatory y-wys
> Into the blys of paradys. (Cotton, 171–74)[64]

The Lambeth version also suggests a foolproof way to avoid one's own damnation. Any believer ("what man or woman") who is buried at the church of S. Andrea will be saved regardless of what sins he or she has committed: "Yf he beleve in God & Holy Chyrche also, / He shall not be dampned *for nought that he hathe doo*" (emphasis added). To anyone skeptical about the validity of such a license to sin, the poem insists, with touching faith in the written word (though not canon law), that this is "the sothe that I the tell" because "on the chyrche dore thou mayst hit see" (Lambeth, 896–905).

Rome as a Conduit of Divine Grace

The mercy available from the churches, relics, and pardons listed in the *Stacions* truly made Rome a "welle of grace / To alle that visyteth that place"

(Vernon Prologue, 21–22). So plentiful were Roman pardons that they surpass even the great number recorded over the course of the poem:

> In Rome is muche pardoun more
> Then I have told here bifore
> Or telle schulde with al my miht,
> Thouh I weore her bothe day and niht. (727–30)⁶⁵

A well of grace for all, the city is presented as an ever-flowing conduit for the absolving waters of heaven that cleanse human souls.⁶⁶

By far the longest narrative in the *Stacions of Rome*, the story of the baptism of the emperor Constantine (241–84), makes explicit the working of divine grace at Rome.⁶⁷ When we first encounter the emperor, he is very different from the heroic martyrs and noble popes honored elsewhere in the poem—he is not even a Christian. Although holding power "in Rome with gret honour" (242), he is an unbeliever, "in Mahoun was al his thouht, / For in Crist ne leevede he nouht" (245–46), and suffering from leprosy: "A mesel forsothe we fynde he was, / Til Crist sende him of his gras" (247–48).⁶⁸ The Middle Ages, as in Robert Henryson's *Testament of Cresseid*, tended to treat leprosy as a moral rather than a physical disease, one that required the "medicyn" of grace mentioned in the Vernon Prologue (11). What is most striking about Constantine's spiritual healing in the *Stacions*, as opposed to that of Henryson's repentant Cresseid, however, is that he appears to have done nothing to earn it. Other medieval versions of the story, such as that in Gower's *Confessio Amantis*, discussed in a later chapter, present the emperor as an ideal pagan leader, so magnanimous that he is willing to sacrifice his own life by refusing the treatment prescribed by his doctors because it would shed the blood of innocent children. In the *Stacions*, Constantine performs no such Christlike act of self-denial, nor, in contrast to other medieval versions of the story, is he rewarded with a vision of Peter and Paul, who send him to Pope Sylvester for instruction. Instead, grace comes directly to Constantine, as soon as he hears and believes Sylvester's preaching:

> Pope Silvestre gon him preche,
> Cristes lawes forte teche.
> So leevede he wel, in Godes sone,
> And Cristene mon wolde he bicome.
> He dude him Cristne, as I [th]ou telle,
> In this miracle thus hit bifelle,

> That the water wesch awey his sinne
> And al the fulthe that he was inne. (249–56)

Constantine is not saved because of any good deed on his part but simply by the grace of God and the words of Sylvester, which kindle a desire in him that "Cristene mon wolde he bicome." When Sylvester, again the active party, baptizes Constantine, a "miracle" occurs, and the emperor's physical and spiritual filth is instantly washed away. Constantine's cure, in fact, is like those promised to sinners throughout the *Stacions*. Pilgrims to Rome receive pardon not because of their own merits but simply out of God's great mercy.

What Constantine does in response to his healing baptism also differs from many other medieval versions of his story. The *Stacions* says nothing about his endowing the papacy with sweeping political power, the so-called Donation of Constantine, which many in the Middle Ages, including Gower, believed had fatally poisoned the church. Instead, more prudently and with more historical accuracy, the emperor in the *Stacions* donates a palace, the Lateran, so that it may be transformed into "Godes hous" (267).[69] His only request is that the pope will bestow his "benyson" on "alle hem that thider come" (272–73), to which Sylvester assents, saying,

> "And as the fulthe fel fro the,
> So clene of sunne schal thei be
> Of alle maner clansyng of synne,
> That non schal dwellen heore soule withinne." (281–84)

This truly is a plenary indulgence, as Christian baptism is supposed to be, which reclaims the first innocence of the soul not through one's own efforts, which are always inadequate, but through the unmerited grace of God. The story of Constantine reminds us that the pardons of Rome are but one manifestation of the supreme "benyson" of Christ's redemption.[70] The mercy that saved a non-Christian emperor is available to all humans everywhere, including the readers of this poem.

The *Stacions of Rome* expresses the yearning for universal salvation found in many Middle English religious writers, as Nicholas Watson has shown.[71] What makes the *Stacions* different from the works Watson discusses is its focus on Rome. The city it imagines is a sacred place of holy martyrs and pious popes, whose pardons pour forth as from a fountain. This Rome is a spiritual Land of Cockayne or Big Rock Candy Mountain, with infinite pardons backed by the full faith and credit of the Creator of the world. The *Stacions of Rome* promises much and demands little. It even suggests that the extravagant pardons of Rome do not even require one's presence in the city but can be obtained by readers in England through their imaginative participation in its artistically limited but spiritually generous poetry. Such readers may have confidence that they, too, will find relief from the burden of their sin because, as *Piers Plowman* more than once quotes the Psalmist as saying, mercy is the greatest of all God's works: *misericordia eius super omnia opera eius* (Ps. 144:9).[72]

CHAPTER 2

The Ruins of Rome:
Pagan Marvels and the *Metrical Mirabilia*

Rome in the Middle Ages was as famous for its ruins as for its relics. In addition to the bodies of early Christian martyrs and other holy objects, the city contained a vast collection of spectacular, if often dilapidated, pagan monuments, largely from the imperial period. The most influential medieval source of knowledge about Rome's ancient ruins was a twelfth-century Latin prose work, the *Mirabilia urbis Romae*, which, in various versions and languages, was known throughout Europe. The *Mirabilia* tradition is more learned and literary than the Latin source of the *Stacions of Rome* discussed in the previous chapter. In contrast to the *Indulgentiae*, whose texts are little more than a list of churches, relics, and pardons, the *Mirabilia*, in addition to its inventory of objects, contains other genres, including stories about individuals associated with some of the city's most famous monuments. As had the *Indulgentiae* tradition, the *Mirabilia* imagines an idealized ancient Rome: instead of a sacred city of martyrs' shrines offering infinite mercy, however, it portrays a golden city of magnificent pagan marvels. Though often erroneous by modern historical standards, the *Mirabilia* claims to present the lost city in all its original glory.

The *Mirabilia*, like the *Indulgentiae*, was eventually translated into Middle English verse. But whereas the *Stacions of Rome* was a relatively popular text and is still extant in nine copies, including some in major manuscript compilations, only two, relatively obscure fifteenth-century English poems, very different in length and achievement, derive from a late Latin version of the *Mirabilia*. The first of these texts, which is found in the same Bicester monastic roll that contains a copy of the *Stacions*, is no more than a brief fragment; the second, a much longer and more impressive poem, is interpolated into the unique copy of the *Metrical Version of Mandeville's Travels*. The *Metrical* interpolation on Rome seems not to have been much read in its own time (and is largely ignored today), but it deserves our attention because of the original and highly conflicted way in which it imagines ancient Rome. Like most Latin versions of the *Mirabilia*, it celebrates the lost splendor of the ancient city, but it also introduces warnings about the dangers that Rome's pagan marvels posed to Christian faith and, in a shocking reversal, it concludes by eagerly endorsing their destruction.

The *Mirabilia urbis Romae*

By the standards of the Middle Ages, though not of later periods, the Latin *Mirabilia* is an impressive antiquarian achievement. No other medieval work contains so much information about what actually survived of the physical fabric of the ancient city or what was remembered and conjectured about it.[1] The earliest version of the *Mirabilia* (composed about 1143) is often attributed to a certain Benedict, a canon at St. Peter's in Rome.[2] The author/compiler, whoever he was, combined his own personal observations of the contemporary city with written and oral knowledge about its past gathered from, among other sources, old catalogues of Rome's regions, Latin histories, Ovid's *Fasti*, Christian saints' lives, papal biographies, legends from the East, and fanciful tales told by the Romans of his own day.[3] The original Latin prose *Mirabilia* did not remain a stable text. Just as it rewrote material from earlier sources, so, too, it was repeatedly rewritten, translated, amplified, and reshaped over the next several centuries, resulting in a variety of versions distinguished one from the other by differences in small details and by the addition or omission of longer passages and episodes. The *Mirabilia* is a prime example of what has been dubbed a medieval "multi-text," though its mutations in form sometimes go unacknowledged by modern commentators.[4]

Manuscript copies of most of the different versions of the *Mirabilia* survive in major English libraries, and internal evidence indicates that many of these were produced for English medieval audiences.[5] I have identified a distinctive form of the Latin text that was especially popular in late medieval England, which I call the Hybrid *Mirabilia*. I shall later demonstrate that the source of the translation of the *Mirabilia* interpolated into the *Metrical Mandeville* (and probably the Bicester fragment as well), though unrecognized until now, must have been a text that closely resembled a specific version of the Latin Hybrid *Mirabilia* that survives in two British Library Harley manuscripts. Understanding the nature of the original twelfth-century *Mirabilia*, and tracing some of the complex changes its text underwent before it became the Hybrid version, will allow us to appreciate both the Hybrid's distinctiveness within the larger *Mirabilia* tradition and, even more significantly, the skill with which the English poet of the *Metrical* interpolation worked with, selected from, and amplified the form of the Hybrid he knew in order to produce his own remarkable account of ancient Rome.

Remembering Rome's Ancient Marvels

The original twelfth-century *Mirabilia* unambiguously admires the pagan monuments of Rome. In his final chapter, the author, speaking for the first time in his own voice, says that his ambition has been to convey to contemporary readers the splendor of the ancient city:

> Quantae etiam essent pulchritudinis auri et argenti, aeris et eboris pretiosorumque lapidum, scriptis ad posterum memoriam, quanto melius potuimus, reducere curavimus. (65)
> (We have endeavored, as best we could, to restore to the memory of posterity by means of writing how great was the beauty of these things [i.e., pagan palaces, temples, etc.] in gold and silver, bronze and ivory, and precious stones. [Nichols, 46])[6]

In contrast to so many other medieval and modern responses to Rome's ruins, from Hildebert to Byron, the *Mirabilia* is not a lament for what has been lost but rather a celebration of the city's past material glories, the memory of which it wishes to preserve.

The Rome of the *Mirabilia* is, of course, a textual city: it exists on the page and in the mind. As such, it describes not only the ruins the author personally saw, which he tries to imagine when new, but also the monuments that he knows (or thinks he knows) once existed in the city. Its thirty-two, mostly brief, chapters tell of ancient objects still in use (such as the city gates), those that had become largely decorative (such as columns), those adapted for Christian use (such as the Pantheon), and those that survived only in fragments or memory (such as baths and temples).[7] The *Mirabilia* can be roughly divided into three sections, each of which uses a dominant literary mode.[8] Chapters 1–10 are lists of different classes of topographical objects, such as arches, hills (unique in being natural and not man-made), and palaces; chapters 11–18 are largely narratives that explain the origins of certain significant monuments, especially memorial statues; and chapters 19–32 are a street-level itinerary through the different regions of Rome, situating previously mentioned structures in relation to one another and introducing new ones.

Much, though by no means all, of the *Mirabilia*'s information about ancient Rome, as we now know, is erroneous in whole or part. For example, many of the structures listed in the *Mirabilia* as theaters were in fact circuses, whereas the one genuine Roman theater still visible today, the Theatre of Marcellus, goes unmentioned. Nine Miedema, who has compiled the most complete inventory of *Mirabilia* manuscripts, argues that the author invented fictional buildings to supplement real ones, but such deliberate falsification has been challenged by Dale Kinney, who argues that even though the identification of several temples cited in the text is not supported by present-day archaeological evidence, none "is without some textual or material justification."[9] For instance, the *Mirabilia*'s claim that there was a pagan temple dedicated to the orator and politician Cicero may not be as ridiculous as it seems, but rather an example of what Kinney calls a "learned solecism," derived from the author's assumption that the Tullianum (actually a prominent Roman jail) was a temple named for Marcus *Tullius* Cicero.[10] In any case, the greatest value of the *Mirabilia* today is not its information about ancient Rome but rather what it tells us about how the city was conceived in the medieval imagination.[11]

The re-creation of ancient Rome in the *Mirabilia* recalls Freud's use of the city in his *Civilization and Its Discontents*. To illustrate the intricacies of the human mind, Freud asks us "by a flight of imagination" to suppose a Rome "in which nothing that has once come into existence will have passed away and all the earliest phases of development continue to exist alongside the latest one," so that, for example, in the place now "occupied by the Palazzo Caffarelli would once more stand—without the Palazzo having to be removed—the Temple of Jupiter Capitolinus; and this not only in its latest shape, as the Romans of the Empire saw it, but also in its earliest one, when it still showed Etruscan forms and was ornamented with terracotta antefixes."[12] Freud acknowledges the literal impossibility of his thought experiment. No real Rome could include all that had been built there over the centuries, but an imagined Rome can because it is a mental concept, not a material reality.

Although the jumble of objects in the *Mirabilia* suggests something of Freud's multiple historical moments, the work's sense of time is quite binary; it recognizes only two broad historical periods: then and now. In the first section of the *Mirabilia*, classes of structures that were still a vital part of the medieval city are described in the present tense, often using the word *sunt*, as in "Hii sunt pontes" (These *are* the bridges) (26, line 7; Nichols, 10, emphasis added), with no indication of (and perhaps no interest in) the specific period in which they had been erected.[13] Structures that had largely disappeared or were in ruins, however, such as baths, palaces, and theaters, are often listed without a temporal verb: "Thermae: Antonianae, Domitianae, etc." (Baths: that of Antonius, of Domitian, etc.) (20, line 4; Nichols, 8–9). The prominent monuments in the middle section of the *Mirabilia* are also described in the present tense (because they still existed), such as "Lateranis est quidam caballus aereus" (At the Lateran there *is* a certain bronze horse) (32, line 3; Nichols, 19, emphasis added), whereas the narratives of the origins of these monuments are firmly set in a distant if somewhat vague past. The bold squire who is commemorated in the bronze equestrian statue just mentioned is said to have lived "tempore consulum et senatorum" (in the time of the consuls and senators) (32, line 5; Nichols, 20), but precisely what historical period is meant and what its temporal relationship to a previous story set "temporibus Tiberii imperatoris" (in the times of the emperor Tiberius) (30, lines 3–4; Nichols, 18) is left unclear.[14] The contrast between now and then is most obvious in the itinerary through the city in part 3 of the *Mirabilia*, which constantly switches back and forth between what is and what was in Rome, for example, "Ubi est Sanctus Petrus ad Vincula, fuit templum Veneris" (Where now *is* S. Pietro in Vincoli *was* a temple of Venus) (60, lines 4–5; Nichols, 44, emphasis added).

Pagan and Christian Rome

The duality of time present and time past expresses the one fundamental division in ancient Rome's history recognized by all versions of the *Mirabilia*: the change from pagan to Christian Rome. The two Romes are evoked in the description of the first of the city's gates in the twelfth-century original: "Porta Capena, quae vocatur Sancti Pauli iuxta sepulchrum Remi" (Porta Capena, which is called S. Paulo and is next to the tomb of Remus) (17, lines

5–6; Nichols, 5).¹⁵ Just as Remus (with Romulus) founded the pagan city, the martyrdom of the Apostle Paul (and Peter) inspired Rome's conversion to Christianity. This juxtaposition does not signal sharp cultural conflict in the original *Mirabilia*, however. Instead, as previous scholars have demonstrated, correspondences between the two eras are repeatedly emphasized. Robert Brentano describes the *Mirabilia* as "a sort of palimpsest with one civilization written over the other," and John Osborne calls attention to the author's effort "to construct a series of bridges between the pagan past and the Christian present."¹⁶ A striking example of this is the *Mirabilia*'s account of the Pantheon, which occurs almost exactly midway through the work (chapter 16), and which Brentano identifies as one of three stories that most carefully join old and new Rome.¹⁷ We are told that the Pantheon was originally built by the victorious pagan general Agrippa in honor of Cybele and Neptune. Much later, Pope Boniface asked for the building from the Christian emperor Phocas (called Foca in the text), and so this "templum ita mirabile" (marvelous temple) (35, line 12; Nichols, 22), once dedicated to Cybele, the "mater deorum" (mother of the gods), on the Kalends of November is reconsecrated at the beginning of the same month to the Virgin Mary, the "mater omnium sanctorum" (mother of all the saints) (35, lines 15–18; Nichols, 22), establishing a feast day still celebrated by the Catholic Church.

A few critics have seen the *Mirabilia*'s references to Christian Rome as the author's assertion of its triumph over its pagan predecessor. Miedema, for example, says that several chapters show the Christian city "as a superior continuation of antique Rome."¹⁸ Jennifer Summit, likewise, says that pagan architecture is valued in the *Mirabilia* primarily because it "prefigures" what is to come: "the sites of pagan Rome are preserved as material prophecies of a Christianity that fulfills and completes them."¹⁹ But the argument that the twelfth-century *Mirabilia* aims to represent pagan Rome as an inferior ancestor of Christian Rome is not supported by the text, in my view, and distorts its attitude toward the earlier city. It is true that the author sometimes identifies pagan buildings by their now Christian names, but his purpose is not so much to argue for (or against) the greater value of their current use as to identify their locations for the medieval reader. As the *Mirabilia* author makes abundantly clear in his final chapter, his ultimate ambition is not to extol Christian Rome at the expense of the earlier city, but instead to call to memory the ancient pagan marvels, whose splendor merits admiration in its own right. This is demonstrated by his praise of the Mausoleum of Augustus or the Circus Maximus, for example, which were never appropriated for

Christian use. The limited role that Christianity plays in the *Mirabilia* is evident near the end of the itinerary in part 3: "In palatio Lateranis sunt quaedam miranda, but non scribenda" (In the Lateran palace are certain things to be marveled at but not to be written about) (59, lines 5–6; Nichols, 44). As we know from the *Stacions of Rome*, the Lateran complex contained more relics than any other place in Rome, but although the author shows his knowledge of such Christian treasure, he is not interested in writing about it here (and rarely elsewhere in the *Mirabilia*) because it is not his real subject.

The original *Mirabilia* avoids the harsh criticism of paganism often found in medieval literature, such as the *Stacions of Rome* and, as we shall see, in the Rome interpolation in the *Metrical Mandeville*. It does occasionally mention hostility between the two faiths, most obviously in a chapter about some of the places where early martyrs were murdered (by pagans, of course), including the sewer where Saint Sebastian's body was discarded (24, lines 6–8; Nichols, 13). The same Sebastian is also said to have destroyed the pagan Olovitreum, a temple containing an *astronomia* with the signs of the zodiac (63, line 6–64, line 2; Nichols, 45).[20] But these passages are not typical of the text's tone. When paganism is found wanting in the *Mirabilia*, it is not so much because of the wickedness of its beliefs and practices but because, as part of the sublunary world, it cannot last. The transitory nature of the pagan world is demonstrated by a statue that Romulus erects in his palace and declares will stand until a virgin gives birth (i.e., forever), though, of course, it falls at the Nativity of Christ (21, lines 4–7; Nichols, 9).[21] Similarly fleeting is the life of even the grandest pagan hero. The *Mirabilia* repeats the legend that a metal globe on the top of the imposing Egyptian obelisk on the Vatican Hill (now in St. Peter's Square) contains the ashes of Julius Caesar, an appropriately lofty resting place for one who had once been so eminent: "ut sicut eo vivente totus mundus ei subiectus fuit, ita eo mortuo usque in finem saeculi subicietur" (just as when he was living the whole world was subject to him, so in death it will lie beneath him forever) (43, line 9–44, line 1; Nichols, 33). The verses that follow, however, stress that such glory is only ephemeral:

> Caesar, tantus eras quantus et orbis
> Sed nunc in modico clauderis antro. (44, lines 5–6)
> (Caesar, you were once as great as the world,
> But now you are enclosed in a small cave.) (Nichols, 33)[22]

No heavenly paradise or pagan afterlife awaited even Caesar—only a modest receptacle for his ashes.

Yet even as the *Mirabilia* shows that golden Rome, like all earthly things, must come to dust, its major theme is celebration of the city's pagan magnificence when new. The *Mirabilia* attempts to answer the question implied by Archbishop Hildebert in his famous poem: if the ruins of the present city are unequalled, what must Rome have been like when whole?[23] Based on the city's ruined remains and on what he has read and heard, the author of the *Mirabilia* imagines an ancient Rome that far exceeds any existing medieval city, perhaps any city that ever was. Although the secular Circus Maximus was already ruined in the Middle Ages, it appears in this work as a richly decorated arena of "marvelous beauty" (*mirae pulchritudinis*), having been constructed with such skill that every spectator had an unobstructed view (58, lines 8–59, line 2; Nichols, 43). The *Mirabilia* also extols a marvelous early warning system on Rome's Capitoline Hill (34, lines 3–9; Nichols, 21). This remarkable mechanism is said to have consisted of a series of statues of the various provinces subject to Roman rule, each with a bell around its neck; the moment any realm became rebellious, the bell of the appropriate image rang, alerting the Senate to take preventive military action.

The *Mirabilia* admires pagan Romans themselves as much as it does their city and notes only a few villains. Although Nero is linked in passing with several sites, his monstrous crimes, a frequent topic of classical and medieval authors, as we shall see in subsequent chapters, go unmentioned. Instead, the *Mirabilia* praises several admirable Romans, especially in the narratives in the middle section of the work. One such is Agrippa, the pious general who built the Pantheon. Another is the bold squire, mentioned previously as commemorated in a bronze equestrian statue, who is first introduced as handsome, virtuous, bold, and prudent (*magnae formae et virtutis, audax et prudens*) (32, line 8; Nichols, 20) and soon justifies such praise by hatching a daring plan to capture the king of an army besieging Rome. The squire is also shrewd enough to make the Senate agree on his reward beforehand, so that he does well for himself by doing good for the city. Another particularly noble Roman, mentioned near the end of the *Mirabilia*, is the heroic leader (*nobilis miles*) who sacrifices his own life by riding into and thus closing an infernal chasm that was damaging the city (56, lines 1–5; Nichols, 41).[24]

Although pagan Romans in the *Mirabilia* cannot expect Christian salvation, their piety is nevertheless treated with respect, as in the story of the vision granted to the emperor Octavian (Augustus Caesar), the first narrative in the second section of the *Mirabilia* (chapter 11). When Rome's senators tell the emperor they wish to deify him, he hesitates and consults the Tiburtine Sibyl, who tells him about a divine king. He then has a vision of a virgin and a child standing on an altar, which a heavenly voice identifies as the altar of the Son of God. The superiority of Christianity to paganism is obvious here, but the spirituality of pagans is not mocked. Although the emperor is human in comparison with the eternal Lord, he is shown to be worthy of admiration. Instinctively modest in responding to the worship of the senators, he follows his faith by consulting the Sybil and is granted a vision of Mary and Christ, to whom he responds with unhesitating reverence: "statim procidens in terram adoravit" (immediately falling to the ground, he worshipped) (28, line 20; Nichols, 18). Octavian never ceases to be a pagan, but he is such a worthy pagan that he is granted a glimpse of the true faith. The author of the *Mirabilia* has little of Saint Augustine's visceral disgust for Rome's ancient religion, but shares something more like Dante's respect for pagan accomplishments and virtues.

The Development of the *Mirabilia* Tradition

The later Latin adaptations of the *Mirabilia* did not fundamentally alter its attitude toward Rome, but they added new material that became part of the textual tradition on which the authors of the English translations drew. The first known adaptation, composed about a decade later, is the *Graphia aureae urbis Romae* (ca. 1150), the most significant additions to which are a fanciful prehistory of Rome (with mentions of settlements by Noah, Saturn, and refugees from the Trojan War) and a long conclusion that purports to describe Roman imperial offices, regalia, and ceremonials.[25] Although the *Graphia* survives in only a single manuscript, much of its material on Rome, reduced but also supplemented and reorganized, was widely available because it was incorporated into the influential thirteenth-century *Chronicon pontificum et imperatorum* (*Chronicle of Popes and Emperors*) of Martinus Polonus (also known as Martin of Troppau or Martinus Oppaviensis).[26] Among the many medieval versions of the Latin *Mirabilia*, two (identified and edited by Carl Urlichs as the third and fourth) are especially important for the English *Mirabilia* tradition because material from both contributed to the previously unnoticed and still unedited late medieval Latin version of the *Mirabilia* that I call, because of its unique combination of elements, the Hybrid *Mirabilia*, whose status as the source of the English translations of the

Mirabilia I demonstrate below. The Hybrid generally follows the third version of the *Mirabilia*, which Urlichs dates to the fourteenth century and which reproduces much of the original twelfth-century *Mirabilia*, with some rearrangement, rewriting, and expansion.[27] One distinctive mark of the Hybrid is an alternative description of the Capitoline Hill, found only in some manuscripts of the third version, that emphasizes the splendor of its monuments and offers a somewhat different account of a special marvel: the images of Rome's provinces whose bells warned the city of rebellion.[28] To this alternate account of the Capitol, the Hybrid adds a unique and elaborate description of the Colosseum as a "Temple of the Sun" from Urlichs's fourth version of the *Mirabilia*, which he dates to the fourteenth or fifteenth century.[29]

I have located five texts of the Hybrid *Mirabilia* in manuscripts all apparently produced for English audiences.[30] Each of these texts differs from the others in some way, but they are alike in generally following Urlichs's third version with the variant account of the Capitol and adding the account of the Temple of the Sun from the fourth version. The texts in Harley 562 and Harley 2321 are exceptional among the Hybrids in beginning with extended prehistories of the city, as do the *Graphia* and Martinus's *Chronicon pontificum*.[31] Because they, too, include prehistories of Rome in addition to other similar details, both Middle English translations of the *Mirabilia* seem to derive from a Hybrid text similar to those in the Harley manuscripts. Harley 2321, in particular, shares many elements with the longer, more important translation of the *Mirabilia* in the *Metrical Mandeville*. As will become clear, however, there are enough differences between the *Mandeville* interpolation and Harley 2321 to suggest that, useful as that manuscript copy is for giving a sense of the material with which the poet was working, it does not represent his immediate source.

The Bicester *Mirabilia*

The briefest of the two Middle English translations of the *Mirabilia* dates from the fifteenth century and is only seventy lines long (twenty-two of which describe the city, and then only its walls and gates); the one surviving manuscript copy of this text immediately follows the full-length *Stacions of Rome* in the Bicester Abbey accounts roll discussed in the previous chapter.[32] The Bicester fragment is as disappointing as poetry as it is brief, though it begins grandly enough by locating Rome within universal history:

> Fro this worlde begynyng,
> Unto that cyte of Rome makyng,
> Four thousand yieres passed be,
> And iiij c iiij xx and thre [i.e., 4,483]. (1–4)

This lofty tone is not sustained, however, and the next six lines, which date the foundation of Rome to 750 years before the birth of Christ, are quite slack, with entire lines whose only function is to round out a couplet: thus "And fro the beginyng of Rome" is followed by "As men tel in ther dome" (5–6), and "There is gone vii c yier and fifti" by "That date witnesse the Romanes aply" (9–10). The fragment lacks the urgent personal address to the reader found in the preceding Bicester *Stacions*. Rather than "Whoso wole his soule leche, / Liste to me, I wolle hym teche" (Bicester *Stacions*, 1–2), there are more perfunctory lines, such as "I wille thow telle or ye gane" (16) or "That tyme as I wille yow tellen" (31).[33]

The first forty-eight lines of the Bicester *Mirabilia* (more than two-thirds of the total) are a muddled account of the Trojan prehistory of Rome that may derive, however fitfully, from the prehistories unique to the Harley manuscripts of the Hybrid *Mirabilia*.[34] Although the poet cites the "clerke Virgile" (20), he does not appear to know the *Aeneid* at all well because he refers to its hero as a woman: "a lauedy that hiht Henye" (13). Further confusion follows. We are told that during the fall of Troy, a lady named "Ylia" survived, that she begot two children, "Remlus" and "Romlus," and that they "were of Rome beginyng" (15–27).[35] A few lines later, however, the poet introduces "Romulus that noble man" (41), who was responsible for walling and naming Rome. This "Romulus" cannot be the earlier "Romlus" because he is said to have lived at least 453 years after the fall of Troy (29–30).[36] Aside from its confusing prehistory, the Bicester *Mirabilia* says little about Rome itself. Only its walls, towers, and gates are described, and the fragment ends before we enter the city itself. The Bicester *Mirabilia* may be a fragment of a fuller text or may always have been intended as a brief supplement to the *Stacions of Rome* that immediately precedes it.[37] Whatever its original purpose, the poem as we now have it is not a significant version of the *Mirabilia*; it uses only a small amount of the information from that tradition and makes little effort to remind the reader of Rome's past splendor.

The Rome Interpolation in the *Metrical Version of Mandeville's Travels*

The *Metrical Version of Mandeville's Travels*

The other translation of the Hybrid *Mirabilia* into Middle English verse is five times the length of the Bicester fragment and far more accomplished. It has never been discussed on its own, however, because it appears not as an independent poem but only as an interpolation within the *Metrical Version of Mandeville's Travels*. The *Metrical Version* as a whole, which was probably composed in the early fifteenth century, has not attracted much scholarly attention either, being an unusual version of the *Travels* that survives in a single manuscript now housed in a small municipal archive, the Coventry City Record Office.[38] Nevertheless, the poet of the *Metrical Version*, employing what Iain Higgins calls "radical overwriting," demonstrates the same energy and originality in translating the *Travels* as a whole that he does in transforming the interpolation on Rome.[39] Most radically, although *Mandeville's Travels*, in whatever language, is usually prose, the *Metrical* poet turns his source, which is probably a Latin prose version of the *Travels*, into three thousand lines of lively Middle English verse, while adding brief learned passages and highlighting the marvelous.[40] Moreover, the *Metrical* adaptor speaks directly to his English readers, replacing the first-person voice of "Mandeville" with his own and addressing his audience with the eagerness of popular Middle English romance (and the *Stacions of Rome*), as in the lines that immediately follow the opening prayer:

> Nowe lordis and ladies leve and dere,
> Yif ye wolle of wondris here,
> A litille stounde yif ye wolle dwelle,
> Of grete mervailis I mai you telle. (11–14)[41]

The poet further appeals to his English audience by including among his additions some on specifically insular subjects, including brief passages on King Cole as founder of Colchester (974–75), on Uther Pendragon, Merlin, and Stonehenge (2131–38), and on the abundance of oaks in England (2419–20). Within the Rome interpolation itself, he adds a few lines on Roman Britain that echo the contemporary English belief that Julius Caesar, who "al this land wan," built the Tower of London and exacted tribute from the island (371–76).

Wonders and marvels are plentiful in all versions of *Mandeville's Travels*, but they are given special prominence by the *Metrical* poet. As others have noted, many of the more serious parts of the *Travels*, such as the Sultan of Jerusalem's criticism of Christianity and other "reflective passages," are simply dropped.[42] The English poet disparages other versions of the *Travels* as "overlonge," even boring, and says he will provide a snappy digest, "a litille tretis" that will nevertheless tell "of alle merveillis . . . That [Mandeville] sawe" and "some thinge elles" (35–46).[43] As this last phrase promises, the *Metrical Version*, despite its many omissions and reductions, contains additions; like other versions of the *Travels*, it seeks to educate as well as entertain. For example, the English poet adds passages on the four elements (air, water, earth, and fire) from Bartholomew Anglicus (2399–2414), on the Seven Sages (549–68), on the Nine Worthies (2585–96), and on the earthly paradise (2675–700) and purgatory (2718–45). The number of new Latin quotations in the text, often from the Bible, suggests that the poet of the *Metrical Mandeville* may have had a clerical education.

The Interpolation on Rome

The interpolation on Rome is the longest single addition to the *Metrical Version*, occupying lines 62–462 of the poem's total of 2,949. Nothing like it appears in any other version of *Mandeville's Travels*, and yet it is introduced into the longer poem with insouciance. After reporting that "Mandeville" set off from Dover on his travels, the narrator suddenly says that from this port to "the cuntre of Rome / Offten times men gone and come" (62–63). Four hundred lines later, the *Metrical Version* finally returns to its hero, who has, in the meantime, reached Hungary (463–67). Rome was never part of Mandeville's supposed itinerary, except in an epilogue to a few versions of the *Travels*, where he stops off to have the pope approve his book, but the English poet is fascinated by the city. After mentioning that travelers often go from Dover to Rome, he generates interest in his Rome interpolation by saying that whereas English travelers say much about the city, "thei knowen nat alle," especially concerning its origins and early development (64–69). Whereas Rome is now the "chief of alle Cristiante" and "hede of Holi Church," once it was a very different capital, the "chieff" of the "empire of alle this worlde rounde" (70–78).

This transition to Rome may appear to be as positive about the dual pagan and Christian heritage of Rome as is the twelfth-century *Mirabilia*, but the continuity the original Latin author traces between the two cultures and his respect for paganism are not, in fact, shared by the English poet. The *Metrical* interpolation on Rome instead puts the old and new religions into existential conflict. In particular, the English poet extensively reworks and expands the two major episodes whose combination distinguishes the Hybrid *Mirabilia* from other versions of the work—the alternate description of the Capitoline from the third version and the Colosseum as Temple of the Sun from the fourth. Both marvels, especially the latter, dazzle the *Metrical* poet even as they unsettle him. Although he gives greater emphasis than the Hybrid to the magnificence and ingenuity of the Capitol and the Colosseum, he is also more fearful of their potential threat to Christians. Instead of emphasizing the continuities between old and new Rome, the poet insists that the most enchanting, and therefore the most dangerous, marvels of pagan Rome had to be destroyed before the city could become truly "chief of alle Cristiante."

The knowledge and cleverness of the poet of the *Metrical* interpolation on Rome are not seen at their best in his own prehistory of the city, which is somewhat more coherent and proportionally less prominent than Bicester's, but equally eccentric (79–158).[44] In contrast to Bicester, Aeneas is given his correct name and sex, "noble kinge Ser Eneas / Captaine and lorde" (97–98), but 450 years of Roman history are casually erased with the claim that this same Aeneas was the father of Romulus and Remus, who are said to have escaped from Troy with seven other kings before its fall (99–108). The result is a perplexing fusion of two separate Roman legends (that the city was founded by Aeneas and that it was founded by Romulus), which ignores the complexities (and temporal span) of the traditional accounts.[45] The poet does reveal once more his command of English legendary history, however, by adding a reference to Brutus, another refugee from the Trojan War, who is said to have conquered and given his name to Britain: "Brute that al this lande wan / That same time fro Troie cam" (109–10).

After the prehistory of the city, the *Metrical* poet demonstrates his desire to portray Rome as "the chief cite undir the sonne" (158) with a topological survey of its ancient pagan objects from the *Mirabilia* tradition that is unparalleled in Middle English poetry. Like the Hybrid text in Harley 2321, the closest approximation I know to its actual source, the *Metrical* interpolation does not include the final chapter of the original *Mirabilia*, with its claim to have preserved in writing the material splendor of Rome, though the English poet achieves a similar effect with some of his small changes. For example, the impregnability of Rome's walls is insisted on more than in the parallel account of them in Harley 2321 by the repeated use of the word "strong." We are told that Rome is encircled by a "stronge stonen walle" (154), whose almost four hundred towers are "of stronge socoures" (160), just as its forty-three "castellis" are "stronge and good" and its seven thousand "barbicans" are "strong," all of which provide "grete strength" for the city's defenders (188–92).[46] Unlike the Bicester fragment, the *Metrical* interpolation takes us through the city's walls and gates and records the magnificent monuments within—Rome's arches, bridges, palaces, and temples—before ending with two long, extensively reworked accounts of the Capitol and the Temple of the Sun.

The Limits of Pagan Achievement

The Rome interpolation in the *Metrical Mandeville* says much about the magnificence of Rome's ancient fabric, but less than earlier versions of the *Mirabilia* about the achievements and virtues of its citizens. The lengthy narratives of admirable Romans, such as Agrippa and Octavian, which make up the central part of the twelfth-century *Mirabilia* and the later third version, are absent in the English poem, probably because they are not in the poem's immediate source, as they are not in Harley 2321.[47] The interpolation also lacks other human stories in the *Mirabilia* tradition associated with places and structures. Thus the English poem mentions "a place men callith . . . helle" (274) but does not go on to tell the story of the brave rider who sacrificed his life to close a chasm so noxious that the place was named *infernus*. Similarly, the bronze equestrian statue, which the original *Mirabilia* and Martinus's *Chronicon* insist does *not* portray Constantine but rather a squire who saved Rome from a besieging army, is said by the *Metrical* interpolation, like Harley 2321, to represent an unidentified "emperoure" and to stand in Constantine's palace (258–62).[48] There is no mention of the squire.

Although the English poem includes only a few tales of noble pagan Romans, it does acknowledge that some performed remarkable feats. One such is as uncanny as anything in medieval romance. The poet repeats the popular legend found in some versions of the *Mirabilia*, including Harley 2321, fol. 116v, of an astonishing getaway by Virgil when he was under restraint in Rome:

> There was taken the grete clerke Virgille,
> And invisible there made hym
> And escaped unto Neapolym. (224–26)

The Virgil evoked here is not the great poet thought by some to have prophesied, in his Fourth Eclogue, the coming of Christ, but rather another medieval persona of him as a pagan magician.[49]

Although the *Metrical* interpolation on Rome mentions pagan structures that became Christian churches (233, 270, 272), it emphasizes destruction rather than continuity. For example, Harley 2321, fol. 116v, like other versions of the *Mirabilia*, tells how Romulus, the founder of Rome, set up his statue in his palace, declaring that it would not fall until a virgin gave birth.[50] The English poet heightens the conflict between the two religions by calling the image a pagan idol instead of just a statue, "And Romulus *his god* there inne sette" (237, emphasis added), and he magnifies the destruction that is caused by the Nativity of Christ. More than the collapse of Romulus's statue, his entire palace is obliterated in a powerful final couplet: "That place that was so stronge and sounde / Alle toflattered and felle to grounde" (243–44).[51] Note the ironic echo of the word "strong," which is repeatedly used at the beginning of the interpolation to describe Rome's walls. Such pagan strength is no protection here. We shall see other, greater destructions, instead of continuities, later in the poem.

From its beginning, the *Metrical* interpolation opposes Rome the "chieff" center of the "empire of alle this worlde rounde" to the city that became "chief of alle Cristiante." The latter is holy; the former is not. Whereas the interpolation gives little praise to pagan rulers, it does frequently remind us of their violent ends. The vile Nero kills himself (250), and even the great Julius Caesar, conqueror of Britain and supposed builder of the Tower of London, is assassinated (379–80). The finality of these pagan ends contrasts with the eternal life of Saint Lawrence, the only Christian whose physical death is mentioned in the interpolation (266). Nevertheless, it is the marvels of ancient pagan Rome that continue to haunt the imagination of the English poet because of their power to unsettle as well as dazzle—to unsettle *because* they dazzle. This mix of fascination and fear is most apparent in two major set pieces about the Capitol and the Temple of the Sun that conclude the final and longest section of the *Metrical Mirabilia*, on Roman temples (295–436).[52]

The Pagan Marvels of the Capitol

All versions of the *Mirabilia* agree that the Capitoline Hill exemplified the material splendor and power of ancient Rome. In the twelfth-century *Mirabilia*, the Capitol is called the center of the world (*caput mundi*), the place where consuls and senators met to govern the empire; its towering walls, richly adorned with gold, silver, bronze, and glass, made it a mirror to all the nations: *speculum omnibus gentibus* (51, lines 1–6; Nichols, 38). Its most remarkable marvel (whose description, in most versions, is part of the chapter on the Pantheon) is the device by which Rome was warned of rebellion in any of its domains by the ringing of a bell on the neck of a statue representing the mutinous province.[53] The Hybrid *Mirabilia* and the poet of the *Metrical Mirabilia* describe the splendor of the Capitol somewhat differently than the original *Mirabilia*, both adding that it was so richly decorated that it was worth a third of all the world (*tertiam partem mundi*) and that its warning system (which they discuss with the rest of the details about the Capitol) was a product of magic (*per artem magicam*).[54]

Unlike other versions of the *Mirabilia*, including the Hybrid, the *Metrical Mandeville* expresses ambivalence about the Capitol by portraying it as both richer in decoration and more disturbingly pagan. Specifically, the poem enhances the opulence of the Capitol's decoration and associates its warning bells not just with magic but also with idols (317–58).[55] In describing the Capitol's lavish decoration, many versions of the *Mirabilia*, including the Hybrid, refer to its *lapidibus pretiosis* (precious jewels), *preciosissimus* in Harley 2321, fol. 117v.[56] In his longest original addition to the Hybrid in the Rome interpolation, the English poet provides an original, precise, and detailed catalogue of the Capitol's many "precious stones" (324).

> With jaspes, beches, and berilles,
> And many othir stones as the boke telles,
> Amatistes, crisolites, and calcidoynes,
> Crapotines, coteices, and sardoynes,
> Diamoundes, dianes ful thik there wore,
> Emeraudes, saphiris, and vermidore,
> Peritotes also and reflambines,
> And carbuncles that bright shines,
> Rubies, topaces, and onicles riche,
> Sardes and garnettis for thei ben liche,
> Smaragdes, ligoyns, and perles fele,
> Moo than I can rekene wele. (325–36)

The brilliant radiance suggested by this extravagant lapidary is almost otherworldly, making ancient Rome appear less like a historical city, however grand, and more like a legendary or heavenly one, such as Priam's Troy, as described in Benôit de Sainte-Maure's twelfth-century romance *Le roman de Troie*, or the heavenly Jerusalem in the book of Apocalypse (21:19–21) and the Middle English alliterative *Pearl*. Although such blinding splendor is appropriate to romance or the divine, there is at least a hint in these lines of worldly excess, perhaps even of immorality, given that the supposed supernatural power of rare jewels was an aspect of medieval astrology, always viewed with suspicion by the church.[57]

The *Metrical* poet further qualifies the Hybrid's positive account of the Capitol by explicitly associating its warning system with idolatry. All versions of the Hybrid *Mirabilia*, including Harley 2321, say that whenever one of the Capitol bells rang to signal a rebellion, the statue bearing the ringing bell turned away from a larger image of the city of Rome.[58] The English poet gives this central image even more prominence by describing it first, before the rest of the marvel, saying that the image was "richeli" set in the middle of a "temple rounde" and calling attention to its great size, which extended all the way "from the rooff unto the grounde" (342–44). The poem, unlike the Hybrid, does not say that the image is of Rome but instead identifies it as a pagan idol: "Hir god that was thair maumette" (341). The term "maumette," which is repeated at the end of the passage (354), is a corruption of the name Muhammed and was a common, and hostile, Middle English term for a heathen idol, such as the one the poet says was erected in Romulus's palace and destroyed at the birth of Christ.[59] Many people in the Middle Ages considered such idols a medium through which devils communicated with human beings, misleading and tempting them into damnation. As admiring as the English poet is of the splendor of the Capitol and its marvelous warning bells, he also introduces a note of caution about supernatural powers and idol worship not found in the Hybrid.

Marvel and Danger in the Temple of the Sun

The conflict between pagan and Christian Rome becomes explicit and destructive during the description of the final ancient marvel in the *Metrical* interpolation: the Temple of the Sun in the Colosseum. The Colosseum is usually mentioned only in passing in the *Mirabilia* tradition, which includes a single brief reference to such a temple that was located in front of the amphitheater.[60] The Hybrid *Mirabilia*, however, adds a new and radically expanded account of the Colosseum taken from the fourth version of the *Mirabilia*, which locates the Temple of the Sun within the Colosseum itself.[61] The temple is said to be huge and beautiful, with a central statue of Phoebus extending from floor to ceiling (like the image of the pagan idol in the interpolation's account of the Capitol) and holding an orb symbolizing Rome's global rule.[62] The most astonishing feature of the temple appears on its vault: a simulacrum of the heavens that causes thunder and lightning and even rain (through tubes), with images of the sun and moon and the signs of the zodiac drawn in chariots: "Erant ibi praeterea signa supercelestia et planetae Sol et Lunae quae quadrigis propriis ducebantur."[63] The temple did not survive long in Christian Rome, however, for Pope Sylvester is said to have ordered it destroyed to prevent pilgrims (*oratores*), tempted by its vain delights, from neglecting their Christian devotions, though he preserved the head and hands of the idol and displayed them before the Lateran, apparently as trophies.[64]

In its presentation of the Temple of the Sun, the *Metrical* interpolation, again reworking a passage quite similar to Harley 2321, fol. 118r, transforms this marvel into something at once more wonderful and more spiritually threatening.[65] Calling the Temple of the Sun the "moost mervailous temple of alle" (386), the poet adds new details that evoke the castles of medieval romance: "hie wallis in everi side, / Proude pynnacles and corven toures" (390–91), while insisting that the heavenly firmament on the temple's vault exceeds mere human skill:

> The rooff was made verament
> Evenliche unto the firmament,
> With sonne and moone and sterris brighte
> That shined both daie and nyghte.
> Thundir and lightenenge, hayle and rayn,
> Whenever thei wolde in certayn,
> Thai shewed it in dede apertly
> And alle through crafft of sorcery
> The sonne to the daie gaff light,
> The mone and the sterris to the nyght. (393–402)

The temple described here is more truly supernatural than that in Urlichs's fourth version or in the Latin Hybrid. The English poet says nothing about man-made pipes producing rain (or hail), and his sun and moon, which are not drawn by chariots as in the Hybrid, are less stage props in a mythological pageant and more like genuine astral bodies able to shine forth "both daie and nyghte."

The Temple of the Sun is a greater wonder in the *Metrical* interpolation than in the Hybrid, but the poet also warns that such pagan marvels may be dangerous. The antepenultimate line of the quotation attributes the firmament to the "crafft of sorcery." *Sorcery* is an especially sinister word in Middle English, denoting black magic or witchcraft, as when Christ is accused of "sorcerie" in *Piers Plowman* because of his raising Lazarus from the dead.⁶⁶ By using the term *sorcery*, whose Latin equivalent is not in Harley 2321 or other Hybrid manuscripts, the *Metrical* poet suggests that the firmament is an idolatrous imitation of God's original Creation, a comparison that is emphasized by the echo of Genesis in the final, vigorous couplet describing celestial light that divides the day from the night.

That the temple is an active threat to Christianity is shown by Pope Sylvester's response to it. Instead of saving pieces of the statue to display triumphantly before his papal palace at the Lateran, as in the Hybrid, he orders that the image, along with the entire temple, be demolished utterly:

> That time that Seint Silvester was pope.
> He fordid that riche mamette
> That so richeli there was sette,
> And distroied that temple of lym and stone
> And othir templis ful many oone. (414–18)

This passage is made especially hostile to paganism, as in the description of the Capitol, by the use of the term for pagan idol, *mamette*, indeed "riche mamette," to characterize the gigantic statue of the sun god.⁶⁷ The English poet goes on to add original lines that make it clear that Sylvester's specific purpose in destroying such temples was to purify the ground in order to build Christian places of worship: "And foundid chirchis many and goode / In the placis there that the templis stoode" (419–20).⁶⁸ These new churches may not be as materially splendid as the pagan temples they replaced, but they offer greater spiritual rewards. The English poet says that Sylvester empowers them to grant "ful grete pardoun," which is done subsequently by "othere popis also" (421–22), among them Pope Boniface, who turns the Pantheon into a Christian church (423–28).⁶⁹

The poet does not change the fate of the Pantheon, perhaps because it was still standing in the Middle Ages, as it is today, but in the lines that immediately follow, which begin a brief account of Christian Rome, there is no question of any general antiquarian respect for pagan houses of worship, but rather an insistence on the sacred duty to raze them: "And thus the templis that were there / With holie men dist[r]oied were" (429–30). The poet makes clear that these pagan temples were destroyed not out of religious hubris but rather from fear of the threat they posed to Christian faith.[70] He goes beyond the statement in the Hybrid that these pagan palaces were demolished because they might prove a distraction by tempting pious Christians to explore such profane buildings (*edificia profana*) instead of devoutly visiting churches.[71] He even goes beyond Harley 2321, which adds the claim that Sylvester eradicated the temples so that pilgrims would be spared the sight of such ancient buildings (*edificia antiqua*) and of the vanities of the pagan gods (*deorum vana*), statements implying that paganism had become outdated and foolish. Instead, the *Metrical* poet insists that such marvels as the Temple of the Sun had to go not because they were distracting, frivolous, or passé, but because they continued to be all too powerfully vital:

> For the pilgrimes that come to toun
> Thai had more devocioun
> To seen the mervailis in that stage
> Than to fulfillen thaire pilgrimage.
> Therefor thoo vanitees thei did cese
> And holie churche thei made encrese. (431–36)[72]

The lesson of the English poem is that pagan material culture, which was celebrated in earlier versions of the *Mirabilia*, must be obliterated if Christianity is to flourish. According to it, these ancient marvels had the power to inspire "more devocioun" (not just distraction or interest, but devotion!) than genuine holy sites, even in pilgrims.[73] The Hybrid generally, and Harley 2321 more specifically, are worried that pagan buildings could get in the way of Christian devotion, but the Rome interpolation in the *Metrical Version* reveals a deeper anxiety that such marvels could actually supplant Christian devotion. The *Mirabilia*'s dream of re-creating ancient Roman splendor has become a nightmare.

The modern reader might well be puzzled that a poet in fifteenth-century England could express such hostility to Roman paganism, which, after all, had been suppressed for a thousand years. Several possible explanations suggest themselves. Perhaps the poet's fascination with Roman marvels, his enthusiasm for antiquarianism, unsettled him. As he neared the end of the interpolation, he might have become uneasy about his own fascination with the Roman past, causing him to react against the glamour of antiquity. Or he might have indulged himself in portraying the Capitol and the Temple of the Sun as greater pagan marvels than in his sources because he knew that later he could always put away such childish fancies. Or he might have thought that the opulence of ancient Rome was too much like the greed attributed to the papacy of his own day, with Pope Sylvester's opposition providing a bracing antidote to such corruption. Lest we too easily assume that the rejection of paganism and all its works at the end of the Rome interpolation is the unsophisticated attitude of a naive versifier, we need only recall a similar, almost hysterical attack in the final stanzas of *Troilus and Criseyde*. After a long and sympathetic exploration of the pagan culture of Troy in the poem, Chaucer (or his narrator) concludes with a ferocious denunciation of "payens corsed olde rites" and of the "rascaille" of their useless gods, which he contrasts to the love of Christ and the mercy of the Trinity.[74]

The interpolation on Rome in the *Metrical Mandeville* ends with this repudiation of the *Mirabilia* tradition's praise of ancient Rome. Instead of a celebration of the city's pagan material glories, which he provides in the early part of his text, the English poet concludes with a lengthy commendation of the contemporary Christian city (437–62). In lines that have no parallel in the Hybrid *Mirabilia* or Harley 2321, but that suggest instead the *Stacions of Rome*, the poet turns away from palaces and temples to salute the city's hundreds of parish churches and its seven principal basilicas, which he lists by name one after the other (437–49).[75] These Roman shrines offer genuine Christian salvation, in contrast to the simulated pagan heaven of the Temple of the Sun. The city is now imagined, as in the *Stacions*, as the source of "moch pardoun" (the word *pardon* is used four times in lines 450 to 460), with, once again, "the grettest indulgences" to be had at the Lateran, for "none hert mai thenke ne tonge rechase / The pardones of that holie place" (450–54).[76] At the end of the interpolation, the poet abandons Rome's pagan objects, despite their splendor and wonders, for the spiritual security of Christian ones. The triumph of the new faith that some critics find (mistakenly, in my view) in the twelfth-century *Mirabilia* is unquestionably proclaimed in the final lines of the *Metrical* interpolation on Rome.

Having left the world of the *Mirabilia urbis Romae* for that of the *Stacions of Rome*, the English poet does not linger but, pleading lack of time and space (455–60), returns to the Mandevillian text he abandoned four hundred lines before: "And therefor ferthirmore wol I wende, / And here of Rome I make an eende" (461–62). The interpolation on Rome in the *Metrical Version of Mandeville's Travels* provides the fullest survey of the city's ancient marvels in any Middle English poem, just as the *Stacions of Rome* provides the fullest survey of holy sites, relics, and pardons, but there are other, more accomplished Middle English poets (Gower, Chaucer, Langland, and Lydgate), who go beyond ruins and relics in their Roman narratives and explore wider cultural, political, and religious questions, including what was gained (and lost) when the pagan city became Christian. To these poets we now turn.

PART II

Narratives of Ancient Romans

CHAPTER 3

Civic Romans in Gower's *Confessio Amantis*

Part 2 of *Imagined Romes* turns from two anonymous Middle English poets to four better-known and more accomplished ones. Rather than survey the pagan and Christian objects of ancient Rome, as do the *Stacions of Rome* and the interpolation on Rome in the *Metrical Version of Mandeville's Travels*, John Gower, Geoffrey Chaucer, William Langland, and John Lydgate focus on people rather than places, on ancient Romans rather than on the fabric of the city. The original *Mirabilia urbis Romae*, it is true, relates a few stories about those associated with prominent monuments (almost all of whom are missing in the English *Metrical* interpolation), and the *Stacions* includes brief episodes from the lives of some early martyrs and popes and a longer account of the emperor Constantine, but the poets discussed in the following chapters are concerned with more than a few individuals. They write intricate narratives of intense human relationships and tell of love, death, faith, bravery, suffering, and salvation.

I begin with the Roman narratives in John Gower's *Confessio Amantis*. As its title announces, Gower's English masterpiece takes the form of a lover's confession. Amans is questioned about his sins against love by Genius, a priest of Venus, who then instructs him with examples from the ancient past, using stories from Troy, Greece, the Holy Land, and especially Rome. Rome is the setting for more narratives in the *Confessio* than any other single location. At least twenty separate stories take place there, far exceeding those in any other fourteenth-century English poem, though in the next century Lydgate's *Fall of Princes* has even more. Chaucer is Gower's only Ricardian rival, but the *Confessio* includes all his major Roman narratives, except the tale of Saint Cecilia, and adds a great many others, often calling special attention to the setting. An extreme case is "The Tale of Virgil's Mirror," about a marvel not unlike the images with bells that warn of rebellion in the *Mirabilia*. "Rome" is the second word in the tale (5.2031), and it is repeated nine more times over the next 165 lines (5.2044, 2047, 2051, 2065, 2068, 2080, 2083, 2107, 2196); moreover, "Romeins" appears three times (5.2199, 2208, 2214) and "Romeward" once (5.2190).[1] Similarly, although Chaucer and Gower both tell the story of Virginia, Chaucer never specifies the location, while Gower does so in the very first words, "At Rome" (7.5131), and cites the city's name three more times (7.5206, 5266, 5283). Rome in the *Confessio* is almost always the ancient pagan city. In contrast to the *Stacions of Rome*, Gower says little about its early Christian martyrs and has only a limited interest in the medieval city.

Some of the best studies of the *Confessio Amantis*, by such scholars as Russell Peck, Judith Ferster, James Simpson, and Alastair Minnis, insist on the poem's underlying political theme, though rarely do they take note of the important role played by "thilke cité chief of alle / Which men the noble Rome calle" (2.2501–2) in developing that theme.[2] Gower's concern in the *Confessio* and elsewhere is with social order and good rule, and, like Dante or John of Salisbury, he looks to ancient Rome for political examples, especially as they concern civic governance. Gower's Roman narratives in the *Confessio* tell of everything from marital love to military triumph to religious conversion, but they always return to the way the ancient city was governed or misgoverned. Unlike his Latin *Vox clamantis*, with its criticism of the fecklessness of the English nobility during the Great Rising of 1381, Gower does not comment directly on English politics in the *Confessio*, but the general political principles, institutions, and practices he finds in Rome make it a valuable mirror for England or any other country. Gower takes two general civic lessons from the ancient city: (1) leaders are strongest when they govern in harmony with the wider community, and (2) a good city is one that is able to sustain itself and its values even when a leader fails, as some inevitably will. Roman governance, as Gower imagines it in the *Confessio*, is no abstract or theoretical system but a flexible realpolitik involving all elements of society working to achieve practical civic solutions.

Winthrop Wetherbee is the only critic, to my knowledge, who has identified something like a Roman theme in the *Confessio Amantis*, though he does so tentatively, arguing that even though Gower's cultural ideals are "referable to no particular historical or religious context," they "tend to organize themselves around a particular place," and "the place is Rome." Wetherbee's interest is not in representations of city itself, however, but in the larger concept of what he calls the "Rome world" of the poem in contrast to its "Troy world," though he acknowledges the imprecision of such formulations when he says that the "'Rome world' is present mainly as a rather vaguely defined ideal." Wetherbee's most valuable insight for my study, though it remains undeveloped, is his observation that "to the extent that it [the 'Rome world'] has a consistent identity it is associated with wise government... and stable institutions."[3] Yet the only Roman tale Wetherbee discusses at length, "The Tale of the False Bachelor," takes place mostly outside the city and deals with personal rather than political issues.

Rome as Civic Paradigm: Mundus and Paulina in Book 1

Gower's Roman stories in the *Confessio* explore civic governance even when their ostensible topic is something different, as in the first such narrative in Amans's confession. Book 1 of the *Confessio* is about the sin of pride in love, and Gower begins with the subdivision hypocrisy. Genius's first illustration of hypocrisy is a lurid tale of how the Roman military leader Mundus deceives the virtuous wife Paulina so that he may have sex with her (1.761–1076).[4] The opening lines of the episode clearly identify the setting as ancient Rome, while hinting that the story will deal with more than deceit in love by introducing the ruler of the city:

> It fell be olde daies thus,
> Whil th'emperour Tiberius
> The monarchie of Rome ladde... (1.761–63)

Tiberius indeed contributes to the restoration of social order at the end of the tale, but he is not alone in doing so. The strength of Rome's governance, in Gower's telling of the story, comes from how many others, high and low, work for the city's common good.

Rome's social order in the tale is disrupted by the crimes of high military and religious officials. Duke Mundus, who is the leader of the "chivalerie / Of Rome" (1.784–85), bribes two priests of Isis to tell Paulina, the wife of a "worthy Romaein" (1.764), that because she is so "chaste and ful of feith" (1.847), the god Anubus will appear to her that night. With the approval of her husband, the pious but naive Paulina goes to the priests' temple, where

Mundus, disguised as Anubus and promising her a child that all the world will worship, has sex with her. Realizing the next day how badly she has been deceived, Paulina laments that her "wifhode is lore" (1.974). She nevertheless is trusting enough to confess all that happened to her husband, who assures her of his belief in her innocence (1.984–87). On the advice of friends, he goes with Paulina and other citizens to seek legal redress from the emperor, who responses immediately: "And [when Tiberius] knew the falshed of the vice, / He seide he wolde do justice" (1.1009–10). The result is that the two priests are condemned to death for betraying their religious order with "privé tricherie" (1.1033), and Mundus, who is judged to be less at fault because "love put reson aweie" (1.1051), is exiled from Rome.

The explicit moral drawn from the tale of Mundus and Paulina is a relatively narrow one about the dire consequences that come from hypocrisy, with a warning not to believe all that one hears (1.1060–63). The blasphemous hypocrisy of Mundus and the priests has indeed caused much pain to a couple who are too credulous, but some critics have also called attention to the political themes of the story: Elizabeth Porter calls it an example of "royal justice in action," while Russell Peck says that it "illustrates superbly" the threat of hypocrisy to common profit and "the ability of a healthy community to repair itself."[5] I agree that Gower praises the actions of both ruler and community in the tale, but, as Peck further suggests, what distinguishes Rome's governance in the story is the way in which the emperor and the community join together to deal with this civic crisis.[6]

All play a part in bringing about a resolution. Paulina and her husband have faith in each other, in their fellow Romans, and in the emperor, and they are brave enough to expose a sordid trick they might have preferred to keep secret. Allowing the personal to become public, they achieve some measure of justice for themselves and reform the city. This only happens, however, because other Romans also contribute. Gower tells us that the couple's friends come together, "in fere" (1.993), to comfort and advise them, and that they are joined by "many a worthi citezeine" in petitioning the emperor, support that Gower emphasizes with a rich rhyme on "citezeine" at 1.1006–7.[7] For his part, the emperor unhesitatingly acts to bring about justice, even though the accused are important Romans, a military leader and priests from a famous temple. This is certainly, in Porter's words, "royal justice in action," but it happens not by royal fiat or force but through the established legal procedures of the city, as Gower carefully explains. The city's "conseil" (1.1018), not the emperor, hears the case and, rejecting the excuses of the priests, convicts them "be lawe resonable / Among the wise jugges there" (1.1030–31). Rome's legal system is even shown to be refined enough to distinguish between the greater wickedness of the greedy priests and the passion of Mundus.

The integrity of the city's governance is preserved by the social acts of individual Romans (Paulina and her husband speak openly of their suffering, their fellow citizens support and advise, and the emperor responds) and by a legal system supported by the general will of the community. If Paulina and her husband will always bear scars from Mundus's crime, Gower shows how Roman civic practices help to heal their wounds and the city's: they are consoled, the guilty purged, and justice reaffirmed. This first tale of the *Confessio Amantis* sets a precedent for the rest of the volume. Without making any explicit connection to the medieval world, this tale set in a pagan city suggests that in the *Confessio*, which Gower calls "a bok for Engelondes sake" (prologue, 24), Rome's civic governance has much to teach Christian states, including his own.

Roman Governance in Book 7

The link between ancient Rome and governance is nowhere more explicit than in book 7 of the *Confessio*. At the end of book 6, Amans suddenly requests that Genius suspend the confession and instead explain what Aristotle taught Alexander the Great concerning "of al that to a king belongeth" (6.2413). The treatise that follows in the next book is not based on Aristotle directly but on medieval texts in the Aristotelian tradition, such as the *Secretum secretorum*, Giles of Rome's *De regimine principum*, and especially Brunetto Latini's *Tresor*, though the formulations, emphases, and choice and shaping of stories are Gower's own.[8] The result is a systematic discourse, whose final part, "Practique" (nearly 70 percent of book 7), is mostly given over to "Policie" (7.1679–5407)—that is, an explanation of how a king "schal sette in governance / His realme" (7.1682–83). The importance of book 7 to understanding Gower's political thought in the *Confessio* has been emphasized by many critics.[9] As Maura Nolan says, it is "the book in which [Gower] most powerfully articulates a vision of political (that is, monarchic) order."[10] What has not been sufficiently recognized is the extent to which narratives of ancient Rome contribute to that vision.[11]

The long final section on "Policie" in book 7 is dominated by Roman narratives. Ten such stories, some quite lengthy, or more than a third of the total of twenty-five, are set in the ancient city.[12] Other Roman episodes concerning governance occur elsewhere in the *Confessio*, including the tale of

Mundus and Paulina in book 1 and others in book 2, as we shall see, but they are unusually concentrated in book 7, befitting the poem's most political book. Perhaps because he is such a monarchist, Gower generally portrays the city in antiquity as ruled by a single powerful figure, usually called king or emperor (sometimes both), even when these titles do not agree with his sources or actual history.[13] At the same time, the poet is no regal absolutist. He rejects the idea that leaders should (or can) rule successfully on their own and pays particular attention to the relationship between ruler and ruled in his narratives of Rome—not only when the city's government operates as it should, but especially when it does not. Unlike his earlier *Vox clamantis*, the *Confessio* does not refer directly to the troubled reign of Richard II, though the poem's first readers knew from experience about the problems caused by a monarch whose personal failings are magnified by an inability to work harmoniously with his subjects. When Gower changed the dedicatee of the *Confessio Amantis* from Richard to Henry of Lancaster, who would become Henry IV, he may have been hoping for an English sovereign better able to realize the virtues of kingship so carefully laid out in book 7.

The five princely points or virtues of policy that, according to Genius, Aristotle told Alexander he should "kepe and holde in observance, / As for the worthi governance" of his kingdom (7.11704–10) are, in order: "Trouthe," "Largesse," "Justice," "Pité," and "Chasteté." None of these virtues is specifically Christian; they derive from the natural law that Gower and many others in the Middle Ages believed to be available to all humans, even nonbelievers, making pagan Rome an appropriate laboratory for studying their application. Only one of the five princely virtues, the first, truth, is not supported by Roman examples in the *Confessio*, but it was so fundamental to Gower's conception of proper governance that he often mentions it in association with the other four. In the following subsections, I discuss each of these four, though not in the order in which they appear in the poem, and what they tell us about Gower's idea of the ancient city as a civic model.

Justice and Roman Rulers: The Good King and the Common Good

The kingly virtue that Gower listed third, or in the very middle of his five points of policy, is justice, which deserves this central place because ensuring that the law was administered well was the chief domestic duty of an ancient or medieval ruler, as we see Tiberius doing in the tale of Mundus and Paulina. To exemplify this crucial virtue, Gower turned immediately to Rome. Three of Genius's first four narratives are about the ancient city's leaders (the other is about a leader of the later Holy Roman Empire). Gower knew that Rome had its share of bad rulers, as we shall see, but those he chose to exemplify justice all use their power for the common good rather than for self-interest.[14] The first of these is the emperor Maximin (7.2765–82), who Gower says is so dedicated to justice that when choosing someone for provincial governor, he would inquire whether the candidate's reputation suggested an inclination "to vertu or to vice" (7.2775) and then he (unlike so many political leaders then and now) would appoint the former. Maximin is something of an exception among the Roman leaders in the *Confessio* because he is shown acting in an imperial rather than a municipal role. More typical of Gower's Roman leaders is Gaius Fabricius, his second example of justice. A "Consul of Rome" responsible for the city's laws (7.2783–86), Gaius rejects a bribe of gold offered by the neighboring Sampnites "to don hem favour in the lawe" (7.2789), using the occasion to teach a civics lesson. Noting that gold is not pleasing to any of the senses ("non of all my wittes fyve / Fynt savour ne delit therinne"), he says that to covet it is foolish because one becomes truly "riche and glorious" only by rejecting material goods and thereby retaining the "liberté / To do justice and equité" (7.2800–816). Gower has Genius then explicitly praise Roman justice by comparing it with the present. Today, there "be nou fewe" such upright judges as Gaius Fabricius, he says, in contrast to the custom in "thilke times" (and implicitly also in that place, unlike contemporary England) that no one was appointed who was "noght frend to comun riht" (7.2818–21).[15]

Pity and Roman Rulers: Pompey and the Benefits of Mercy

Justice alone is not sufficient for good government, and Gower reflects traditional political (and religious) thought by showing that it must be combined with mercy, which he calls pity, the fourth virtue needed by a king. Once again, Genius looks to ancient Rome and the explicit testimony of four of its rulers to illustrate this virtue. He begins with the words of Constantine, who says that not until an emperor becomes the servant of pity is "he is worthi to ben a lord" (7.3137–41), and this is followed by Trajan's refusal to treat his people with harsh justice, because it is better "With love here hertes to him drawe, / Than with the drede of eny lawe" (7.3148–56). A thousand lines later, near the end of the discussion of pity, Emperor Antonius is the third Roman to explicitly recommend pity, declaring that he would rather save one of his subjects than slay a thousand enemies, a sentiment he learned from a fellow Roman, Scipio, a "consul of Rome" (7.4181–88). Genius concludes by stressing the need for a ruler to combine pity with the virtue he discusses next: "Pité is the foundement / Of every kinges regiment, / If it be medled with justice"; only together do they "make a kinges regne stable" (7.4196–202).

Gower includes a narrative earlier in the section on pity about one of Rome's most famous generals, Pompey the Great, to demonstrate that this virtue can be effective governmental policy as well as morally good. After conquering the king of Armenia, Pompey brings him back to Rome and puts him in prison (7.3215–26). When he sees that his captive endures his adversity with "humilité" and "pacience," Pompey feels "pité with conscience" and restores his captive to his throne, saying, "it was a more goodly thing / To make than undon a king," leading to a peace agreement between the former adversaries (7.3227–41). Genius then draws the political lesson that rulers have practical reasons to practice such pity, because God has overthrown many a tyrant who lacked it, while upholding kingdoms "wher Pité the regne ladde" (7.3254–59).

Largesse and Roman Rulers: Caesar's Prudence Versus the Excesses of Flattery

The central governmental virtues of justice and pity in the discourse on policy are bookended by two other virtues that are also heavily supported with Roman examples: largesse, the second virtue in the list, and chastity, the fifth. Gower's argument for largesse, as for pity, is that it protects a ruler from the worst vices of power (largesse guards against avarice and covetousness, as pity does against cruelty and tyranny), while promoting the general good (see 7.1985–2024). Most of Genius's stories about largesse are Roman, and the first and penultimate ones feature the leader Gower most admires in the *Confessio*, Julius Caesar.[16] Earlier, in the prologue to the *Confessio*, Gower praises Caesar for healing the political divisions between realms after the death of Alexander and for achieving "of al this world the monarchie" (prologue, 714–24). Now, in the section on largesse, Caesar reveals himself to be equally skillful in dealing with civic affairs. The "Tale of Julius and the Poor Knight" (7.2061–114) says that Caesar is in court one day when a "worthi povere kniht" comes to Rome "to poursuie his riht" (7.2061–62). Seeing his former commander, the knight appeals to him as ruler of the city: "O Julius, lord of the lawe," he pleads, "do thin office / After the lawes of justice" and support "the truthe of mi matiere" (7.2075–80). Although Caesar provides an advocate, the knight continues to reprove him as "unkinde" and lacking in gratitude: though the knight had once suffered wounds for Caesar fighting in Africa, as "thou wost," Caesar now refuses to reciprocate by expending either his own speech or money (7.2086–99). Recognizing the truth of the complaint, Caesar takes over the legal case himself and gives the knight enough money to support himself for life, showing largesse to one who is both deserving and needy (7.2107–10). Gower concludes with an additional point. Like the other kingly virtues, largesse must be practiced prudently. Caesar is generous, but not reckless: "He gaf him good ynouh to spende / Forevere into his lives ende" (7.2105–6). The knight is granted a sufficient annuity but not a windfall, an example of Caesar's practicing the "discrecion" that "it sit wel every king to have" (7.2115–16).[17]

Caesar's good judgment is further shown in a penultimate, more comic narrative on largesse (the final one is biblical). One day, Caesar is sitting on "his real throne" when a man comes up and first worships him as a god before sitting next to him as an equal (7.2449–90). The man boasts of his cleverness: if Caesar is indeed a god, he has been properly pious, but if Caesar is only a man, he is right to have treated him with more familiarity. But Caesar turns the tables by replying that the man is a fool to sit next to one who may be a god and to worship one who may be only human. The Romans are so impressed that from then on they hesitate to say anything that is not "trouthe and reson" to so wise a ruler (7.2486).

Although there are positive examples of largesse in book 7, as in Caesar's generosity to the knight, Gower's primary emphasis is negative, dwelling on the lack of truth and reason produced by the excesses of flattery, which "many a worthi king deceiveth" (7.2169).[18] Such inflated, insincere use of language would have especially disturbed a moral poet like Gower, and after Genius tells two other ancient stories about flattery and deplores its prevalence in contemporary royal courts, he offers ancient Rome as a superior alternative model. Long ago, he says, when "Rome was the worldes chief," its citizens cherished the "sothseiere" because he would "noght the trouthe spare" but instead spoke to the emperor in "wordes pleine and bare" (7.2346–54).

Genius declares that his discourse on policy in book 7 will instruct Amans about the virtues that belong to a king, but the Roman narratives in this section do more than extol exceptional individual leaders like Caesar. They also detail the ways in which the city as a whole protected itself from rulers who might be susceptible to flattery. Rome's civic strategies to counteract human imperfection are one of the principal reasons that it is the chief exemplar of governance in the *Confessio*. A striking example of such strategies is found in Gower's extended description of a Roman triumph, which occurs in the middle of the discourse on largesse (7.2355–411), an episode that concludes not with flattery of the triumphant hero but with a sobering call to duty.[19] While describing the conqueror as he parades in his chariot through the city "in al his glorie," Gower calls the reader's special attention to the Roman custom of placing "a ribald" next to the victor to warn him: "For al this pompe and al this pride / Let no justice gon aside, / But know thiself, what so befalle" (7.2383–89), a reminder to the hero of his humanity and of his responsibilities to the city.[20] Gower reinforces this message by describing two related civic customs in Rome. On the day of a triumph, the ribald was not the only one licensed to speak "pleinly as the trouthe stod" (7.2402): the whole Roman community was free to address the hero openly, even critically, like the soothsayer already noted, so that "whil he stod in that noblesse, / He scholde his vanité represse" (7.2409–10). The following "Tale of the Emperor and the Masons" (7.2412–31) further stresses the value ancient Rome placed on speaking truth to power. In this story, on the very day when a new emperor is installed in power, while he is feasting and hearing what "most was plesant to his ere," workmen arrive to enquire where he wishes to be buried and what decoration he wants on his tomb. Although Charles Runacres says that this story "does no more than reiterate the message" that all men must die, the context shows it to be another instance of many in the poem that reinforce Rome's lessons on good government.[21] Wisely recognizing the temptations that might befall any human faced with such power, the ancient city, according to Gower, had procedures in place to forestall or at least mitigate such hubris.

Chastity and Roman Rulers: The Corruption of Civic Power

Chastity, the last of the five points of princely policy in book 7, seems a virtue to be practiced (or flouted) more by a lover like Amans than by a political ruler, but Gower discusses it in the section on policy to demonstrate that one who cannot govern himself should not govern others. Once again, Rome is prominent, and the well-known stories of Lucretia and Virginia, both of which are also retold by Chaucer and Lydgate, take up well more than half of the lines devoted to this virtue.[22] But personal chastity, or rather its abuse, is not Gower's primary interest here. In addition to depicting the terrible suffering of his two female victims, these stories explore a variety of civic issues: the misuse of political power, the danger that even civic virtues may become destructive, and, as we see elsewhere in the *Confessio*, the communal response of the city to governmental breakdown.

Roman leaders' lack of chastity in the narratives of Lucretia and Virginia are especially shocking because just two books earlier, Genius, in his somewhat curious praise of virginity (he is, after all, a priest of Venus), notes the respect for such sexual purity among Roman officials (5.6359–417), beginning with the claim that emperors were required to give way on the streets of Rome to virgins of either sex, and ending with mention of Emperor Valentinian, who, when praised for his military conquests, replied that they were easier than conquering his own flesh and remaining a virgin.[23] The stories involving Lucretia and Virginia, by contrast, describe Roman leaders who are as wanton as they are tyrannical. The first narrative is a long double episode of the parallel crimes, one military and the other sexual, committed by Rome's royal family, the Tarquins: the deceitful conquest of a neighboring city and the rape of a noble wife (7.4593–5123).[24] In the first of these stories, Aruns, son of King Tarquin, after pretending to have been exiled by his father, is taken in by the neighboring Gabines, who make him their ruler, a generosity Aruns repays by beheading their leaders and opening the city to a waiting Roman army led by his father, which "tok and slowh the citezeins / Withoute reson or pité" (7.4698–99).[25] The same deceit, violence, and cruelty occur within Rome itself in the second story, in which Aruns brutally violates Lucretia after she has welcomed him into her house as a friend of her husband's.[26]

Gower describes the Tarquins' crimes as social and political. The father is introduced as a "proude tirannyssh Romein" who as king "wroghte many a wrongful thing," while Aruns is said to be "lich to his fader of maneres," and both are accused of "tresoun," "tirannie," a lack of "justice," and failing their duties according to "the reule of governance" (7.4594–605).[27] Gower shows that Aruns violates all five of the points of policy necessary for a good king.[28] He mocks justice and perverts truth in lying to both the Gabines and Lucretia (7.4647–49, 7.4929, and 7.4935–36), and he lacks largesse, not to say common decency, in betraying the hospitality both show him, just as he has no pity for any of his victims (cf. 7.4643 vs. 7.4699). Finally, of course, he corrupts his own chastity and Lucretia's at the point of a sword (7.4965; cf. 7.4980) because of the "blinde maladie" of his lust (7.4855).

In the penultimate narrative on chastity (as with largesse, the last is biblical), Gower tells another well-known story of a sexually corrupt Roman leader who abuses his civic power. Apius, whom Gower calls "governour of the cité" (7.5133) rather than a judge, as in other versions, is, like Aruns, lacking in chastity and he, too, is inflamed by the "blinde lustes of his wille" (7.5147), in this case for the "gentil maide" Virginia (7.5135). This false governor concocts a plan whereby his brother will get legal control of the innocent young woman while her father, Virginius, is away at battle. Apius persists even after Virginia's friends protest that what he is doing is against the "comun lawe" and that it is especially outrageous because her father is fighting on behalf of Rome's "comun riht" and the "profit of hem alle" (7.5185–96). The contrast between Apius's sexual self-interest and the general good of Rome is stark. In order to gratify his lust, Apius is willing to pervert the civic duty for which he is himself responsible—the honest administration of the law of the city. Seeking to corrupt Virginia, he corrupts Rome itself.

Chastity and Civic Virtue as Vice

The condemnation that Gower heaps on the civic vices of the Tarquins and Apius is also present in classical versions of their stories. The English poet is more original, however, in challenging any assumption that civic virtues are automatically commendable. In his political poem "Easter, 1916," Yeats says that the hearts of those "with one purpose alone," however high-minded, may eventually "seem / Enchanted to a stone." Gower likewise suggests that those who go too far in pursuing a single civic virtue, however admirable that virtue may be and however much is sacrificed for it, can become something inhuman. Although chastity is a noble Roman virtue, as seen in the opening tale of Mundus and Paulina and in Genius's praise of virginity, it may exact too high a price—as Gower shows in the case of Lucretia. Unlike Paulina, Lucretia is unable or unwilling to be reassured by her husband and friends and refuses to let herself be reintegrated into society or to seek legal redress (with some justification, because the ruler here is not her defender but her abuser). Instead, with zealous righteousness, Lucretia quickly kills herself so that "nevere afterward the world ne schal / Reproeven hire" (7.5063–64). Her reputation for chastity is preserved and her death results in a new, improved government for Rome, but the toll is heavy on herself, her father, her husband, and her children. Given the viciousness of Tarquin and his son, it is hard to fault Lucretia for her desperate act, but her solitary suicide hardly accords with Gower's praise of collective civic behavior elsewhere.

The tragedy of Lucretia is replayed in an even more grisly way in the tale of Virginia, which immediately follows, and here the negative lesson is explicit. Virginius saves his daughter from certain sexual violation by Apius and thus puts in motion the process that ends the leader's tyranny over the city. Yet, for all that, one more good Roman woman is dead by the sword, killed this time by her own progenitor. Moreover, Virginia, unlike Lucretia, dies at the hand of another and without her consent. Gower leads the reader to wonder whether Virginius could not have found a less peremptory solution, portraying the slaughter of his daughter as both rash and savage:

> Riht as a leon in his rage,
> Which of no drede set acompte
> And not what pité scholde amounte,
> A naked swerd he pulleth oute,
> The which amonges al the route
> He threste thurgh his dowhter side. (7.5240–45)

The language Gower chooses is especially shocking because it associates Virginia's father with Lucretia's rapist. Both wield naked swords against a helpless woman, and the simile comparing Virginius to "a leon in his rage" echoes the earlier image of Aruns pursuing Lucretia like a "tigre . . . / In hope for to cacche his preie" (7.4944–45).

More damning still is the speech Gower gives Virginius after he has cut down his daughter, in which he expresses as much concern for his own self-image as for her life, proclaiming that he would rather be the "fader of a maide, / Thogh sche be ded" than that "men saide" that "in hir lif sche were schamed / *And I therof were evele named*" (7.5249–52, emphasis added).[29] Gower's description of Virginius taking his "swerd droppende of [Virginia's] blod" (7.5263) back to the army to ask for aid in seeking revenge mimics Brutus's pulling the "blodi swerd" (7.5085) from Lucretia's body and stirring up outrage against the Tarquins, but with a significant difference. Before Lucretia's suicide, Brutus, along with her father and husband, attempted to console her, insisting that her innocent life was more important than her violated body, whereas the only violation of Virginia is carried out by a father who prefers her death to her (and his) dishonor. In defending chastity and pursuing justice, Virginius exhibits two of the five points of policy that Gower argues are needed for a leader to govern the state. The virtue that Virginius most conspicuously lacks, however, is pity, for in his bestial rage he has forgotten "what pité scholde amounte." Despite his admiration for Rome's governance, Gower recognizes that the city's sterner virtues, like justice and chastity, if unalloyed and taken to extremes, can lead to tragedy. His stories of ancient Rome suggest that civic life succeeds best when it is in the hands of a wise leader working with the advice and consent of his people to achieve practical ends. Like Bertolt Brecht, the English poet seems to pity the land that requires heroes, at least heroes like Lucretia and

Virginius, for their fierce dedication to their own virtue brings about both personal and civic misery.

Chastity and Roman Civic Self-Correction

Gower's general view of ancient Roman governance is far from negative, however, even in these grisly stories of violated chastity. For all its faults, the city as imagined in the *Confessio* is strong enough to overcome the abuses of leaders like the Tarquins and Apius and find solutions to civic disruption that are more effective than the anguished responses of Lucretia and Virginius. Gower is well aware that ancient Rome was sometimes led by vicious rulers, among them the emperor Caligula, who "berefte the virginité" of his three sisters before exiling them (8.199–207), and the monstrous Nero, whose social rather than sexual crimes are emphasized in the *Confessio* (6.1151–227), in particular, the self-indulgent cruelty with which he gives a feast for three men simply to satisfy his curiosity about which after-dinner activity (riding, walking, or resting) best aids human digestion, which he discovers by dissecting each guest (the answer turns out to be walking). Yet despite the ineptness, corruption, and in some cases pure evil of Rome's worst leaders, Gower again and again reminds the reader of the resilience of its civic culture. In this sense, Gower's Rome exemplifies some of the late medieval political ideas that Paul Strohm and David Wallace see as influencing the art of Chaucer's *Canterbury Tales*. In his influential *Social Chaucer*, Strohm argues that the *Canterbury Tales* form "a mixed commonwealth of style" that challenges existing hierarchies with its variety of different voices and viewpoints; similarly, Wallace in his *Chaucerian Polity* shows the importance in the *Tales* of associational social groupings, such as monasteries or parish and guild fraternities, which resist the domination of secular and ecclesiastical rulers at their most absolutist.[30] Gower honors such horizontal governance in the *Confessio* and describes it as standard practice in ancient Rome. Although he regularly presents the city as a monarchy and advocates the benefits of a good, strong king, the ultimate health of civic Rome, as he depicts it, depends on the vigilance of its citizens.

Such communal self-correction results in positive political resolutions to the two harrowing Roman stories we have been discussing. When the raped Lucretia commits suicide in front of her family, her cousin Brutus pulls the sword from her dying body and vows "vengance" (7.5085–87). Despite this apparent call to arms, what Brutus actually instigates is a more peaceful and communal effort to put Rome right, a series of civic actions undertaken by the city as a whole to which Gower gives much more attention than does his source, Ovid's *Fasti*.[31] The *Confessio* describes how Brutus displayed Lucretia's dead body in "the marketplace / Of Rome," presumably the Forum, a specific location not mentioned by Ovid, and, after the assembled city is told what has happened, the poem stresses the unity of public response: "every mannes herte is trembled / Whan thei the sothe herde of the cas" (7.5101–5). Ovid reports only that the Tarquins were then banished, but Gower adds a careful account of the civic process that brings this about. First, the entire populace is canvassed: "the conseil was / Take of the grete and of the smale" (7.5106–7); next, "the comun clamour" of the city rehearses the past crimes of the Tarquins (7.5109–16); and, finally, a consensus is reached about what to do: "al the toun began to crie" as with one voice, "Awey, awey the tirannie / Of lecherie and covoitise!" (7.5117–19). Only after these extended communal consultations among the citizens of Rome do "thei exile" the Tarquins and "taken betre governance" (7.5120–23).[32]

Similar civic action to cure a Rome that has been compromised by its leader is detailed at the end of the *Confessio*'s tale of Virginia. Having been forced (as he sees it) to kill his daughter to save her from ravishment, Virginius initiates a more general and considered response to Apius's crime by persuading his troops in the field to first right wrongs at home before fighting a foreign enemy (7.5269–72). This is the first step in the communal healing that Gower carefully describes in the *Confessio* but makes no mention of in his Latin marginal summary of the story.[33] Swearing that "thei wol stonde be the riht," the soldiers return to Rome, where they publicly discuss the "tirannye" of Apius and "every man seith what he couthe," with the result that the wicked leader's "privé tricherie" is revealed "openly to mannes ere," prompting the "comun feere" that Apius may commit further outrages (7.5280–92). To prevent this, however, the citizens agree, "thurgh comun conseil of hem alle," to depose this "wrongfull king" and punish those who aided him "be lawe" as a warning to those that "scholden afterward governe" the city to avoid the "lust of vice and vertu suie" (7.5293–306).

In book 7 of the *Confessio Amantis*, and especially in the account of chastity, we see Roman rulers betraying the public trust and civic virtues becoming vices, but even so the ancient city remains Gower's primary example of good governance. As a human institution, civic Rome has its failures and excesses, but, as the poet shows, it is successful in good times and resilient in bad. Ideally, ruler and community work together to solve their problems, as in the tale of Mundus and Paulina. If the ruler is corrupt, however, Gower depicts the Roman citizenry as capable of reasserting the city's values and replacing its failed leadership, as they do after the deaths of Lucretia and Virginia. The genius of civic Rome in the *Confessio* is its ability to integrate vertical and horizontal sources of power. Gower praises the wise, strong leadership of a Julius Caesar but also the established civic customs of the city, such as the ribald of the triumph who challenges the victor's vanity and reminds him of his humanity. If a Roman ruler becomes tyrannical and threatens the governmental order of the city, as the Tarquins and Apius do, Gower shows a community confident enough to redress abuses and preserve the integrity of the city.

Christianity and Roman Governance

Gower's positive view of ancient Rome's governance is not affected by the city's paganism, because, unlike the Rome interpolation in the *Metrical Version of Mandeville's Travels*, the poet does not regard pagans as potentially devilish or unworthy of imitation in secular matters. If anything, Gower suggests that the civic, if not religious, arrangements of pagan Rome were superior to those of the Christian city that replaced it, especially because of the potential abuses of unchecked papal power. Pagan and Christian governance are contrasted in Gower's narrative of Emperor Constantine the Great, which concludes book 2 of the *Confessio*, and in two other tales set in Christian Rome from the same book that portray good and bad Christian rule in the city.

Constantine was the first Christian emperor of Rome, but Gower, surprisingly, portrays him as a wiser and more benevolent ruler before his conversion than after. While still a pagan, Constantine displays exemplary pity, whereas as a Christian, his misguided bestowal of temporal power on the church corrupts it by allowing the pope to become an absolute ruler. Gower's Constantine is a different and more complex figure than the emperor described at length in the *Stacions of Rome*. The Constantine of the *Stacions* is the beneficiary of the bountiful divine mercy that the poem associates with Rome. First seen as a pagan unbeliever suffering from leprosy (probably meant to suggest his sins), Constantine in the *Stacions* obtains God's grace not because of his own merits but only because of the intervention of Pope Sylvester, who heals the emperor in mind and body, in response to which Constantine builds Christian churches and donates one of his palaces, the Lateran, so that it might become a place that offers others the unmerited pardon from sin that saved him.

In contrast to this Constantine in the *Stacions*, the emperor in Gower's tale of Constantine and Sylvester is saved not gratuitously but as a reward for his own pagan virtue (2.3187–496). Before his conversion, Gower portrays Constantine as the worthiest of ancient Romans (whose leprosy seems the result of bad luck, "infortunes," rather than any fault of his own [2.3190]), and he is certainly the most selfless. The *Confessio* includes a scene from hagiography not found in the *Stacions* in which Constantine consults learned men who tell him that the only cure for his leprosy is to bathe "in childes blod" (2.3206).[34] Infants are gathered to be slaughtered for this purpose, but faced with their crying and the grief of their mothers, Constantine chooses to put his people before himself, and in a long philosophical soliloquy, often admired by critics and greatly developed from the poet's source (2.3243–73), he declares that Providence has created all men alike so that no rank is morally superior to another: "The povere child is bore als able / To vertu as the kinges sone" (2.3258–59).[35] These are the words of a righteous pagan with the capacity, generally recognized in the Middle Ages, to understand the natural law of good and evil without the aid of Christian revelation.[36] The pity that Constantine displays toward the threatened mothers and children is also the virtue that Gower attributes to him in a later poem, "In Praise of Peace."[37] In the *Confessio*, the emperor chooses "his oghne bodi for to lese" rather than see "so gret a moerdre wroght / Upon the blod which gulteth noght" (2.3290–94). He further declares that pity is not just an ethical ideal but a necessary requirement for good rulers: "Who that woll maister be, / He mot be servant to pité" (2.3299–300)—almost exactly the words attributed to Constantine in the section on pity as a princely virtue, at 7.3138–41, as previously noted.

Gower's Constantine behaves like an ideal Christian even when he is still a "hethen emperour" (2.3435). Sparing mothers and children makes him the antitype of Herod, who massacred the innocents to preserve his own power, and instead a type of Christ, who sacrificed his life to save others. In addition to being a man of pity, the *Confessio*'s pagan Constantine also practices three of the other four points of policy that Genius in book 7 says are required of a good ruler: truth (he knows his true place in the universe and is loyal to the most vulnerable), justice (he does the right thing despite the peril to his health), and largesse (how could anyone be more generous?). Chastity is the only point of policy not explicitly mentioned one way or the other in connection with Constantine. Leprosy was often seen as punishment for lechery or other sins in the Middle Ages, but that does not seem to be the case here.[38] Gower's Constantine is a model ruler, one who is instinctively just and piteous and has the magnanimity of a good king. As a reward for his outstanding virtues (in contrast to the automatic pardons of the *Stacions*), Constantine is granted a vision of the patron saints of Rome, Peter and Paul, who declare that his behavior has earned him a heavenly reward from God: "for thou hast served / Pité, thou has pité deserved," and therefore "God thurgh pité woll thee save" (2.3339–42), with the result that he is simultaneously healed and converted.[39] The vision granted to the pagan emperor Constantine suggests the vision granted to the pagan emperor Octavian in the Latin *Mirabilia*, but Octavian is permitted only a glimpse of the true God to come, whereas Constantine gets to become a Christian.

The tale of Constantine and Sylvester ends happily for the emperor, but, in contrast to his story in the *Stacions*, not for the church. After he is instructed in the faith, baptized by Pope Sylvester, and cleansed in "the bodi and the soule also" (2.3464), Gower's Constantine shows his gratitude by constructing two great churches "for Peter and for Poules sake" (2.3478). But then, in a further, fatal act of generosity, he goes beyond largesse to prodigality by giving the pope temporal power, "possessioun / Of lordschipe and of worldes good" (2.3480–81). Although Gower insists that the emperor's "will was good" (2.3482), such ill-judged selflessness is ruinous, as the poet immediately confirms by introducing a voice from on high "of which al Rome was adrad," which declares:

> "Today is venym schad
> In holi cherche of temporal,
> Which medleth with the spirital." (2.3489–92)[40]

The so-called Donation of Constantine, as Gower says in the prologue to the *Confessio*, though an act of "pure almesse" on the emperor's part (prologue, 742), is poisonous because it unites temporal and spiritual authority, abolishing the previous balance of horizontal and vertical power in Rome, which, as we have seen, served the pagan city so well, according to the *Confessio*. After Constantine's gift, the pope becomes the supreme political ruler of Rome, unchecked by any of the city's traditional political customs or the participation of the wider community.

The possible consequences of Constantine's ill-considered gift are seen in two tales about Christian Rome, one set in the ancient and the other, unusually, in the medieval city, that occur earlier in book 2 and are explicitly linked to the tale of Constantine and Sylvester: one portrays the pope and emperor in their proper roles, as Gower thought they should be, and the other shows the folly of unlimited papal rule. The first is the tale of Constance, in which Constance's father, a Christian emperor in late antiquity, arranges for her to marry the Muslim sultan, which causes her much hardship until she finally returns to Rome, where her son becomes emperor himself (2.587–1598). This long story, which is linked to Constantine's by the similar name of its heroine and by Gower's referring to her father as "Tiberie Constantin" (2.590), is discussed at greater length with Chaucer's version in the next chapter, but its significance here lies in what it says about the relationship between church and state.[41] Introduced as "a worthi kniht in Cristes lawe" (2.587), the father of Constance in the *Confessio*, unlike his counterpart in Chaucer's *Man of Law's Tale*, is never blamed for sending his daughter away from Rome but is instead shown to be a good ruler in addition to a good father.[42] In a division of responsibility that Gower thought was right and proper, the emperor is the political leader of the city and the pope its spiritual head, though they work together to advance Constance's marriage and the conversion of the sultan (2.634–39).[43] In addition to the separation of powers between church and state, the emperor's role in Gower's tale seems to be subject to civic control. When Constance's son becomes emperor, his authority is confirmed by "a parlement" (2.1549).

In contrast, a second, shorter narrative set much later historically in Christian Rome, the tale of Boniface VIII (2.2803–3040), which occurs just before the tale of Constantine and Sylvester, details the worst fears of papal tyranny announced by the voice from on high at the Donation of Constantine.[44] The opening words identify the setting as "At Rome" (2.2803), though this is, of course, the medieval city, less than a century before Gower composed the *Confessio*, a rare example of a "modern" story in the poem. When first seen, the papacy appears to be uncorrupted by its temporal power, for the reigning pontiff is a modest, "holy clerk reclus," who "full was of gostli vertus" (2.2817–18). Such innocence is no match, however, for the ambitious Boniface VIII, the supplanter of this good pope and one whose damnation Dante anticipated so gleefully in canto 19 of the *Inferno*. Gower shows that Boniface's lust for power equals that of the worst rulers of pagan Rome. Employing a "wonder wyle" (2.2847) and words that are "slyhe and queinte" (2.2853), he achieves the papal throne by means of a nasty "jape" (2.2933). Foreshadowing the true heavenly voice that bewails the Donation described in the following tale and recalling the feigned divinity of Mundus in the first Roman story of the *Confessio*, Boniface rigs up a speaking trumpet in the elderly pope's chamber to persuade him that God wants him to renounce his office, which he does. Boniface's papacy, achieved so corruptly, is marked, according to Gower, by "Envie, which is loveles, / And Pride, which is laweles"

(2.2961–62). Finally, his "misgovernance" (2.2965) causes a quarrel with France, whose troops remove him (2.2992–3032). This allows Gower to call attention to another negative result of the Donation: abuses in the Christian papal city are now corrected by outsiders rather than by the Roman people themselves, as in pagan times.

The fraud, vaulting ambition, and chaos associated with Boniface did not die with him. The prologue to the *Confessio* rails against the propensity of the present-day church, whether based in the city or elsewhere (as it was for most of the fourteenth century), to engage in simony (prologue, 204, 241ff.), war (212–16, 242, 252ff.), covetousness (263), and avarice (315), all stemming from the pollution of the spiritual by the temporal (846–64). The communal values and practices that Gower associates with the governance of ancient pagan Rome, which allowed the city to repair its faults, are lacking in Christian Rome. This is not a problem when the city is ruled by a good emperor like Tiberius Constantine or by a good pope like Boniface's predecessor, but Gower demonstrates the helplessness of Christian Rome before the rule of a wicked pope, for the grant of absolute power to the papacy precludes the intervention of an engaged civic community, as happened in antiquity. Medieval Christian Rome possesses the true religious faith that its pagan ancestor lacked, but the ancient city provided better answers to the questions of governance that feature so centrally in the *Confessio*. The Rome imagined in Gower's poem is a crucial element in this deeply political work, being its principal model of civic responsibility and cooperation. The English poet uses the ancient city to inform and, he must have hoped, to reform his countrymen, from the king to the commons. The ancient Rome that Gower imagines in the *Confessio* is not a substitute for the lost golden age he extols in the poem's prologue, but it does offer a workable system of human governance.

CHAPTER 4

Heroic (Women) Romans in Chaucer's *Canterbury Tales* and the *Legend of Good Women*

All but one of Geoffrey Chaucer's principal narratives of ancient Rome also appear in Gower's *Confessio Amantis*, yet the cities imagined by these two literary friends and rivals could not be more different. Gower's Rome is a model of resilient, communal governance, whereas Chaucer's city is a place of unrelenting oppression. The *Confessio* contains many examples of broad-based civic action by high- and low-ranking Romans, women as well as men, whereas Roman power in Chaucer's poems is vertical and gendered, with dominant men repeatedly using state authority to victimize women. Instead of finding political lessons in ancient Rome, Chaucer in the *Canterbury Tales* and the *Legend of Good Women* describes the heroic suffering of its noble women. Ancient Rome is thus feminized, in the sense that the poet depicts the city's pagan and Christian women as the most important and admirable figures in these narratives.[1] Chaucer's Roman women never achieve political power in the ancient city (indeed, they rarely survive for long within it), but their perspective is the one from which events are seen, and it is they whose inner lives are most honored.[2] In contrast to these good women, Chaucer's male leaders are wickedly malicious when not simply ineffectual. Perhaps the most accomplished of Chaucer's Roman men is Gower's favorite, Julius Caesar, but, despite his many conquests, even he is represented ultimately as a failure because of his ignominious assassination. In the relative absence of positive male exemplars, it is the women of Chaucer's Roman tales who embody the city's traditional values. Armed with little more than their unshakeable virtue, they demonstrate the bravery and moral fortitude that classical and medieval authors often attributed to illustrious Roman men. Although Chaucer's women, pagan and Christian alike, practice Roman virtues, they do not do so on behalf of Rome or to shore up its political order—far from it. They are victims rather than supporters of the city, and what they seek is freedom from it and its male oppressors, even to the extent of welcoming the release of death.

Chaucer's Roman Tales

Critics have often recognized Troy and other classical cities as important topics in Chaucer's poetry, while all but ignoring the theme of ancient Rome. There are certainly reasons why Chaucer's Roman stories have been so little analyzed (or even recognized) as a coherent group: some, like the *Physician's Tale*, are among his most puzzling, and all but one, the *Man of Law's Tale*, are quite short, in contrast to the lengthy *Knight's Tale* set in Athens and Thebes and the even longer Trojan *Troilus and Criseyde*. Of the few critical essays that discuss Chaucer's use of Rome, each considers only a couple of tales, even though four narratives and two briefer sketches take place in the city.[3] All six works appear in either the *Legend of Good Women* or the *Canterbury Tales*, suggesting that Rome became important to the poet late in his career. Chaucer's four Roman narratives occur at different moments in the city's history, though the poet himself, like Gower, seems largely indifferent to exact chronology. According to ancient Roman historians, the story of Lucretia's rape in the *Legend of Good Women* is the earliest, set in the last days of the city's monarchy, whereas the next in time is the republican *Physician's Tale*, which tells of the murder of the maiden Virginia by her own father. The third, the *Second Nun's Tale* of Saint Cecilia (the only one of Chaucer's major Roman tales not also in the *Confessio Amantis*), occurs during the imperial persecution of Christians, and the last and longest of these narratives, the *Man of Law's Tale*, which is about the exile and trials of the emperor's daughter, Constance, takes place in late antiquity, after Rome became Christian. Two biographical sketches, of Julius Caesar and Nero, appear among the brief historical tragedies of the *Monk's Tale*.

Perhaps critics have overlooked the theme of Rome in Chaucer's works because the physical descriptions of the city are not as vivid as those of his other ancient sites, especially Troy in *Troilus and Criseyde* and Athens in the

Knight's Tale, which Lee Patterson calls "Chaucer's two major essays in classical historiography."[4] There are no Roman public spectacles to equal the elaborate Athenian tournament held to decide who will marry Emelye in the Knight's Tale or the original Trojan parliament scene in book 4 of Troilus and Criseyde, during which the exchange of Criseyde is agreed upon.[5] The Physician's Tale does not even explicitly say that its story of Virginia occurs in Rome, though the mention of Livy would be a signal to readers that it does.[6] Unlike the detailed depiction of Theseus's amphitheater in the Knight's Tale, especially its individual temples to the gods, or the careful accounts of Troy's structures in Troilus and Criseyde, there is little description of physical places in Chaucer's Roman tales. At the beginning of the Legend of Lucrece, the heroine's husband is said to ride to Rome with other soldiers, and, at the end, her corpse is taken "thurgh al the toun" (1867), but there is no mention of a specific gate or market as in the Confessio. The Second Nun's Tale includes the most topographical information among Chaucer's Roman tales, but even that does not amount to much: a misleading claim that the "Via Apia" is three miles from the city (8.172–73), a reference to the catacombs as "seintes buryeles" (8.186), and the statement that Cecilia's house later became a church.[7] Likewise, the domestic interiors of Rome in which most of the action takes place in these narratives have none of the specificity of the rooms and gardens in the palaces of Criseyde, Pandarus, and Deiphobus in Troilus and Criseyde.[8]

Although Chaucer's Rome has been largely ignored by previous critics and is portrayed less precisely than his other ancient cities, it is exceptional in one way. Nowhere else in Middle English poetry do Roman men in power treat good women with such unrelenting nastiness. In the Confessio, Gower tells of male Romans who act badly, but they are balanced by good Roman men and a wider civic community of both sexes. But Chaucer has little interest in the virtues of Roman governance; his emphasis is instead on the suffering of the city's exemplary women. Rulers in Chaucer's other ancient states are also patriarchal, of course, but none is as thoroughly oppressive as his Romans. Theseus is the unchallenged master of Athens in the Knight's Tale and never thinks to ask Emelye whom she would like to marry, yet when the Theban widows and later Hippolyta, along with Emelye, beg his favor (admittedly on their knees), he listens attentively to their requests and changes his behavior accordingly. Although Trojan women are not equal to men in Troilus and Criseyde, they are shown to have some social and even political influence. Helen seems to be able to sway Paris and consults with Deiphobus over matters of state. Although Criseyde feels vulnerable as a single woman (and the daughter of a traitor), she nevertheless enjoys the support and friendship of the royal family and of Hector in particular, who offers his protection and attempts to keep her from being traded to the Greeks.[9] In his argument that Chaucer is critical of antiquity for its subjection of women, Robert Edwards's primary examples are Trojan and Theban, but he could have found even more pointed Roman ones.[10] Whatever the male privilege of Theseus and Troilus, they lack the unhinged cruelty toward women of Chaucer's worst Romans.

The female victims of male oppression in Chaucer's Roman tales, by contrast, are portrayed with sympathy and admiration. Whereas Gower's Roman stories are fundamentally political, Chaucer's are hagiographical in the contrasts they draw between good women and bad men. Chaucer's one genuine saint's life, the *Second Nun's Tale*, takes place in Rome, and, even more revealingly, each of his other major tales set in the city is modified to make the principal women resemble Christian martyrs, even though two of them are pagan. Chaucer also draws on secular texts to defend Rome's women and indict its male leaders, especially those by his favorite Latin poet, Ovid.[11] James Simpson calls attention to "the voice of experiential narrative" that the English poet found in his Roman predecessor: "This frequently female voice, often the victim and relic of empire, is invested, via small but immensely significant shiftings of perspective, with the power to unsettle and even undo the impersonal solidities of epic, and the assurance of accepted, masculine, imperial ideals. Ovid's poetic shapes a fundamentally skeptical viewpoint with regard to large-scale civic endeavor."[12]

Chaucer echoes Ovid's challenges to traditional male power and interest in women's perspectives even in Roman stories that are set outside the city and thus not directly part of this study. As Gavin Douglas noted in the prologue to his translation of the *Aeneid*, Chaucer shows himself "ever, God wait, wemenis frend" in his disapproval of the desertion of Dido by Aeneas, whose descendants will eventually found Rome.[13] Chaucer's first use of the episode occurs early in the *House of Fame*, with an imitation of Virgil's heroic presentation of Aeneas at the very beginning of the *Aeneid*: "I wol now synge, yif I kan, / The armes and also the man" (143–44). Soon, however, as John Fyler points out in his notes to the *Riverside Chaucer*, "Chaucer complicates Virgil's account of Dido and Aeneas by adopting Ovid's perspective (in Heroides 7), which wholeheartedly takes Dido's view of the affair."[14] By the end of the poem, the narrator's sympathy is entirely with Dido because Aeneas has "betrayed hir" (294). He describes in detail desperate appeals that her lover stay and her piteous suicide (315–74), blaming it on Aeneas's "untrouthe" (384), with no mention, as mitigation, of the gods' order that he leave Carthage to lay the foundations of Rome.[15] When the same events are retold as the *Legend of Dido* in the *Legend of Good Women*, Chaucer follows Ovid more closely and, as befits a work in praise of women, is even more compassionate toward the abandoned queen. Once again, the English poem refuses to accept the excuse in Virgil that divine command forced Aeneas to discard Dido and instead, as in Ovid, calls him a deceitful "traytour" (1328). Even before the walls of Rome are built, therefore, Dido stands as a warning of what other women can expect from the city.

Another victim of Roman male oppression occurring outside the city walls is the first woman whose story is told in the *Legend of Good Women*, Cleopatra. That the wily Egyptian queen begins the roll of good women may seem to take Ovidian sympathy too far (though Chaucer also includes a good deal of Ovidian irony), but Rome's relentless persecution of Cleopatra, whatever her faults, is a further example of what Simpson calls its "masculine, imperial ideals." Once Cleopatra is crowned in Egypt, Rome sends Marc Anthony to compel her obedience, only to have him fall under her spell. The city sees their liaison as treason and judges Marc Anthony a "rebel unto the toun of Rome" (591) because he chooses to "love and serve" a foreign woman (604). Such emotional attachment to a woman is bad enough, as the example of Dido shows, but subservience to one is fatal in Roman eyes. The city responds to this betrayal of manhood by sending a more cold-blooded commander, Octavian, supported by a host of "stoute Romeyns, crewel as lyoun" (627), a macho force that soon defeats its effeminate enemies and drives them to suicide.[16] In Chaucer's narratives that take place in the city itself, as we shall see, Roman women more virtuous than Cleopatra suffer worse fates at the hands of Roman leaders more vicious than Octavian.

Chaucer's Roman Men

Oppressors of Women

Chaucer's tales set in Rome are concerned with personal rather than political matters. The poet rarely shows his Roman leaders engaged, positively or negatively, in running the city. Even though the men in these tales hold various high offices, we see them using their power not to govern but to subject women to their will.[17] None of the stories of the Roman tales in the *Canterbury Tales* or the *Legend of Good Women* is original, and all but one are also found in the *Confessio Amantis*, but Chaucer so constructs his versions that they are consistently more hostile to the city's men than Gower's versions, and also, to varying degrees, more hostile than his sources.

A clear example of Chaucer's greater emphasis on female exploitation at the hands of powerful men can be seen in the *Legend of Lucrece*, the fifth of the female biographies in his *Legend of Good Women*.[18] The *Legend of Lucrece* is based on a long section in Ovid's *Fasti* about Rome's last royal family, which is also used by Gower in the *Confessio*, but Chaucer eliminates much of Ovid's extended account to concentrate on Lucretia's rape by the king's son, Tarquin (whom Gower calls Aruns), and its immediate aftermath. Both Ovid and Gower present the attack on this chaste wife as the last in a long series of outrages committed by the Tarquins, father and son, which finally incites the city to overthrow their monarchy. Chaucer, however, ignores the Tarquins' earlier, more public crimes, such as their deception and slaughter of the neighboring Gabines, to tell of the private violation of Lucretia, which he treats as a moral rather than a political crime. After Tarquin has ravished Lucretia, Ovid's narrator in the *Fasti* addresses him rhetorically: "Quid, victor, gaudes? Haec te victoria perdet./ Heu, quanto regnis nox stetit una tuis" (Why, victor, do you rejoice? This victory will ruin you. Alas, how much a single night will cost your regal power).[19] The narrator's longer address to Tarquin at this point in the *Legend*, however, says nothing about the serious political consequences of his act (the loss of the throne) and instead condemns the social and ethical degeneracy it reveals:

> Tarquin, that art a kynges eyr,
> And sholdest, as by lynage and by ryght,
> Don as a lord and as a verray knyght,
> Whi hastow don dispit to chivalrye?
> Whi hastow don this lady vilanye?
> Allas, of the this was a vileyns dede. (1819–24)

Chaucer disregards the threat to Tarquin's power to dwell instead on the moral disgrace that such a high-born man should so foully treat a respectable woman. Lucretia is called a "lady," but Tarquin, whose royal status should make him behave like a "verray knyght," has debased himself to the level of a churl by his attack on the helpless Lucretia. The use of both "vileyn" and "vilanye" emphasizes that Tarquin's sin is against both his rank and his humanity. In addition to disgracing his lineage by behaving like a social inferior, or *villein*, he has also, more damningly, violated basic human decency. The condemnation of him as a noble and as a man is absolute.

This scornful judgment is in keeping with the treatment of Tarquin throughout the *Legend of Lucrece*, where he is revealed to be a counterfeit knight. The initial mention of his attraction to Lucretia, because of her "beaute and hyre cheere, / Hire yelwe her, hire shap, and hire manere" (1746–47), might seem to suggest a chivalrous lover, a role appropriate for "this proude kynges sone" (1745), but events soon prove otherwise.[20] Tarquin's pride is really selfish arrogance, and the "desyr" that burns in him "so wodly that his wit was al forgeten" (1750–52) is basely carnal. Chaucer's language makes clear that Tarquin does not seek Lucretia's heart, just her body. His only concern is the crudely expressed worry that "she wolde nat ben geten," in other words, that he will be unable to possess her physically, which is reinforced by the use of forms of the rapacious word "covet" twice within two lines (1753–56). Although Ovid had referred to Tarquin's being goaded by an "unjust love" for Lucretia (*iniusti stimulis agitatus amoris*), Chaucer makes Tarquin an even greater sinner against love by showing that his desire is not only immoral, "unrightful talent," but also scornful; he thinks of her "with dispit" (1771).[21] Tarquin's contempt is seen in the vow he makes in the very next line: "For, maugre hyre, she shal my leman be" (1772). Brutally dismissive of her own wishes, he regards this good wife as just a plaything, simply a "leman," the most churlish Middle English term for a female sexual partner. Having degraded himself by vicious lust, he regards her similarly.

The rape of Lucretia is horrible in Chaucer's sources and analogues, but worse in the *Legend*. The English poet amplifies Tarquin's violence by having him violate Lucretia's marital house as well as her body.[22] In Ovid's *Fasti* and Gower's *Confessio*, Tarquin first encounters Lucretia when her husband, a fellow soldier, brings him to their home in Rome. Inflamed with desire, Tarquin later visits Lucretia on his own; he is received as an honored guest and invited to stay, which permits him access to her bedroom that night. Chaucer makes Tarquin's second visit more depraved by having him dispense with even the forms of politeness. Instead of pretending to pay a friendly call, Tarquin in the *Legend* sneaks covertly into Rome, "in the nyght ful thefly gan he stalke" (1781), breaks into Lucretia's house, and, in a further act of trespass, invades her bedroom and rapes her. In another original and chilling moment, Chaucer has the sleeping Lucretia, who has been wakened by Tarquin climbing into her bed, utter her only spoken words during the whole ordeal, which emphasize her intruder's wildness and physical bulk: "'What beste is that,' quod she, 'that weyeth thus?'" (1788). Ovid's and Gower's narrators compare Tarquin to a wolf and Lucretia to a lamb, as in the *Legend* (1798), but Lucretia's own reference to him as a beast is a Chaucerian addition.

The account of Lucretia's violation in the *Legend* ends by giving less emphasis than other versions to the civic benefit that is said to result from Tarquin's crime. Although Chaucer follows Ovid in stating briefly that the rape caused the abolition of the monarchy in Rome (1869–70), he does not, like the Latin poet, mention the republic that replaced it.[23] As a monarchist, Gower plays down the end of Roman kingship by saying only that the Romans "taken betre governance," but Chaucer is finally not all that interested in the civic life of the city. Instead, he ends the tale with an extended, nonpolitical conclusion on the difference between the sexes in love, contrasting the truth and stability of women to the unreliability of men (1874–85).

Tarquin's behavior is extreme even by the low standard of Chaucer's Roman men (he is the only actual rapist), but it fits a pattern of villainy toward women practiced by other male leaders of the city. Apius, in the *Physician's Tale*, also wants to debauch an innocent, Virginia, as he desires in both Chaucer's source, Jean de Meun's *Roman de la Rose*, and in Gower's version of the story in the *Confessio*. Once again, however, Chaucer intensifies Roman masculine iniquity. When Apius first notices Virginia going to a temple with her mother, the *Physician's Tale* contains an original speech in which he vows to possess her despite the opposition of others: "This mayde shal be myn, for any man" (6.129), and Chaucer alone characterizes Apius's lust as literally devilish, saying that "the feend into his herte ran" (6.130). Unlike Tarquin and Apius, the Roman prefect Almachius in the *Second Nun's Tale* has no apparent sexual designs on Cecilia, but he is just as eager to victimize female innocence by ordering the young holy woman to be killed for thwarting his will and that of the city's "myghty princes" (8.470). Nor does male oppression cease when Rome becomes Christian. The emperor in the *Man of Law's Tale* is neither a rapist nor an executioner of women, but he sends his own daughter into a long and dangerous exile during which she escapes a massacre and is saved from execution and rape only by God's intervention. Neither Nicholas Trevet's *Chronicles* nor Gower's *Confessio Amantis*, Chaucer's two primary sources for the *Man of Law's Tale*, criticizes the Roman emperor for arranging a marriage between Constance and the sultan of Syria to bring about his conversion to Christianity, but Chaucer's narrative voice does so in a number of original emotional responses that stress the great anguish her father's plans cause Constance, as when the narrator refers to her departure from the city as "the woful day fatal," on which she is "with sorwe al overcome" (2.260–64). In an added complaint of her own, Constance protests to her father that she, "thy wrecched child," is being sent away "unto the Barbre nacioun" without regard to the dangers she might face: "I, wrecche womman, no fors though I spille" (2.274–85).[24] Constance concludes her speech by declaring that, despite her imperial rank, she shares the oppression of all her sex at the hands of domineering men, a view supported by Chaucer's other Roman stories: "Wommen are born to thraldom and penance, / And to been under mannes governance" (2.286–87). Chaucer's emperor makes no response to his daughter's unhappiness, but years later, when she returns to the city after her many trials and finally reveals herself, she has still not forgotten what her father caused her to endure, and she implores him, "Sende me namoore unto noon hethenesse" (2.1112). The emperor in the *Man of Law's Tale* is not sexually depraved, like Tarquin or Apius, nor is he murderous, like the prefect who martyrs Saint Cecilia; nevertheless, his indifference to Constance's feelings and fate demonstrates that, in Chaucer's view, even after Rome becomes Christian, its male leaders continue to disregard the well-being of good women and make the city (and the world) a place of misery for them.

Chaucer's most sadistic persecutor of women is undoubtedly the emperor Nero, whose life is one of the brief historical biographies in the *Monk's Tale* (7.2463–550). Nero was a major exemplar of general Roman depravity for classical and medieval writers, but Chaucer, in contrast to Gower, stresses his crimes against women. Whereas the *Confessio*, as we saw in the previous chapter, tells of Nero's killing three men merely to learn about their digestion, the *Monk's Tale* records trespasses against his two closest female relatives: sexual intercourse with his sister and, told in some detail, the cutting open of his mother's womb just to see where he had been conceived—after which, her dead body elicits no tears from her son but only the cool comment "A fair womman was she" and a request for wine (7.2489–92). The narrator's judgment of Nero applies to Chaucer's other Roman leaders: "Whan myght is joyned unto crueltee, / Allas, to depe wol the venym wade" (7.2493–94).

Julius Caesar, who also appears in the *Monk's Tale* and is so admired by Gower, is the only Roman ruler whom Chaucer does not accuse of oppressing women (7.2671–726), perhaps because he is presented as in some ways like a woman. True, Chaucer's Monk praises Caesar for his "wisedom" and "manhede" and for rising from humble origins to "roial magestee" (7.2671–73), but this glory ends in tragedy, as Caesar, in common with so many of the city's good women, becomes the victim of male power when he is stabbed to death by a "conspiracye" of senatorial enemies (7.2699). Although Chaucer insists that Caesar dies in a "manly" way, he explains at some length in this short narrative how the ruler's "honestee" caused him to arrange his clothing to preserve the modesty of his body even as he collapsed because of his deadly wounds (7.2711–18), which is precisely what Lucretia does during her suicide in the *Legend* (1856–60).

Ineffectual Men

It should be acknowledged that some other Roman men in Chaucer's tales are not active oppressors of women and even make efforts to help them. These are almost always secondary characters, however, and despite their best efforts, they achieve little in the way of relieving female suffering. Although not villains, they are ineffective.[25] For instance, as in all versions of the story, Chaucer's Lucretia is comforted after her rape by her husband, father, and friends (1847–50), yet nothing they say or do is able to prevent her from taking her own life. The most active of Lucretia's male supporters in the *Legend of Lucrece* is Brutus, who vows to avenge her "chaste blood" (1862) and, in the presence of her corpse, tells the city about Tarquin's "horryble dede of hir oppressyoun" (1868). Yet Chaucer's Lucretia receives noticeably less consolation from Brutus than she does in other versions of the story. Ovid and, more explicitly, Gower have the dying woman signal that she has understood and approves of Brutus's promise.[26] Not so Chaucer. When Brutus is first mentioned in the *Legend*, Lucretia is already dead, so there is no last communication between them and thus no comfort for her in knowing that she will be avenged. Virginius, in the *Physician's Tale*, is more prominent and active than family members in the *Legend of Lucrece*, but no more capable of bringing about a happy ending. He does succeed in keeping his daughter from being debauched by Apius, and a few critics have suggested that he does so from noble and generous motives, but, even if so, the cost is appalling.[27] Like the village in the Vietnam War that an American officer claimed had to be destroyed in order to save it, Virginia's purity is preserved only by paternal extermination, though Chaucer does not make Virginius as crazed and self-regarding as he is in Gower's *Confessio*. In the *Man of Law's Tale*, the one obvious good Roman is the senator who rescues Constance and her son at sea after their years of exile and brings them back to live with him in the city. While he is certainly more nurturing than the father who sent her away, the senator plays only a minor role in her story: ignorant of her real identity, he does not recognize, let alone repair, her alienation from father and husband. The best of Chaucer's Roman men are those in the *Second Nun's Tale* who choose to be "feminized" (in a positive sense) by becoming the followers of a good woman rather than the leaders of bad men.[28] Cecilia's husband, her brother-in-law, and the sergeant Maximus are among the Christian converts who renounce their traditional male privilege to obey the holy woman's teachings. Although these believers earn a heavenly reward, they are ineffectual on earth. Like Pope Urban, another good Roman but one forced into hiding beyond the city's walls, Cecilia's male converts have no active civic power and are incapable of preventing pagan persecution of Christians, leaving Saint Cecilia alone to oppose Almachius.

But if the good men in Chaucer's Roman tales are shown to be largely ineffective, the city's oppressors of women are even greater failures. Not only do they come to wretched ends, but the poet insists how little they succeed in accomplishing their evil desires. Murderous cruelty, like Nero's, and illicit sexual desire, like Tarquin's, end in frustration and misery. Tarquin succeeds in violating Lucretia's body, but he cannot touch her heart. She spurns him before the act and, in a scene original in both Chaucer and Gower, falls unconscious during it, making her incapable of any response, however involuntary, to his lust. Apius, for all his judicial conniving, never lays a hand on Virginia, let alone succeeds in debauching her, and, after being imprisoned by a popular revolt, kills himself. The Christian emperor of the *Man of Law's Tale* is eventually reunited with Constance, but not before his plan to use her to convert Syria ends in slaughter and in separation from his daughter (and his grandson) for many long years. Even Almachius in the *Second Nun's Tale*, for all his supposed power and threats, gains only ridicule from Cecilia, while his desperate efforts to eliminate Christians have the opposite effect of producing mass conversion among his own officers. Nero, the most coldly vicious of Chaucer's rulers, suffers the most wretched end of all. In a nightmarish final scene (7.2527–50), the city rises up against him, forcing him to flee alone in the dark and to beg for refuge from one former ally after another: "and ay the moore he cried / The fastere shette they the dores alle" (7.2531–32). Driven almost mad by repeated cries of "Where is this false tiraunt, this Neroun?" (7.2537), he prays "pitously" to his gods for help, also in vain (7.2539–40). The homeless emperor is finally reduced to imploring two churls to behead him and put him out of his misery, but they too fail, and he has to kill himself: "he koude no bettre reed" (7.2549). His suicide has none of the nobility of Dido's or Lucretia's, and his end is treated with mockery: "Of which Fortune lough, and hadde a game" (7.2550). Chaucer's Roman women are oppressed, but none dies as horribly as Nero.

Chaucer's Roman Women

Feminizing Roman Heroism

Chaucer most obviously "feminizes" ancient Rome by making women, not men, the protagonists of his narratives. It is their struggle, subjectivity, and valor, not that of their male oppressors, that are central in his Roman tales. As has often been recognized, pathos is a major element of Chaucer's poetry, from the *Book of the Duchess*, to *Troilus and Criseyde*, to the *Clerk's Tale*, and it should come as no surprise that three of his major Roman tales (the *Legend of Lucrece*, the *Physician's Tale*, and the *Man of Law's Tale*) contain more pathos than Gower's versions of these stories in the *Confessio Amantis*.[29] Harry Bailly, who can always be relied on for the conventional literary response, is accurate when, in the introduction to *the Pardoner's Tale*, he calls the previous tale of Virginia "a pitous tale for to heere" (6.302; cf. 6.317), and the narrator of the *Man of Law's Tale* powerfully solicits our pity for Constance when she is falsely accused of murder (2.631–58) and when she is adrift on the sea alone with her son (2.918–45).[30] Somewhat less flamboyantly, but no less emotionally, the narrator of the *Legend of Lucrece*, in lines original with Chaucer, describes the response of Lucretia's family and friends as they listen to her, disheveled and distraught, reveal what Tarquin has done to her:

> Al hadde folkes hertes ben of stones,
> Hyt myght have maked hem upon hir rewe,
> Hir herte was so wyfly and so trewe. (1841–43)

As the last line of this verse suggests, Chaucer, in addition to pitying Roman women, also admires them for their virtue and courage. As he portrays them, they become more than passive victims, for each also demonstrates her own kind of active moral integrity. Lucretia's truth in marriage is explicitly announced as the theme of her *Legend*. The poet says that, in contrast to other versions of her story, his will not deal with the "horible doinges" of kings (a reference to the political crimes of the Tarquins that Chaucer, unlike Gower, omits from his Ovidian source), but instead will focus on "the verray trewe Lucresse," who is first glimpsed busily engaged in domestic work so as to avoid "slouthe and idelnesse" (1681, 1686, 1722).[31] Chaucer praises both Virginia and Constance for their physical attractiveness, but even more for their unshakeable righteousness. In original additions to its source in the *Roman de la Rose*, the *Physician's Tale* says that whereas Virginia's beauty was "excellent," "a thousand foold moore vertuous was she" (6.39–40), a judgment that is supported with a detailed catalogue of her humble, patient purity (6.41–71) and, in an echo of 2 Corinthians 3:2, by comparing her to a book in which other virgins might read "every good word or dede / That longeth to a mayden vertuous" (6.108–9; cf. 6.114).³² Chaucer does something similar in the *Man of Law's Tale*. Using language not found in Gower's version, he cites "the commune voys" of Rome in praise of Constance because "to rekene as wel her goodnesse as beautee, / Nas nevere swich another as is shee" (2.155–59), just as the poet later has the Roman senator who rescues Constance declare that she is "so vertuous a lyvere" that "I dar wel seyn hir hadde levere a knyf / Thurghout hir brest, than ben a womman wikke" (2.1024–28). Cecilia, who asks for and receives the least pity of Chaucer's Roman women, is the most exemplary, as befits a saint.³³ The prologue of the *Second Nun's Tale*, like its sources, interprets Cecilia's name as an expression of her virtues of "chaastnesse of virginitee," "honestee," "conscience," and "good fame," and concludes by praising her good deeds: "ful swift and bisy evere in good werkynge" and "brennynge evere in charite ful brighte" (8.88–90, 116–18). From her wedding night to her dying days, Cecilia is always working to convert others to the Christian faith, prompting Pope Urban to extol her as "a bisy bee" (8.195). Even after her neck is fatally sliced, she does not cease her pious activities and teaching (8.533–46).

Chaucer represents his Roman women as practicing the fortitude traditionally associated with Roman men. Although they are not warriors like Caesar, who in the *Monk's Tale* is called a "conquerour," who "wan al th'occident by land and see, / By strengthe of hand, or elles by tretee" (7.2673–75), they are equally resolute when forced to resist the men of their own city rather than foreign armies. Lucretia is physically overwhelmed and terrified by Tarquin's surprise attack, but she never consents to his desires. In other versions of the story of Virginia, such as that in the *Confessio Amantis*, the heroine is silent in the face of Apius's lust and her father's fatal blow. Chaucer, however, gives her a voice with which she consents to death so that she may preserve her honor: "Yif me my deeth, er that I have a shame" (6.249). The most protracted example of fortitude in the Roman tales is Constance, who endures the slaughter of her first husband and her accompanying countrymen by the sultaness, two long sea voyages in a rudderless boat, a false sentence of death, a long separation from her second husband, attempted rape, constant worry about her little son's safety, years of lonely exile (some in Rome itself), and, finally, the deaths of both her husband and her father. Calling attention to the steadfastness she exhibits throughout her ordeals,

Chaucer gives Constance original speeches that express her trust in God's protection (e.g., 2.451–62, 639–44). Among Chaucer's Roman women, Cecilia is the most like a martial hero, though she never resorts to violence.[34] The saint battles the Roman prefect, Almachius (using words rather than weapons), and, with an intensity not found in other versions of her life, mocks the great power he claims to wield, calling it nothing but "a bladdre ful of wynd" (8.439). She opposes the prefect with a spiritual army of "Cristes owene knyghtes leeve and deere" (8.383), who conquer souls rather than territory and whose ranks grow larger the more they are persecuted.[35] Cecilia achieves a victory far greater than those celebrated during any Roman triumph, for, in addition to winning eternal life for herself, her perseverance in the faith presages the conquest of the pagan city itself, along with its empire, by Christianity.

Pagan and Christian Female Saints

Although the *Second Nun's Tale* is Chaucer's only true saint's life, his three other principal Roman tales all have strong hagiographical elements with heroines to match, as other critics have often noted. Constance in the *Man of Law's Tale* is not formally canonized, but she is a model of Christian faith and works, one who converts others and wholly trusts in God during her many trials.[36] More surprisingly, and unlike his immediate sources, Chaucer also borrows motifs from the lives of the saints to describe his two pagan Roman heroines. Lucretia's story appears in the *Legend of Good Women*, which the Man of Law calls "the Seintes Legende of Cupide" (2.61), and its conclusion describes her as if she were indeed sanctified. The poet uses explicitly Christian terms in adapting Ovid's commemoration of her in the *Fasti*: he tells us that she was considered "a seynt" in pagan Rome, where the citizens "ever hir day yhalwed dere," though he historicizes this with the qualifying phrase "as in hir lawe" (1870–72).[37] Among the original speeches Chaucer gives Virginia in the *Physician's Tale* is one in which she compares her situation not with that of a classical heroine, as we might expect, but with that of Jephthah's daughter in the Old Testament (6.240–44), and elsewhere he portrays her as if she were a Christian virgin martyr, as in her dying declaration, which is original with the poet: "Blissed be God that I shal dye a mayde" (6.248).[38]

Like medieval female saints' lives, Chaucer's Roman tales feature women of virtue and courage who both speak and act. This is as true of his pagan "saints" as of his Christian ones. Lucretia, of course, had long been a symbol of female valor in classical and medieval literature, and the *Legend* largely follows Ovid's *Fasti* in having her forthrightly announce to her family the outrage done her and explain why she feels she must kill herself. Chaucer emphasizes Lucretia's resoluteness in seeking death before dishonor in a powerful couplet whose repetition of personal pronominal words underlines her agency, just as the striking rhyme insists on the brutal finality of her act: "But pryvely *she* kaught forth a knyf, / And therewithal *she* rafte *hirself hir lyf*" (1854–55, emphasis added).[39] As already noted, Virginia, unlike Lucretia, with whom she is often linked, is usually portrayed as silent and passive as she meets death, but not in the *Physician's Tale*, to which Chaucer adds an exchange with Virginius in which she takes responsibility for what happens.[40] When her father tells her that she must die so as to avoid Apius's lust, Chaucer initially describes her as a little girl, which she is in age, one who helplessly begs her parent to take care of her. Her first words are "O mercy, deere fader" (6.231), and she then weeps as she embraces his neck and cries, "Goode fader, shal I dye? / Is ther no grace, is ther no remedye?" (6.235–36). When he replies that there is none, however, she quickly puts away childish things and accepts her fate. Now all she asks is the leisure to lament what must happen, and, after swooning from the emotion of it all (she is courageous but human), her final words, which remain those of a loving daughter, are mature and resolute, as she aligns her will with that of her parent in the name of God: "Dooth with youre child youre wyl, a Goddes name" (6.250). Chaucer's Virginia is no mute victim, as in other versions of her story, but, like the poet's Lucretia, a morally responsible woman who does not flinch from death, however much she regrets it, choosing instead to accept what she recognizes is necessary to preserve her own integrity.

The Tragedy of Rome's Pagan Heroines

For all their bravery, the two pagan heroines of Chaucer's Roman tales, Lucretia and Virginia, are finally tragic figures, whose valor benefits neither themselves nor anyone else. In contrast to other versions of their stories, Chaucer's narratives do not show these good women having much positive effect on the civic affairs of Rome. At the end of his tale of Lucretia in the *Confessio Amantis*, Gower explains that in response to her death, the people of Rome exiled their king and his son and established "betre governance" (7.5123). Not even such a vague claim of political improvement is made by Chaucer in his *Legend of Lucrece*. Although he briefly notes that Rome never had another king, he does not say whether this was a good thing for the city or worthy of imitation in England (doubtful, given the poet's royal associations). Chaucer concludes the *Legend* by presenting Lucretia less as a civic reformer than as a pagan saint, as we have seen, and then adds extended praise of her as one who was "of love so trewe" (1874) and a model of female loyalty, in contrast to the "tirannye" of men (1883). This "tirannye" (the only appearance of the word in the *Legend*) does not refer to Roman political abuses, as it often does with the Tarquins in Gower's story of Lucretia, but rather to the general faithlessness of men in their relationships with women (as Dido also discovered).

The Roman oppression of women in Chaucer's tales is not caused by any one form of government but continues to be emphasized long after the city's kings are no more. In the postmonarchal *Physician's Tale*, for example, a central institution of Rome, its legal system, is used to oppress Virginia, as Apius manipulates it in attempting to possess her. Unlike Livy or Gower, but following his immediate source, the *Roman de la Rose*, Chaucer says nothing about how Apius's misbehavior led to specific civic changes.[41] The rather odd moral drawn at the end of the *Physician's Tale* addresses spiritual, not political, reformation: "Forsaketh synne, er synne yow forsake" (6.286).

Such religious language suggests that the ultimate tragedy for Chaucer's pagan heroines, Lucretia and Virginia, is not that their deaths fail to effect political change but that their faith offers no remedy or even consolation for their suffering. Gower is largely indifferent to religious practices (pagan or Christian) in ancient Rome (as opposed to the corruption of the medieval church) because his attention is on the city's lessons about government. Chaucer, however, like the Latin and English authors of the *Mirabilia*, is alert to the contrasts and continuities between the two kinds of belief. Although Chaucer says that Lucretia was considered a "seynt" in Rome and her day was "yhalwed," the festival he refers to is not, of course, a Christian holy day but a civic commemoration of the overthrow of the Tarquins (1870–71). Chaucer's reference to Lucretia as a saint indicates his respect for her as one of "these Romeynes wyves" who "lovede so here name" (1812), but the evocation of Christian sanctity here points to the limitations of her own religion.[42] As good as she is, Lucretia, as a pagan, has no hope of achieving Christian salvation; the most she can expect after death is that her good reputation, which she guards so carefully, will be celebrated, as it was by Roman chroniclers, Ovid, and, centuries later, Gower and Chaucer. Her only postmortem existence is a textual one. She survives as an exemplum from the distant past, but one lacking the power of the Christian saints, as seen in the *Stacions of Rome* and the tale of Saint Cecilia, to work miracles or to intercede for the living.

However true her love for her husband, Lucretia knows nothing of the love of the true God and his saving grace.[43]

Like Lucretia, Virginia (despite the biblical imagery in the *Physician's Tale*) is also a secular heroine. By describing her as if she were a virgin martyr, Chaucer emphasizes her difference from the real thing. When Chaucer has Virginia begin her first speech to Virginius by asking for "mercy" and end it by looking for "grace" (6.231–36), he reminds us that any succor must come from her earthly rather than her heavenly father. Likewise, when, in the same speech, she asks, "shal I dye?" (6.235), it is physical, not spiritual, death that she means. Virginia's acceptance of her fate is a measure of the courage with which she, like Lucretia, upholds Roman ideals of honor, but the tragedy of these two women, from the perspective of Chaucer's readers, is that their virtues as pagans were insufficient for their salvation, though Langland challenges this general view, as we shall see in the next chapter.[44] Like Theseus in the *Knight's Tale*, Lucretia and Virginia are portrayed as proto-Christians at best, good women whose values and behavior suggest that they might well have accepted the true faith that eventually prevailed in Rome had they been given the opportunity. But they were not.

The Triumph of Rome's Christian Heroines

Because they are Christians, Chaucer's two other Roman heroines, Constance and Cecilia, are able to transcend the city in ways unavailable to Lucretia and Virginia. The Christian coloring of the *Legend of Lucrece* and the *Physician's Tale* is replaced by the faith itself. The most forceful of Chaucer's Roman women is one whose story Gower does not tell: Saint Cecilia in the *Second Nun's Tale*. In the words of Karen Winstead, Cecilia "is in command of every situation and always in action."[45] Chaucer chooses as his only true saint's life the story of a woman who dominates each of the male Romans she encounters, with the fugitive Pope Urban the only possible exception. On her wedding night, she persuades her husband, Valerian, in the bridal bed no less, to forgo his marital rights and accept a radically new form of chaste marriage under the watchful eye of her guardian angel (8.141–82); later, she encourages her brother-in-law, Tiburce, to overcome his natural fears about the danger of belonging to a religion outlawed by the city (8.319–32); and, finally, in the three days while she is dying, she continues to teach others and prepare them for the future (8.537–46). Cecilia's most direct and scornful rejection of Rome occurs during her dispute with the city's prefect, Almachius. Chaucer shapes their one-sided debate so that, as Paul Beichner says, "Cecilia had never before been quite so contentious or belligerent, nor had Almachius been so obtuse or stupid."⁴⁶ She ridicules the hapless prefect as a "lewed officer and a veyn justise" (8.497), declaring that the "myghty princes" from whom he claims to possess "power and auctoritee" over the lives of others (8.470–72) have given him the capacity only to destroy, making him a "ministre of deeth," not life (8.485), just as the gods to whom he wants her to sacrifice are lifeless, mute stones "nat worth a myte" (8.498–511).

Cecilia is the only Chaucerian heroine who directly opposes a male leader of Rome, and she alone creates an alternative society in the city. She redefines Roman marriage, and, as Chaucer makes clear by his choice of words, redefines kinship as well. She treats her husband's brother not so much like a relative as like a fellow spiritual warrior, calling him "myn allye" (8.292, 297), and she refers to those she has inspired to become Christians as her children, whom "she hadde fostred" (8.539). The Roman community that Cecilia creates is no lasting city, however, but one that she is happy to abandon. Gower's relatively optimistic civic conclusion to the story of Lucretia shows Romans responding to her death by creating a "betre" government (7.5123), but Cecilia speaks instead of a "bettre lif in oother place" (8.323). Rather than a reformed Rome, she looks to the heavenly city of God, that "oother lyf ther men may wone," proclaimed by "heigh Goddes Sone, / Whan he was in this world" (8.330–32).

With her confidence in future glory, it is no wonder that death has none of the tragic sadness for Cecilia that it has for Lucretia and Virginia. Her challenge to the masculine regime of Rome is only the first step in rejecting the earthly city for the more abundant city of God, a destination not available to Chaucer's pagan heroines. Indifferent to bodily death, Cecilia urges her husband and brother-in-law to rejoice in their martyrdom, which will allow them to trade this life for "the corone of lif that may nat faille" (8.388). When Cecilia asks God for a period of respite before she dies, it is not so that she may declare how she has been abused, like Lucretia, or lament her coming end, like Virginia, but to "recomende" the "soules" of believers to Pope Urban and to arrange for her house to become a church (8.542–46). In Chaucer's time, a church dedicated to Saint Cecilia still stood on the supposed site of her house in the Trastevere section of Rome (as it does today), a representation of the faith that would eventually conquer the city and make it its seat.

Cecilia's victory is over more than Rome; it is over earthly existence itself. Her tale places little value on the things of this world, including her own corruptible flesh. In contrast to Lucretia's pagan corpse, which is publicly displayed by Brutus, and unlike the Christian relics so cherished by pilgrims in the *Stacions of Rome*, once Cecilia leaves her body, it is quickly and discreetly, if reverently, interred by the pope:

> Seint Urban with his deknes prively
> The body fette and buryed it by nyghte
> Among his othere seintes honestly. (8.547–49)[47]

Cecilia's physical death is given so little attention in the *Second Nun's Tale*, in contrast to those of her pagan sisters, because it marks not the sad end of her life but rather its full flowering in heaven, though in the Middle Ages, as the *Stacions of Rome* demonstrates, her divine power was believed to be still accessible to all at her shrine in Trastevere.

Constance in the *Man of Law's Tale* is a less flamboyant Christian than Cecilia, but one equally devout and close to God.[48] When her father the emperor forces her to leave Rome to marry the sultan of Syria, it is her heavenly father from whom she seeks protection, to whom she constantly prays, and by whom she is supported during her trials, as when he directly intervenes to declare her innocent when she is accused of a murder she did not commit (2.673–76). Perhaps because Rome is now a Christian capital, Constance's rejection of the city is less absolute than that of Chaucer's other Roman heroines. The faith can safely be practiced in the city, even if some of its adherents, like her father, may be far from exemplary. After the tribulations of her long exile, she is rescued by a Roman senator and brought back to the city, but she does not reveal her identify until her converted British husband, Alla, arrives in the city to receive absolution from the pope. She goes back to Britain with Alla, but after his death she again returns with her son to Rome to spend her last few years there.

Constance is not in open rebellion against Rome, as Cecilia is, but her whole life is a rebuke to its militant propagation of the faith, which imitates the coercive practices of the earlier pagan city, as seen in Almachius's bullying in the *Second Nun's Tale*. The Roman Christians of the *Man of Law's Tale* arrange a dynastic marriage for the reluctant Constance to secure the conversion of the Muslim sultan and his people. When that scheme ends disastrously with the sultan's death (at the hands of his mother), along with the deaths of the many Roman Christians accompanying Constance, her father the emperor responds with overwhelming and pitiless military force. He sends a senator with a large armada to take "heigh vengeance" on his would-be religious allies: "They brennen, sleen, and brynge hem to meschance / Ful many a day" (2.964–65).

A less aggressive Christian missionary than her models in Trevet and Gower, Chaucer's Constance, in her gentle way, proves herself an effective ambassador for the faith, as she shows in her reclamation of a lapsed Britain. The distinction between Constance's modest, feminine Christianity and the more assertive form practiced by Rome's male leaders is briefly but sharply dramatized when the returning Roman armada comes across Constance's rudderless boat:

> This senatour repaireth with victorie
> To Rome-ward, saillynge ful roially,
> And mette the ship dryvynge, as seith the storie,
> In which Custance sit ful pitously. (2.967–70)

The Roman senator "saillynge ful roially" suggests the imperial power and authority that Almachius had once attributed to "the mighty princes" of the pagan city, just as the "victorie" of this armada, like Almachius's execution of Cecilia, is one more example of state violence. Constance's little boat, by contrast, stands as a rebuke to the use of force in the name of faith. Unlike the triumphant Roman fleet confidently making for home, Constance sits "ful pitously" in a vessel wholly subject to the ocean's currents and God's will.[49] Constance's craft is surely the weaker in military might, but she is the more successful Christian. She kills no one but converts many, including her father the emperor, whom she teaches, in their final days together, to live "in vertu and in hooly almus-dede" (2.1156).

The stories of Cecilia and Constance are less tragic than those of Lucretia and Virginia, but Rome itself has not been much improved by their achievements and sanctity. Although Cecilia creates a strong alternative community that includes converted men, the structures of the pagan city are unaltered, and Almachius is still in charge after her death. The martyr Cecilia and her church point to the Christian future of the city, though it is one that will not always match her absolute trust in the power of God. Constance lives in that future Rome, and while her own faith is as absolute, if more quietly expressed, as Cecilia's, the leaders of the now Christian city, like their pagan predecessors, continue to oppress women, including her, and pollute the church itself with their imperial ambitions, which though undertaken in the name of religion result in forced marriage, slaughter, and bloody revenge. The medieval reader looking for a positive message about Christian Rome in the *Man of Law's Tale* may hope that Constance's Maurice will become the truly Christian emperor that his grandfather was not, but Chaucer's Roman tales offer little cause for optimism that any male ruler could equal the moral and spiritual heroism of the city's women, whether pagan or Christian.[50]

The generous if ironic tone so often attributed to Chaucer's poetry is absent from his harsh treatment of Rome. At the end of *Troilus and Criseyde*, the narrator asks his little book to kiss in homage the steps where mostly Latin poets once trod, but for those who ruled Rome during the time of these ancient writers and immediately after, Chaucer, unlike Gower, seems to have only contempt. He does not necessarily have a more positive view of medieval Christian Rome, though that is harder to judge because, unlike the ancient city, it is mentioned infrequently in his poetry. One striking reference to the contemporary city's ecclesiastical abuses, however, occurs in the portrait of the egregious Pardoner, who is introduced in the General Prologue as having just arrived from the "court of Rome" (1.671), bearing, along with his false relics, a wallet full "of pardoun comen from Rome al hoot" (1.687), an attack on the indulgences treated reverently in the *Stacions of Rome*. More indirectly, the uncompromising purity of Saint Cecilia's (and Constance's) faith offers a strong, if implicit, criticism of the corruptions and limitations of the Church of Rome in Chaucer's day. While it was true that fourteenth-century popes no longer had to live hidden in the catacombs, Chaucer's medieval readers might have wondered whether the inhabitants of the grand papal palaces and churches in the contemporary city shared the same fearless sanctity and desire for a "bettre lif in oother place" shown by Cecilia.[51] Chaucer's occasional and oblique criticisms of medieval Rome, however, do not begin to equal his unremitting hostility to the ancient city. It has no parallel in the work of any other Ricardian poet and is a remarkably unexplored element of Chaucer's profound interest in the classical world.

CHAPTER 5

Virtuous Romans in *Piers Plowman*

Ask most Middle English scholars about ancient Rome in William Langland's *Piers Plowman* and, after some hesitation, they will probably mention the emperor Trajan and say that a fair amount has been written about his escape from hell. And yet Trajan's relative prominence in Langland scholarship obscures how singular this Roman figure is. When Rome is mentioned elsewhere in the poem, it is almost always with reference to the contemporary city, and the verdict is not very positive. In contrast to the somewhat later *Stacions of Rome*, which extols Rome as an overflowing well of mercy because of its innumerable holy martyrs and pardons, *Piers* suggests that Christians should look elsewhere for salvation. In a sermon to the field of folk, Reason argues against their making a pilgrimage to Saint James Compostela in Spain or to the "seyntes of Rome" and urges them instead to seek Saint Truth (5.56–57).[1] Sloth, by the end of his confession in the same passus, comes to agree with Reason when he vows, "I shal seken truthe erst er I see Rome" (5.461), though, given his nature, Sloth is probably happy to have any reason to avoid such an arduous journey. The conclusion of the *visio* in *Piers Plowman* acknowledges that the Roman pontiff has the power to grant a plenary (that is, total) indulgence for one's sins (7.174–79), but the value of such papal dispensations is qualified by the lines that immediately precede and follow. Just before this passage, the dreamer/narrator remembers the priest's assertion during the tearing of the pardon that, at the Day of Judgment, Dowel "passeth al the pardon of Seint Petres cherche" (7.168–73), and, shortly thereafter, we are warned that however many indulgences and bulls we might have acquired, unless "Dowel yow helpe, / I sette youre patentes and youre pardon at one pies hele" (7.194–95). Later in the poem, the Samaritan, who personifies charity, echoes this advice by telling the dreamer that if he is "unkynde" to his fellow Christians, he will surely be rejected by the Holy Ghost regardless of whatever else he may have done, even if he has managed to "purchace al the pardon of Pampilon and Rome" (17.251–53).

Although medieval Christian Rome is viewed skeptically in *Piers Plowman*, it appears several times, whereas the ancient pagan city, like the ancient world in general, is barely noticed. The Trajan episode excepted, almost nothing in the poem is taken from Roman literature, history, or mythology. Even the most ingenious graduate student desperately seeking a dissertation topic will not get very far with one titled *Piers Plowman and the Classics*. For instance, Langland shows no knowledge of or interest in the material splendors of the ancient pagan city that are so carefully catalogued in the *Mirabilia* tradition. Apart from the poem's frequent allegorical dreamscapes, such as the route to Truth described by *Piers* at the end of passus 5, its geographical settings are largely biblical or English—Jerusalem, Malvern, and London. Langland's indifference to Roman history and culture sharply distinguishes him from his fellow London Ricardian poets, Chaucer and Gower. They are both attracted especially to the wit and subtlety of Ovid and to his sympathy for women, but it is hard to think of a poet whose interests and tone would have appealed less to Langland. The Latin that fills *Piers Plowman* comes overwhelmingly from the Bible or other Christian writing and not from classical texts, and this imbalance also holds true for the sparse references in the poem to secular Roman figures. Thus Caesar (Julius or more likely Augustus) appears in the poem only in Holy Church's citation of Christ's command at Matthew 22:21 to render unto Caesar what is Caesar's and unto God what is God's (1.46–53). Likewise, the Cato who is quoted several times in *Piers* is not a historical Roman figure, neither Cato the Elder nor Cato the Younger, but rather the convenient name under which was gathered a series of practical maxims in an important medieval school text.[2] Virgil, whom Chaucer knew and imitated as a major poet, is mentioned only once in *Piers*, probably in his medieval guise of mage. His name (and only his name) appears in a list with other famous biblical and classical figures, such as Lucifer, Solomon, Job, Aristotle, Hippocrates, and Alexander, simply to point the moral that, for all their wealth and intelligence (their "catel and kynde wit"), each met a wretched end (12.40–45).

And yet, despite the almost total absence of references to ancient Rome in *Piers Plowman* and despite its repeated warnings not to look to the city or its papacy for salvation, both a famous pagan emperor and a famous Christian pope from late antiquity are featured at the very heart of the poem. In passus 11 of the B-text, while the first-person narrator is wrestling with questions about whether or not learning helps one get into heaven, Trajan (called "Troianus" in the poem), who was Roman emperor from A.D. 98 to 117, bursts into the poem.[3] Unlike the narrator, who has been merely speculating about salvation, here is a figure from the distant past who has truly been to hell and back. Langland's Trajan declares that he was rescued from damnation not by the learning, liturgy, or prayers of the Christian church but because of his own virtuous actions, which were admired by Gregory the Great, a Roman aristocrat and eventually a saint who was pope from 590 to 604. At this crucial moment in the poem, and only here (though Imaginatif confirms Trajan's place in heaven in the next passus), ancient Rome is prominent and thematically significant.[4]

Langland devotes many fewer lines to Rome and Romans than does either Gower or Chaucer (or, as we shall see, Lydgate), but brevity does not always mean disparagement; the single episode he includes in the middle of *Piers* is wholly positive. In a poem full of narrative surprises, this is one of the most astonishing: an esteemed pagan Roman emperor and a great Christian Roman pope demonstrate their admiration for each other's virtue despite all the differences in time and belief that separate them. No other Middle English poem imagines such a personal and profound reconciliation of pagan and Christian Roman values. Gower, as we saw in chapter 3, admires elements of Roman governance, but he is largely uninterested in its pagan beliefs (the one exception being the moral goodness of Gower's Constantine before his conversion), and Chaucer and Lydgate show that even the best and most saintly Roman pagan women (Lucretia and Virginia) have no hope of heaven. Only Langland, for all his moral sternness and the frequent spiritual despair of his Christian characters (the narrative "I" and Haukyn, for instance), not only imagines but also vividly dramatizes the salvation of a nonbeliever who lived after Christ.

In what follows, I pay special, though not exclusive, attention to the B-text of *Piers Plowman*, whose Trajan/Gregory episode is somewhat longer than the parallel lines in the C-text (the A-text ends too soon to include it at all). Unusually, Langland cites a specific source for the story of Trajan and Gregory (the life of the latter in the influential thirteenth-century collection of saints' legends by Jacobus de Voragine, the *Legenda aurea*), even though he transforms what he found in the *Legenda* to produce his own unique retelling. In his most radical departure from the *Legenda*, Langland tells events from Trajan's perspective and gives the emperor his own voice to speak about himself and Gregory.

Although relatively short, and uncharacteristic of the rest of *Piers Plowman* in its use of ancient Roman material, the episode reflects some of the poem's deepest concerns, especially the major theme of how to balance justice and mercy (or the related concepts of truth and love), a question that appears again and again throughout *Piers*. Scholars have rarely called attention to Trajan and Gregory as fellow Romans or analyzed the meaning of their bond, even though Langland specifically identifies Trajan as "an Emperor of Rome" (11.153) and "a paynym of Rome" (11.162), and Gregory was an important enough Roman pope to be called "the Great." My argument is that the city that Trajan and Gregory share is essential to what the poet is doing in the episode. The respect that two such exemplary Romans have for each other despite their dissimilarities foreshadows Langland's hope that nonbelievers as well as Christians may be saved and looks forward to the final reconciliation of the virtues each represents in the remarkable Harrowing of Hell scene at the end of passus 18.

Introducing Trajan

The Trajan/Gregory episode in *Piers Plowman* calls attention to itself with its dramatic opening. The first-person narrator has been expressing worries about whether learning can help save one's soul, when, after he has received some reassurance from Scripture, a new voice suddenly breaks into the poem with four short, sharp words: "Ye, baw for bokes!" (11.140). That this intervention is significant is indicated by its resemblance to the entrance of Piers the Plowman himself, who, with almost equal abruptness, suddenly appears to the pilgrims who are blundering around in search of Saint Truth: "'Peter!' quod a Plowman, and putte forth his heved" (5.537). The demotic voice in B 11, however, is not that of a local plowman or of one of Langland's many moral personifications, but of an ancient Roman who claims to have "broken out of helle" (11.140). The speaker is soon identified as Trajan, "a trewe knyght," and he cites a Christian pope (later identified as Gregory) as witness that, though "dampned to dwellen in pyne" because he was a pagan, he was eventually freed because of love, "leautee," and his own good decisions (11.141–45). Trajan further claims that although Gregory desired his salvation because of "my werkes," his actual release from hell was brought about not by Christian prayers or masses but by the righteousness of his own conduct, "my lyvynge in truthe" (11.146–52). An unspecified commentator, who may be the narrator/dreamer, continues with praise of this "Emperour of Rome," whose "pure truthe" saved him when learning and law could not, citing Saint Gregory again as testimony (7.153–56). The commentator then addresses English "lordes" who are responsible for keeping the laws, urging them to imitate Trajan's example and act truthfully to the people (11.157–58). Noting that a more complete version of this story is to be found in the legends of the saints, the voice blesses the "leel love" and "lyvyng in truthe" that saved this pagan from Satan, and asserts that "love and leautee is a leel science," a "book blissed of blisse and joye," that is, the Ten Commandments that God gave Moses to teach us all (11.159–69). Finally, Trajan himself reappears to close the episode by declaring that "lawe withouten love" is worthless (11.170).

Langland's Trajan is clearly an admirable figure, even if he does brag about his central virtue. He is a pagan paragon in contrast to the mix of good and bad Roman leaders in Gower's *Confessio Amantis* and the consistently awful ones in Chaucer's tales. The Trajan of *Piers* is more like the pious Roman exemplars in the *Mirabilia* tradition, such as Agrippa, who built the Pantheon, or Octavian, who was granted a vision of the Virgin and Child. Trajan also resembles them (and Gregory) in being a genuine figure from Roman history. Both emperor and pope were leaders of ancient Rome: one ruled the pagan city and empire in the late first and early second centuries, the other, the Christian papal city in the late sixth and early seventh centuries. In contrast to most of the dreamer's previous mentors in *Piers*, who, as Elizabeth Salter observes, are "really nothing but chapter-headings in a medieval text-book of faculty psychology," Trajan is a "literal, historical character," with the result that his "irruption into the allegory is startling and impressive" and his "testimony is fresh and irrefutable."[5] Andrew Galloway is justified in calling Trajan "the poem's only speaking human figure from the ancient past apart from Jesus," though other biblical characters in *Piers*, such as Abraham and the Samaritan, albeit also representing allegorical concepts, would undoubtedly have been considered historical by Langland and his original readers.[6] Langland insists that Trajan and Gregory are Romans, but he does not therefore go on to show any interest in the reality of the physical city itself. We hear of Gregory's admiration for Trajan, but not that he expressed that at any particular Roman place (Jacobus's *Legenda aurea* says that this first occurred while the pope was walking in Trajan's Forum), and Trajan, no longer in hell, speaks in *Piers* from a discursive, perhaps heavenly, space that is not linked in any way with the city of Rome.

The Trajan/Gregory episode in *Piers Plowman*, from the emperor's first statement to the last words that are unambiguously his, is relatively short, just thirty lines (11.140–70). Unlike some other critics, I do not attribute to Trajan the long, passionate speech, primarily about patient poverty and false clerics, that immediately follows and occupies much of the rest of B 11 (171–318). This extended statement has been attributed to a number of different speakers, an example of the modern critical tendency, challenged so powerfully by A. C. Spearing, to assign any first-person textual narration to a single coherent speaker.[7] In his edition of the B-text, Schmidt attributes 11.171–318 to Trajan, while acknowledging that not all of it "would be strictly apt to the Roman emperor."[8] Other modern critics also assume that these lines are Trajan's.[9] But I consider George Kane and Talbot Donaldson more convincing in their punctuation of the Athlone edition of the B-text, which attributes to Trajan only those lines where he is clearly identified as speaking in the first person (11.140a, 143b–152, 170, and also his indirect speech at 141b–143a), though I acknowledge that this makes his voice end at 11.170 almost as abruptly as it first began.[10] I take lines 11.140b–141a and 153–69, which occur within the Trajan/Gregory episode, to be textual commentary, or what Spearing calls the "I" of the text, which need not be attributed to a fully personalized narrator or the poet himself.[11] The continuation after 11.170 I take as the utterance of a speaking textual agent whose identity, even if it were discoverable and consistent (neither of which is certain), is irrelevant to my argument because it does not deal directly with the rescue of Trajan from hell or with his relationship with Gregory, and it moves far away from Rome. Not attributing 11.171–318 to Trajan also avoids the difficulty of having the pagan emperor, albeit now saved, quoting extensively from scripture and discussing such anachronistic and parochial topics as parish priests. In the C-text of *Piers Plowman*, this continuation is assigned to an original character, Rechelesnesse, which suggests that Langland may never have considered these lines to be Trajan's.

The Medieval Legend of Trajan and Gregory

The story of Trajan and Gregory, which seems to have originated in a life of the saint written by an anonymous English monk at Whitby early in the eighth century, was retold throughout the Middle Ages.[12] Gordon Whatley, who has made the most thorough study of the different versions of the legend, observes that its longevity "seems to have been due, in part at least, to its flexible adaptability to the evolving patterns of medieval thought and culture."[13] As a result, the story appears in nonhagiographical texts as well as in numerous forms of the life of Gregory. For example, John of Salisbury, in his twelfth-century *Policraticus*, presents Trajan as the ideal Roman imperial ruler, superior even to Julius Caesar or Augustus, because, in addition to his military successes, he "built the majesty of his reign solely upon the practice of virtue" and he was admired by the saintly Gregory.[14] In his *Commedia*, Dante represents Trajan as an example of humility in *Purgatorio* 10.73–93 and of justice in *Paradiso* 20.43–48, 106–17.[15] In the *Paradiso* lines, Dante, apparently following one of the medieval explanations for Trajan's salvation, says that Gregory caused the emperor to be briefly restored to life so that he could accept Christianity and qualify to enter heaven.[16]

Langland may possibly have known other versions of the Trajan/Gregory story, but his primary source, as he himself announces, is the "legende *sanctorum*" (11.160), which scholars agree is a reference to Jacobus de Voragine's *Legenda aurea*.[17] The English poem's first-person commentary at this point admits that *Piers* provides only a selective version of Jacobus's fuller legend, with the result that its meaning may be obscure to some readers: "This matere is merk for many of yow" (11.159). To fully understand the unique portrayal of Trajan and Gregory in *Piers*, we must respond to the commentator's observation that the "legende *sanctorum* yow lereth more largere than I yow telle" (11.160) and compare Langland's presentation of their relationship with what is in the *Legenda*. Jacobus, in his life of Gregory, as he is recounting the saint's many deeds and miracles, pauses to tell about Trajan. One day when the emperor is preparing to leave Rome for war, Jacobus says, he is approached by a widow in tears demanding that he avenge her son, who has been put to death despite his innocence. Trajan promises to attend to the matter on his return, but the widow objects, asking how she can be certain of justice if he were to die in battle. Trajan reassures her that his successor will deal with the matter, but the widow says that it would be better for Trajan himself to act now and thus receive credit for the good deed. Moved by compassion for this woman (we are told) and perhaps by concern for his good name, the emperor dismounts and sees to it that the widow's innocent child is avenged.[18] Jacobus goes on to explain how, centuries later, when walking through Trajan's Forum in Rome, Gregory remembers the story of the emperor's kindness. Proceeding to St. Peter's Basilica, he laments with bitter tears that such a good man was a pagan. While at the church, Gregory hears the voice of God proclaiming that his petition has been granted (though no such formal petition has been mentioned) and that Trajan has been spared, though the saint is warned never again to pray for a damned soul. This narrative in the *Legenda* is followed by a long survey of the various opinions about precisely what Trajan's final fate was.

Langland's Reformulation

Although the Trajan/Gregory episode in *Piers Plowman* is based on the *Legenda*, Langland alters it significantly. His encounter with the widow is not mentioned at all in the poem, for example, and whereas Gregory is the major character in the *Legenda* (it is, after all, his legend), in *Piers* the episode is told from Trajan's perspective and often in his voice, for the emperor's life and fate is Langland's main subject.[19] The episode begins with Trajan and his first dramatic words, which insist (like Chaucer's Wife of Bath, whose assertiveness he shares) that his own experience is more relevant than bookish authorities. The attention remains on Trajan, who is given a name, though an as-yet-unidentified pope is also mentioned, as he goes on to report, in indirect speech, how he was damned:

> "Ye, baw for bokes!" quod oon was broken out of helle
> Highte Troianus, a trewe knyght, took witnesse at a pope
> How he was ded and dampned to dwellen in pyne
> For an uncristene creature. (11.140–43)

In the lines that follow, Trajan gives his one substantial speech in the poem, which is only nine and a half lines but differs in several important respects from Jacobus's original. In the *Legenda*, the emperor's good deed to the widow is first reported objectively and then recalled by Gregory. But in *Piers*, Trajan steps forward himself to announce that he was rescued by his good works, though without providing any specific examples:

> "Clerkes wite the sothe—
> That al the clergie under Crist ne myghte me cracche fro helle
> But oonliche love and leautee of my lawful domes.
> Gregorie wiste this wel, and wilned to my soule
> Savacion for the soothnesse that he seigh in my werkes.
> And after that he wepte and wilned me were graunted grace,
> Withouten any bede biddyng his boone was underfongen,
> And I saved, as ye may see, withouten syngynge of masses,

> By love and by lernyng of my lyvynge in truthe,
> Broughte me fro bitter peyne ther no biddyng myghte." (11.143–52)[20]

Trajan's claim that intercessory prayers and liturgical services were powerless to free him from hell is in accord with standard church doctrine that damned souls, unlike those in purgatory, were beyond such assistance, however devoutly performed.[21] According to Trajan, his salvation is due to his own actions when alive and, secondarily, to Gregory's endorsement of them after his death. Some critics believe that Langland's Trajan gives himself too much credit for his rescue; whatever his good deeds, he is, after all, initially sent to hell.[22] But given that Trajan is an "uncristene creature," albeit one now in heaven, perhaps he should not be expected to know the precise mechanism by which he was saved, and it is natural that he should see it as a reward for his merits. As already mentioned, even medieval explanations of his rescue differ as to how much he contributed to it, and modern criticism has continued the debate. Nor is Langland's Trajan quite as vainly self-congratulatory or self-righteous as his words may at first suggest. He does, after all, acknowledge that another person, Saint Gregory, was involved.

The most substantive change in Langland's Trajan episode from all other medieval versions is the mutual respect the poet portrays between the pagan emperor and the Christian saint. In the *Legenda aurea*, the respect goes only one way. Gregory admires Trajan and laments his fate, but this is never reciprocated. Jacobus's emperor is the passive recipient of the saint's sympathy, about which, as about the saint himself, Trajan appears to know nothing. Gregory is aware of Trajan's virtue, but Trajan, even after he is saved, remains ignorant of Gregory's role in his rescue. Things are quite different in *Piers* because Trajan, not Gregory, is the focus of the episode, and Langland has him acknowledge the pope's concern and express his thanks for it. By eliminating so many other narrative elements in the traditional legend, such as the widow's request and Gregory's walking through the forum, Langland's focus is squarely on Trajan and Gregory themselves and the mutual respect the poet creates between them.

The gratitude that Langland's Trajan feels toward Gregory helps to explain his denial of any institutional role for the church in his salvation.[23] To be clear, the emperor does not argue that "al the clergie under Crist" ("clergie" here meaning both Christian learning and clerics) or Christian prayers and services ("bede biddyng" and "syngynge of masses") lack any efficacy at all (would he have been allowed into heaven if this were his view?), only that they were irrelevant in his own case. It is Gregory's personal response that Langland's Trajan values, and he refers to him neither as pope nor as saint but only by his given name. For Trajan, Gregory is more than simply a neutral "witnesse" (11.141), but, as he himself says, one who even though aware that the emperor had been damned as a pagan ("wiste this wel") nevertheless wished for his salvation because of admiration for his works. The word Langland uses for Gregory's desire is "wilned," a form of *will*, which is a key term in *Piers*. In contrast to Langland's source, his Trajan, while remaining a pagan and not brought back to life so he can convert, as he is in some forms of the medieval story, is shown to recognize the extraordinary Christian compassion in Gregory, who "wepte" and "wilned" (the second use of this word in a short speech) that a nonbeliever in hell be granted salvation. Trajan's salvation is brought about both by the emperor's own actions and by Gregory's compassion, though of course the ultimate agent is divine grace.

The Debate About Trajan's Salvation

Critical discussion of Trajan in *Piers Plowman* has not focused on his Romanness, or even much on his relationship with his fellow Roman, Gregory, but rather on the theological justification for his release from hell. As early as 1924, R. W. Chambers insisted that Langland used Trajan to challenge conventional medieval church doctrine that good works alone are insufficient to secure salvation.[24] Others disagreed with Chambers, among them T. P. Dunning and later Britton J. Harwood, who both argued that Trajan's salvation is not exceptional but fully in accord with standard Catholic teaching.[25] In one of the most original treatments of the whole question, "The Trouble with Trajan," Frank Grady divides the critics who write about Trajan's salvation, perhaps a little too neatly, into those who see it as "orthodox" and those who see it as "heterodox," and he quotes Robert Adams as predicting that "this debate is likely to continue."[26] Adams himself had earlier attempted to transcend and reframe the debate by citing Trajan's salvation as an example of Langland's semi-Pelagianism, the belief, which Adams says most theologians held by the thirteenth century, that good works were meritorious, even for nonbelievers.[27] Adams argues that Langland "believed fervently in man's obligation to do his very best (*facere quod in se est*) and in its guaranteed complement, divine acceptation." As proof of this, he offers Trajan's insistence that he was freed from hell on account of his righteous deeds, rather than as a result of intercessory masses or prayers: "No episode in the poem marks Langland more clearly as a semi-Pelagian than this one." Adams also points out that although Trajan's good works were not enough to keep him out of hell initially, they did attract Pope Gregory's subsequent admiration; thus his works, though not sufficient alone to achieve salvation, "were, in some sense, a cause of the mercy granted him."[28] Many subsequent discussions of Trajan, such as those by John Burrow, James Simpson, and Emily Steiner, accept, at least in general, Langland's semi-Pelagianism, although a substantial attack on that conclusion has been made by Alastair Minnis.[29]

It is understandable that modern academic opinion should differ about the nature of Trajan's salvation, because ideas about it were not fixed in the Middle Ages. Langland's source, the *Legenda aurea*, concludes its account of Trajan with an extensive survey of different views of the emperor's fate, as noted above.[30] It reports that some say that Trajan was restored to life so that he could become a Christian and receive grace; others, that his punishment was only temporarily suspended; others, that he was sent to hell with the knowledge that Pope Gregory would eventually pray for his release; and still others, that even if Gregory did not actually pray for him, God often grants unexpressed wishes, though in any case Trajan was only granted relief from infernal pain, not heaven itself. Two starkly opposed views about Trajan's salvation in the popular English universal history the *Polychronicon* indicate the range of late medieval opinion on the issue.[31] In the original Latin *Polychronicon*, Ralph Higden gives a straightforward account of Trajan's deliverance because of his good works. The Middle English translation by John Trevisa reproduces Higden's account, modifying it only by adding the qualifying phrase "it semeth" in the concluding sentence: "For so greet rightwisnesse it semeth that Seint Gregorie wan his soule out of helle." But then, under his own name, Trevisa contemptuously rejects Higden's view, declaring that belief in the salvation of a damned soul is ridiculous and contrary to Christian doctrine, though "so it myghte seme to a man that were worse than wood, and out of right bileve."[32]

The question of Trajan's final location seems to be settled in *Piers* when the personification Imaginatif refers to him again in the next passus during a long and important discussion of the salvation of the righteous heathen. Imaginatif first explains that because "Troianus the trewe knyght" was not put very deep into hell (presumably because of his virtue), the Lord could more easily pluck him out, but, correspondingly, he now resides only in the "loweste" part of heaven (12.209–12). Later, Imaginatif makes a final statement about the emperor's religious status and eternal destination. Describing

Trajan once again as "a trewe knyght," though one who "took nevere Cristendom," Imaginatif declares that nevertheless "he is saaf, so seith the book, and his soule in hevene" (12.280–81).

Pagan Truth and Christian Love

The continuing debate among modern Langlandians about how and in what fashion Trajan was rescued from the pains of hell has diverted attention from the emperor's behavior while on earth and his relationship with Gregory, which are what Langland emphasizes in *Piers*. Langland's reimagining of the episode identifies each of these two ancient Romans with a specific virtue appropriate to his own historical period: the emperor's pagan *truthe* and the pope's Christian *love*. From his entrance into the poem, we are told of Trajan's truth. Initially characterized as "a trewe knyght" by the commentating voice, the emperor himself echoes and deepens the concept by turning the adjective into a noun at the end of his speech, when he refers to "my lyvynge in truthe." In Middle English, *truthe* is a powerful and profound concept, as Richard Firth Green has explicated in his magisterial *Crisis of Truth*. In addition to denoting what is factually accurate, *truthe* for Langland and his audience also meant, as it still sometimes does for us, righteousness, honesty, justice, loyalty, and even divinity. In his speech in *Piers*, Trajan's central claim is that he showed *truthe* as a Roman leader, as the *Legenda* confirms in its account of his response to the widow who demanded justice for her son. Langland's Trajan does not mention the widow or any other specific situation, but he instead speaks more generally of the "leautee of my lawful domes" (11.145), which might be paraphrased as "the justice of my equitable judgments."

After Trajan's speech, further commentary in the text, which repeats some of the emperor's own phrases, declares that the *truthe* of this ancient Roman is a model for contemporary English leaders who administer the law:

> Lo! ye lordes, what leautee dide by an Emperour of Rome
> That was an uncristene creature, as clerkes fyndeth in bokes.
> Nought thorugh preiere of a pope but for his pure truthe
> Was that Sarsen saved, as Seint Gregorie bereth witnesse.
> Wel oughte ye lordes that lawes kepe this lesson to have in mynde,
> And on Troianus truthe to thenke, and do truthe to the peple.
> (11.153–58)

As already noted, Schmidt, in his editions, like some other critics, assumes that Trajan is still speaking here despite the switch to the third person.[33] But another reason why the lines seem inappropriate to Trajan is that they refer to Gregory as a saint, a term not used by the emperor in his own speech; as already noted, he refers to Gregory only by name (11.146). The corresponding lines in the C-text are explicitly not by Trajan, for they begin the long passage that is eventually attributed to Rechelesnesse.

Whomever we take the speaker to be, the thrust of the lines quoted is that the ancient emperor's *truthe* is a good model for contemporary English authorities. *Piers Plowman*, even when most spiritually exalted, never wholly forgets the concerns of this world. Trajan may have achieved paradise, but Langland does not want his readers to overlook his earthly virtues. And now, for the first time in the poem, Trajan, previously identified in the episode only by name or as a knight, is explicitly linked with his imperial office. The "lordes" addressed in the first line of the verse quoted above are urged to consider what was accomplished by another leader, this "Emperour of Rome." Although Trajan was indeed "an uncristene creature" and a "Sarsen" (an even more loaded term), those who wield political power in England ("ye lordes that lawes keep," as he once did in Rome) are told to keep the "lesson" of his story "in mynde." These Christian leaders are urged to imitate the central virtue of a pagan and "on Troianus truthe to thenke." Moreover, they ought to put that truth into practice for all, high and low: "do truthe to the peple." The admonition in *Piers* is as arduous as it is stark, and, while ostensibly offering practical political advice in the tradition of those medieval mirrors for princes that lie behind book 7 in the *Confessio Amantis*, it goes further than John of Salisbury's praise of Trajan as a ruler to imagine an ideal civic community of truth beyond even Gower's hopes.

If Trajan's root virtue in *Piers Plowman* is *truthe*, that of Gregory, his fellow Roman, is *love*. This virtue is hardly surprising in a saint and gratifying to find in a pope, but Langland is unique among medieval writers in having Trajan himself twice give testimony about Gregory's love. The word first appears when Trajan says that no "clergie" could snatch him out of hell, "but oonliche love and leautee of my lawful domes" (11.144–45). The line might be read as Trajan's self-praise, in which the two alliterative words, "love" and "leautee," are parallel and both refer to himself: his own "love," as in his kindness to the widow (though this incident is not mentioned in *Piers*), and the "leautee" of his own lawful judgments. But it is more reasonable to take "love" here as referring to Gregory's merciful compassion for Trajan, which along with Trajan's "leautee" brought about his rescue. This interpretation is supported two lines later by Trajan's reference to Gregory's strong desire for his "savacion," as shown by the pope's weeping (11.147), and, even more firmly, by a second use of the word "love," when Trajan declares that he was "saved" not by the singing of masses but instead "by love and by lernyng of my lyvynge in truthe" (11.150–51). The love spoken of here must be Gregory's. The two words alliterating on the letter *l* ("love" and "lernyng") are clearly parallel here—the one who loves is also the one who learns about Trajan's exemplary conduct (he loves because he learns). Since that one can only be Gregory, it implies that the first use of the word "love" in the passage also refers to him. As Gregory praises the emperor's truth, so Trajan praises the pope's compassionate, saving love, his mercy.

The mercy of Gregory is found throughout the texts discussed in chapter 1 of this study. The *Indulgentiae ecclesiarum urbis Romae* and its Middle English verse translation, the *Stacions of Rome*, describe Rome as a place offering pardon and Gregory the Great as a major papal agent of that grace. Some Latin texts of the *Indulgentiae* name Gregory in the opening sentence as granting special pardons for pilgrims who visited St. Peter's and other principal basilicas of the city.[34] All versions, including the English *Stacions*, anachronistically attribute many of the specific pardons at individual churches to Gregory.[35] Even the extraordinary release of Trajan from hell that results from Gregory's intervention has a parallel in at least some versions of the *Stacions*. Although a number of Roman churches are said in such texts to grant to pilgrims at certain times the ability to free someone from purgatory, the Lambeth *Stacions* also claims, as noted in chapter 1, that "Seynt Gregory purchased syche grace" for the church of S. Andrea that any believer buried there "shall not be dampned for nought that he hathe doo, / But be saved frome the payne of hell."[36]

Although the *Indulgentiae* tradition shares the desire for God's grace found in Langland's Trajan episode, the understanding of that grace is radically different. The *Indulgentiae* promises that the problem of human sin and damnation can be remedied by the abundant pardons of Rome, whereas in *Piers Plowman*, the efficacy of such indulgence is repeatedly questioned. As already noted, a voice in the poem tells us that, at the Last Judgment, even a "pokeful of pardon" will be as useless as an old pie crust unless "Dowel yow helpe" (7.192–95). Unless, that is, you count on something like Trajan's "soothnesse" in works and "lyvynge in truthe"—the righteous behavior that earned him Gregory's love.

Trajan and Gregory, as Langland portrays them in *Piers Plowman*, appreciate each other's virtuousness, though one is pagan and the other Christian. In contrast to the *Stacions of Rome* and the interpolation on Rome in the *Metrical Version of Mandeville's Travels*, which are fundamentally hostile to paganism, this scene in *Piers* is not. As a Roman nobleman (in addition to a churchman), Gregory admires Trajan's upright moral integrity, a value prized by the city from the early days of the republic, many examples of which are presented in the Latin *Mirabilia*, such as the noble Roman who sacrificed his life by riding into a noxious chasm to save the city.[37] Correspondingly, Langland's Trajan admires the merciful love Gregory shows him, a more personal and focused compassion than the abundant, almost automatic pardons available at the city's many churches and shrines in the *Stacions of Rome*. Each of Langland's two ancient Romans not only embodies a virtue central to his own culture, but also esteems the virtue of the other. Gregory respects the pagan righteousness of Trajan, "the soothnesse that he seigh in my werkes," and Trajan likewise respects Gregory's Christian pity, which extends even to a nonbeliever like himself, for whom he "wepte and wilned me were graunted grace."

Roman Virtue and God's Grace

The C-text of *Piers Plowman* ends its Trajan/Gregory episode with the admonition to contemporary guardians of the law to follow truth (at B 11.158), but the B-text continues the episode.[38] After identifying the *Legenda* as its specific hagiographical source, the commentary voice returns to the exemplary virtues of Trajan and Gregory, which, though representative of the different periods of Rome in which each leader lived, are now seen as complementary, transcending the earthly city and reflecting divine grace:

> Ac thus leel love and lyvyng in truthe
> Pulte out of peyne a paynym of Rome.
> Yblissed be truthe that so brak helle yates
> And saved the Sarsyn from Sathanas and his power,
> Ther no clergie ne kouthe, ne konnyng of lawes!
> Love and leautee is a leel science,
> For that is the book blissed of blisse and of joye:
> God wroughte it and wroot it with his on fynger
> And took it Moises upon the mount, alle men to lere. (11.161–69)

In these lines, neither Trajan nor Gregory is called by name or title (though the former is referred to as a "paynym" and once again as a "Sarsyn"), but their distinctive virtues, already established in Trajan's own speech, are linked in the first line of the quotation. Both the "leel love," which Trajan has previously associated with Gregory, and the emperor's own "lyvyng in truthe" are together said to have "pulte out of peyne a paynym of Rome."

For all their individual merits, however, Trajan and Gregory are human beings. The next line in the quoted passage begins to suggest the divinity that was the real power behind the rescue of Trajan, a divinity identified as the highest manifestation of the emperor's characteristic virtue: "Yblissed be truthe that so brak helle yates." This is a reference to nothing less than divine Truth itself, and if Middle English manuscripts followed our system of capitalization, the word would be in uppercase. The Truth described here is indeed "yblissed," a supernatural force that, rather than merely rescuing a single figure like Trajan from hell (remarkable as that was), destroys the very gates of the infernal kingdom. But in addition to combatting evil, more awesome still is Truth's loving mercy, which "saved the Sarsyn" from the clutches of "Sathanas and his power." Truth does what human effort, however holy or just, cannot: "Ther no clergie ne kouthe, ne konnyng of lawes!" Trajan's rescue depends on more than just the virtues of the emperor himself ("konnyng of lawes" suggests his "lawful domes") or the virtues of the other exemplary Roman in the episode ("clergie" suggests both Gregory's learning and his papal office). Instead of the human justice that English secular lawgivers are urged to practice just a few lines before, we are now introduced to a more profound, sacred power: the "leel science" of "love and leautee." Love, of course, is Gregory's virtue and "leautee" a form of Trajan's truth, both of which are linked once again and then traced back to their divine source. Long before Trajan or Gregory, the eternal God wrote this "science" in a holy book with "his on fynger." It is a "book" that cannot be dismissed with a "baw" because, in addition to being "blissed," it tells "of blisse and of joye" in the form of the Ten Commandments given to Moses on Sinai and applies to "alle men"—that is, rich and poor, powerful and lowly, Jews, Christians, and pagans alike.

Trajan appears once more in this episode to speak, in the racy, colloquial style of his first words, a final line that sums up his relationship with Gregory: "'Lawe withouten love,' quod Trojanus, 'ley ther a bene'" (11.170). Although the epigram may appear to praise love at the expense of law, it is another example of the convergence of the virtues of our two exemplary Romans.[39] Trajan is not denying the value of the law he upheld so justly—a law that might have also suggested to Langland's Christian readers the divine law of the Ten Commandments. Rather, he is saying, as Saint Paul and Saint Augustine did, that following the law, even divine law, is of little worth without the generous human love demonstrated by Gregory, a love that reflects God's love for all.

Unlike some medieval versions of the Trajan legend, Langland's does not bring the emperor back to life so that he may be baptized a Christian. He remains a pagan, and so his salvation must come from outside his own world. To indicate this, Langland gives Trajan a vocabulary that, while appropriate to an "uncristene creature," contains Christian resonances. Thus Trajan says that his salvation is due to "my lawful domes" and to the "soothnesse" of "my werkes" (11.145–47). It is for just such law-giving and good works that John of Salisbury considered Trajan the best of Roman emperors. Yet Trajan's words would also have suggested Christian concepts familiar to Langland's readers. The word "domes," for example, while applicable to imperial judicial rulings, is a form of the common Middle English word for the Last Judgment, the Doom. Trajan risked having his initial damnation confirmed for eternity on the Day of Doom, but because of his truthfulness (and because of Gregory's love), he will receive the divine grace that might well be denied, according to *Piers*, to professed Christians who rely only on pardons to save them. Similarly, Trajan's use of the word "werkes" evokes the dictum in the Epistle of James (2:26) that faith without works is dead, which is quoted in Latin earlier in *Piers* and memorably rendered as "feith withouten feet is feblere than nought, / And as deed as a dorenail but if the dedes folwe" (1.186–87). The good works of Trajan, despite his lack of faith, are what attract Gregory's respect and lead to the rescue of this "Sarsyn" from the pit of hell into the bliss of heaven. Langland's Gregory does not use his papal office to recite intercessory masses for Trajan, nor does he grant pardons as in the *Stacions of Rome*, for we are explicitly told that the emperor was not saved "thorugh preiere of a pope" (11.155). Instead, Gregory more humbly weeps out of his own human sympathy for Trajan and awaits the mysterious workings of divine mercy, like any other Christian.

The Resonance of the Trajan/Gregory Episode

Appearing near the very center of the poem, the conjunction of Trajan and Gregory contains, in Nevill Coghill's brilliant formulation, those "foretastes and echoes" that make *Piers Plowman* such an intricate and subtle work.[40] In addition to being historical figures of pagan and Christian Rome, respectively, Trajan and Gregory are also symbols of the dialectic between justice and mercy that occupies so much of Langland's poem and is perhaps its major theme. That Trajan is a representative of justice is seen in his insistence on the equity of his "lawful domes" and in the comparison of him with those in England who "lawes kepe," though the word Langland most often uses to evoke his justice, as we have seen, is the much richer Middle English word *truthe*. Truth in this sense is a traditional Roman virtue, as exemplified by Lucius Junius Brutus, cousin of Lucretia, who executed his own son because he was a traitor to the republic, yet it is, of course, even more central to Christianity, as in Christ's claim that he is the way, the truth, and the life (John 14:6). Truth in all of these senses is a central topic from beginning to end in *Piers Plowman*, a poem John Alford has labeled "a poetic *summa* on truth."[41] In passus 1, Holy Church, who is the dreamer/narrator's first instructor, explains that the tower on the field of folk is the location of Truth ("Truthe is therinne"), whom she identifies with the deity, the "fader of feith, formed yow alle" (1.12–14). Holy Church goes on to advocate a just way of living characterized by "mesure," in contrast to the unlawful extravagances of Meed, an argument she frames with the statement "Whan alle tresors arn tried, Truthe is the beste" (1.85 and 1.135). Truth is also, of course, the figure whom the folk seek after the confession of the sins in B 5 and whom Piers the Plowman, as he enters the poem, claims to know "as kyndely as clerc doth his bokes" (5.538). After the failure to plow the half acre, Truth also sends the pardon that Piers tears in frustration. Thus, well before the appearance of Trajan in the poem, truth has been established as a high, even divine ideal, perhaps unrealizable by humans on earth. Yet whereas Piers's relationship with truth is somewhat troubled, the same is not so with the pagan Trajan. He claims to go beyond knowing truth to having lived it, and because of that to have achieved heaven. Later in the poem, after he confirms Trajan's salvation, Imaginatif makes the case, in language that depends more on poetic wordplay than strict logic, that God must reward truth like Trajan's: "Ne wolde nevere trewe God but trewe truthe were allowed" (12.287), though this is expressed as a "hope" rather than a certainty (12.289). When Trajan is lauded by Gregory for his truth, he manifests a virtue already deeply embedded in the poem.

Piers Plowman is a summa on truth, but it could as easily be called a summa on love. The poem twice says that the emotion Gregory feels for

Trajan is love; it is the pope's root virtue in the episode. Like Trajan's truth, Gregory's love also participates in the foretastes and echoes of *Piers Plowman*, serving to link the Trajan/Gregory episode to other key moments in the poem. Love is a word also used by Holy Church, who justifies her claim that truth is the best of all treasures with the text *Deus caritas* (1.86) from 1 John 4:8: "He that loveth not, knoweth not God; for God is charity." Later, in the face of the dreamer's protestation that he lacks "kynde knowynge" of her teaching (1.138), Holy Church attempts to edify him by means of the extraordinary "plant of peace" passage, which begins by firmly linking truth and love, "For Truthe telleth that love is triacle of hevene" (1.148). The *Stacions of Rome* talks about the "medicyn" of pardon, as discussed in chapter 1, but Holy Church advocates divine love as an even more powerful cure in this world and a sure road to the next:

> "Love is leche of lif and next Oure Lord selve,
> And also the graithe gate that goth into hevene." (1.204–5)

Gregory's love, which helps Trajan on his way to heaven, also looks forward to the Good Samaritan in B 17, who practices the mercy and love of Christian charity. Just as Gregory wished ("wilned") for Trajan's salvation, the Samaritan concludes his speech by insisting that there is no man so wretched that he cannot love and

> "bothe wisshen and wilnen
> Alle manere men mercy and foryifnesse,
> And lovye hem lik hymself." (17.348–50)

Anomalous as the episode featuring the Romans Trajan and Gregory may seem when compared to the characters and settings in the rest of *Piers Plowman*, their two specific virtues, often combined as a pair, anticipate important moments later in the poem. The truth and love, or justice and mercy, represented by Trajan and Gregory are most fully realized in B 18 of *Piers Plowman*, the spiritual climax of the poem in which Christ rides to a death that will bring eternal life to men and women. It is one thing for Gregory or any being, however saintly, to desire the salvation of someone else; it is quite another to bring it about for all humankind, as Christ does so spectacularly in the Harrowing of Hell after his crucifixion. In freeing the souls imprisoned in the pit of hell (just as Trajan himself will later be both imprisoned there and freed), the Lord declares that he acts with both justice and mercy: "I may do mercy thorugh rightwisnesse, and alle my wordes trewe" (18.390). Earlier in the passus, Christ had been called "Truthe" by a fiend (18.294), and the same name and ability to break "wide open the yates" of hell (18.323) have already been announced in the Trajan episode: "Yblissed be truthe that so brak helle yates" (11.163). As he engineers this blessed jailbreak, Christ also declares that "love is my drynke" (18.366). He performs mercy and justice simultaneously during the Harrowing, combining the principal virtues of Langland's Gregory and Trajan.

The fraternal relationship between Trajan and Gregory, fellow ancient Romans who respect one another despite their different historical periods, also looks forward to the sisterly kinship of the Four Daughters of God in B 18, whose reconciliation Langland uses to frame the Harrowing of Hell. The two most prominent of the daughters, Truth and Mercy (comparable to Trajan and Gregory, respectively, as are the two other daughters, Righteousness and Peace), are first shown debating the meaning of what they see happening in hell. Truth and Righteousness, who argue for strict divine justice, are unwilling, like Trevisa in the *Polychronicon*, to accept that any rescue of the damned is possible, insisting, as Truth puts it, that if a soul is "ones in helle, out cometh it nevere" (18.148). Their belief is challenged by Peace's announcement that her sweetheart, Love, has said that she and her sister Mercy "mankynde sholde save" (18.182). The two compassionate sisters are right, but their stricter siblings are not wholly wrong in that Langland's Christ, as the poet makes clear, also acts justly at the Harrowing, though not in the narrow way they expect. In a more intimate and more joyous version of the mutual affection of Trajan and Gregory, the Four Daughters of God kiss one another at the end of B 18 while dancing a carol, as Love sings about brotherly unity until Easter dawns. This resolution of apparent differences, reminiscent of the end of a Mozart opera, implies, once again more through art than through argument, that Christ's vow during the Harrowing to "have out of helle alle mennes soules" (18.373) applies not just to exceptional cases like the Jewish patriarchs and Trajan. In the sole Roman episode of *Piers Plowman*, Langland portrays Trajan as a paradigm of pagan justice far exceeding any of the *Mirabilia*'s civic heroes, and Gregory as an example of Christian mercy more reliable than the papal pardons of the *Stacions*. The dual legacy of ancient Rome, pagan and Christian, is explored more profoundly here than in the tales of either Gower or Chaucer—and reconciled. The exercise of truth and love by Trajan and Gregory, and their respect for each other, is a *figura* of the brotherhood and blood relationship that Christ says he shares with all his human kindred. Trajan and Gregory were each eminences in ancient Rome, but the truth of the one and the love of the other are finally combined, fulfilled, and salvific not in the earthly city each led but in the heavenly city of God.

CHAPTER 6

Tragic Romans in Lydgate's *Fall of Princes*

John Lydgate's *Fall of Princes*, as the first word of its title proclaims, is a record of catastrophes, and none are given more attention than those that befell ancient Rome and Romans. Lydgate's last major poem (written 1431–38) and his longest, at 36,365 lines, the *Fall* echoes, sometimes deliberately, elements of many of the Middle English poems on ancient Rome already discussed.[1] It includes descriptions of the physical city and its customs found more extensively in the *Mirabilia* tradition, and a long, positive account of the first Christian emperor, Constantine, as in the *Stacions of Rome*, though there is no evidence that Lydgate knew either of these poems.[2] He did, however, know the poetry of Chaucer and Gower well, and he retells some of their Roman tales in the *Fall*. What may be unexpected in a poet so easy to underrate, however, is the skill with which Lydgate develops the topic of Rome by reshaping episodes from his principal French source and by adding new material of his own. Two powerful examples of this are the long original Envoy to Rome on the ruin of the ancient city that ends book 2 and the radical reworking of the story of the violation and death of the noble Roman wife Lucretia found in both books 2 and 3.

The daunting length of the *Fall of Princes* has often discouraged analysis, but the poem has recently attracted renewed attention and respect.[3] Nigel Mortimer, in the first book-length study of the *Fall*, reminds us of the esteem in which it was held by Renaissance writers and demonstrates the learning and labor Lydgate put into the poem, especially its early books.[4] Maura Nolan argues for the "aesthetic" achievement of the *Fall* (and that of Lydgate's earlier prose Roman work, *The Serpent of Division*), by which she principally means the poet's awareness of the intertexual and didactic complexity of writing about the past.⁵ Others have encouraged us to look more carefully at the literary influence of the *Fall of Princes*; Paul Strohm notes its many contributions to fifteenth- and early sixteenth-century English literature, and Larry Scanlon contends that it anticipates Renaissance tragedy.⁶

Because Rome is not mentioned in the title of the *Fall of Princes*, and because stories about it are mixed in with so many others, the city's importance in the poem is easy to underestimate.⁷ Yet more of the *Fall*'s narratives are set in Rome than in any other ancient city, and no other Middle English poem begins to equal the number of these episodes. Given the sheer amount of Roman material in the *Fall*, it is not surprising that Lydgate does not achieve even the generally consistent view of the city found in Gower (Rome as civic model), Chaucer (Rome as oppressor of noble women), or Langland (Rome as site of pagan truth and Christian love). If Lydgate's Rome, and the *Fall of Princes* as a whole, has any general lesson to teach, it is a monkish one about the vanity of this world. As in Augustine's *City of God*, ancient pagan Rome in the *Fall* stands for the ephemeral earthly city as opposed to the heavenly one. Lydgate's patron, Humphrey, Duke of Gloucester, requested that the poem instruct princes about how to avoid the kinds of downfall from power it records. But if the poem's narratives and envoys demonstrate anything, it is that the calamities that beset human life are too many and too varied to render any such cautionary advice useful.⁸ As James Simpson says, "The sheer density, variety, and rapidity of noble descents in this work finally beggars any ethical account of why kings fall; they just do, whatever their ethical status."⁹ Those who are good and prudent fall as surely as those who are bad and foolish, and Rome provides the richest source of such tragedies.

Rome in Laurent and Lydgate

Stories about ancient Rome were already prominent in Lydgate's principal source, Laurent de Premierfait's prose *Des cas des nobles hommes et femmes* (1409), the second version of his translation of Giovanni Boccaccio's prose *De casibus virorum illustrium*, one of the vast Latin encyclopedic works of the Italian writer's later career.¹⁰ Although Lydgate frequently announces that he is following "Bochas," there is no evidence that he knew the Latin work, which does not seem to have achieved wide circulation in England.¹¹ Laurent's translation, by contrast, was extremely popular. Its nine books generally follow Boccaccio's *De casibus*, retelling most of its stories while generally amplifying them.¹² Ancient Rome first appears in book 2 and is a major subject throughout most of books 3, 5, 6, 7, 8, and the beginning of book 4. The Romans Boccaccio and Laurent mention include those we have already met in this study, Lucretia, Virginia, Julius Caesar, Octavian, Trajan, and Nero, along with a considerable number of additional figures, including Marcus Manlius, Regulus, the Scipios, and Galba and other late emperors.

Had Lydgate done no more than mechanically translate Laurent's *Cas des nobles hommes* into English, he would have performed a great service by making so many ancient stories about Rome and other places available in the vernacular. But instead of merely reproducing what he found in his source, Lydgate was an active and innovative translator. He turned Laurent's prose into poetry, for example, and replaced the first-person speeches of Fortune's victims with his own third-person narration. Lydgate's most obvious additions in the *Fall* are the formal envoys that follow many of his stories, whose metrical ingenuity and rhetorical power have been praised even by those most skeptical of the poet's skills. The English poet constantly modified what he found in Laurent. Sometimes, especially in the later books, Lydgate abridged, but more often, as we would expect from his other work, he amplified, just as Laurent had amplified Boccaccio.

As part of this general expansion in the *Fall*, Lydgate provides antiquarian knowledge of Rome that far exceeds anything in the works of Gower, Chaucer, or Langland. Although some of his material about the ancient city is taken more or less directly from Laurent's *Cas des nobles hommes*, such as accounts of Romulus's Asylum for fugitives by which the city was first populated (2.4166–83) and of Nero's richly decorated *Domus aurea* (7.659–69), the English poet also adds new information, such as mention in his Envoy to Rome (discussed below) about three famous Roman monuments also found in the *Mirabilia* tradition, though that work does not appear to be the poet's immediate source.¹³ The first of these structures is the statue, "clere of golde shining," erected by Romulus in his palace (2.4481–83), also found in chapter 6 of the original *Mirabilia* (though Lydgate says nothing about its collapse at the birth of Christ). The second is a temple of gold and crystal displaying "the heavenly spheres" (2.4484–87), most probably the astrological Olovitreum in chapter 30 of the *Mirabilia*, but just possibly the Temple of the Sun that so fascinates and frightens the English poet of the

Metrical Mandeville. The third structure is the temple that contained images of Roman provinces with bells around their necks that warned the city of rebellion (2.4495–501), which is described in chapter 16 of the *Mirabilia* and attributed here to Virgil.[14]

Such passages are often ignored by modern critics as digressions, but they are crucial examples of the English poet's efforts to provide a more complete account of Roman life than that found in Laurent's *Cas des nobles hommes*. The long narrative about the rise and fall of Marcus Manlius, who defended the Roman Capitol from invaders but was later executed for abusing his power (4.211–637), is an excellent example of Lydgate's thick or at least abundant description of ancient Rome. To Laurent's bare fact that Manlius was awarded certain crowns as a reward for his great deeds, for instance, Lydgate adds ninety lines naming the seven different kinds of Roman crowns (triumphal, obsidional, mural, naval, castrence, oval, and civic), identifies the materials from which each was made, and explains the particular achievement each honored (4.232–322).[15] A more impressive example of Lydgate's antiquarianism is the extended description of a Roman triumph (4.512–74) added to the Manlius episode. Lydgate says that he is following "John Bochas" here, but neither Boccaccio nor Laurent includes any such account.[16] The lines seem to draw from what is said about triumphs in Gower's *Confessio Amantis* and in the monk's own earlier *Serpent of Division*, but the *Fall of Princes* also contains its own unique information, such as that a triumph had to be approved by all three estates of Rome (4.519–25).[17] As in the *Serpent*, but not the *Confessio*, the destination of Manlius's triumph is precisely located in the Roman cityscape: "To the Capitoile so he shal be brouht" (4.562). This added detail enables Lydgate to make a grimly ironic point. The same Capitol that Manlius once saved and is now being brought to in triumph will later be the site of his downfall (both figuratively and literally), when he is sentenced to be thrown from its heights (4.484–90, 575–603).[18] In his description of Manlius's fatal punishment, Lydgate supplies further topographical detail not in his source. He identifies the precise location on the Capitoline Hill from which the condemned were flung to their deaths as the Tarpeian Rock, which, he then informs us, was named after a condemned woman, though he adds that this place was also known as "Carmentoun," after another woman who built the Capitol and first invented the Roman alphabet (4.603–16).[19] Such supplementary information about Roman locations and practices suggests how much trouble Lydgate took to describe the ancient city for his readers.

Lydgate's Ambition: Translation Theory in the Prologue

In the prologue to book 1, under cover of various expressions of deference and humility, undoubtedly learned from Chaucer, Lydgate suggests his lofty ambitions for the *Fall of Princes* by asserting the value of translations that transform their originals, as he is about to do in the work that follows.[20] He repeats Laurent's claim that it is proper for a writer to alter a literary work to make it better, as a potter breaks an old vessel to refashion it anew (1.8–14).[21] Building on Laurent's image, Lydgate develops the idea of innovative translation by mentioning "artificeres" (the word denotes skilled craftsmanship) who "chaunge and turne" the "shappis" and "formys" of an inherited work "and newli hem devyse" (1.9–11). The adverb "newli" suggests not just a better work but a different one (forms of the word *new* appear five times within three stanzas, at 1.11, 14, 18, 23, and 28). Lydgate here envisions a literary re-creation undertaken by "men off crafft" who are "inventiff," even visionary, because they are able to "fantasien in ther inward siht / Devises newe thoruh ther exellence" (1.15–18).[22] Lydgate then echoes Chaucerian language to declare that the ideal translator/writer takes a work "maad of auctours hem beforn" and renders such "old chaff" into "ful cleene corn" (1.22–24).[23] This image suggests a transformation that goes far beyond adaptation: the waste of old chaff is somehow reborn as fresh, wholesome wheat.[24] Having anticipated Ezra Pound's famous modernist injunction to "make it new" with his own bold declarations, Lydgate more modestly concludes his own original statements about authorial transformation by returning to Laurent's cautionary admonition that translators should have "no presumpcioun" but rather, in a nicely paradoxical phrase not in Laurent, should take care that "meeknesse have dominacioun" (1.29–31).[25] The literary alchemy that Lydgate imagines here is, in fact, attempted in many of his Roman episodes in the *Fall of Princes*, as we shall see, though, as in this initial prologue, their originality is often camouflaged.[26]

Lydgate's ambition and skill are evident later in the prologue to book 1 in his praise of his great poetic predecessor, Chaucer, and of his royal patron, Gloucester. Despite the deference he expresses to both, Lydgate also makes an artistic space for himself by indirectly claiming that he is worthy both to continue Chaucer's work and deserve Gloucester's respect.[27] Halfway through the prologue, in one of the most famous passages in the *Fall of Princes*, Lydgate stops to lament the death of Chaucer:

> My maistir Chaucer, with his fresh comedies,
> Is ded, allas, cheeff poete off Breteyne,
> That whilom made ful pitous tragedies;
> The fall of pryncis he dede also compleyne. (1.246–49)

Lydgate's praise of Chaucer is undoubtedly sincere, but he expresses it in such a way that it serves to elevate his own reputation as well. After mentioning Chaucer's "fresh comedies," Lydgate notes that the older poet also wrote "ful pitous tragedies" about the "fall of pryncis." Since Chaucer is dead, that leaves a vacancy for "cheeff poete off Breteyne"—and who better to fill it than the author of the *Fall of Princes*? As if to make absolutely clear what sort of poet ought to be Chaucer's successor, Lydgate goes on to name three other literary paragons (two Roman and a third who was made a laureate in the city), each of whom, along with Boccaccio, wrote tragedies—Seneca, Tullius (Cicero), and Petrarch (1.253)—and by so doing achieved "famous renoun" and "gret worshipe dede unto ther nacioun" (1.272–73).[28] In a long catalogue of Chaucer's works (1.281–357), the title Lydgate names last is the *Monk's Tale*: "how the Monk off stories newe & olde / Pitous tragedies be the weie tolde" (1.349–50).[29] If the handful of tragedies of past worthies in the *Monk's Tale* helped to bolster Chaucer's exalted literary reputation, what must be the effect of the greatest collection of such tragedies yet attempted in English?

The second encomium in the prologue to book 1, to the Duke of Gloucester, is even more obsequious than the one to Chaucer but equally confident about Lydgate's role as poet.[30] He praises Gloucester for, among other things, his power, his royal birth, his prudence, his command of language and knowledge of books, and his stout defense of the church against Lollardy and heresy (1.372–413). Even before he names him, Lydgate compares Gloucester to Gower's hero, Julius Caesar, who, despite "his conquest & renoun," paid "gret attendaunce" to books and took "joie and gret pleasunce" in stories (1.365–71). But, as with Chaucer, Lydgate's praise of Gloucester also reflects well on himself.[31] After all, this royal paragon chose him to turn "the noble book off this John Bochas" (1.423) into English, and even as he presents himself as a client of the duke, the poet asserts his literary independence. The duke believes in the positive effects of reading books; they "bryngith in vertu," suppress vice, and help a prince "to knowe hymsilff" and correct his errors (1.416–20). But Lydgate has already shown himself to be less certain of literature's moral benefits, as he will further demonstrate in many of his Roman narratives. Earlier in the prologue, he suggests a more modest, less practical benefit of reading literature: it can teach us not to overvalue human accomplishment and instead accept that "in worldly worshepe may be no surete" (1.56).

The Tragedy of Pagan Rome

The envoys that Lydgate added to many of the narratives in the *Fall of Princes* have no precedent in Laurent's *Cas des nobles hommes*.[32] The most admired of these, and the one that often appears as an independent extract in medieval manuscripts, is the long and intricate Envoy to Rome that concludes book 2 (2.4460–592).[33] A virtuoso performance, the Envoy to Rome uses only three rhymes throughout, as do all of Lydgate's envoys, but this one sustains such a restricted rhyme scheme for a full nineteen stanzas of seven lines each, rather than the usual three to five stanzas. Derek Pearsall, who is sometimes dismissive of the poetry in the *Fall*, concedes that the Envoy to Rome is "an extraordinary technical achievement" and, "apart from one or two lapses, maintains a tone of lofty eloquence."[34] According to Lydgate, Gloucester requested that "everi tragedie" be followed with a "remedie" to teach princely readers how "bi othres fallyng thei myht themsilff correcte" (2.146–54). Yet, unlike his other envoys in the *Fall*, the Envoy to Rome is addressed not to the reader or to Gloucester's princes but to the ancient city itself in the form of an *ubi sunt* lament (the early stanzas of which begin "wher be" or "wher is"). Nor does the envoy provide the practical advice Gloucester sought that would assist a ruler in self-correction.[35] Instead, ending each stanza with the refrain word "ruin," the Envoy to Rome tells of the fall of the ancient city.

Although the word "tragedie," used eighty-five times in the *Fall of Princes* according to Mortimer, does not appear in the Envoy to Rome, the fall of the ancient city is a tragedy by the definition Lydgate gives later in the poem—"For tragedie, as poetes spesephie, / Gynneth with joie, eendith with adversite" (5.3120–22)—an adaptation of Chaucer's words in the *Monk's Tale*: "Of hym that stood in greet prosperitee, / And is yfallen . . . / Into myserie."[36] Both Lydgate and Chaucer associate tragedy with personal calamity (such as Adam's fall or the assassination of Caesar at the height of his power), but in the Envoy to Rome, ruin is even more devastating. Not just individuals but what Lydgate later calls the "cite of cites" (8.2542) is swept away. The fall of ancient Rome from "joie" and "prosperitee" into "adversite" and "myserie" is total: the ancient city's dazzling marvels, its worthy deeds, and its wickedness, like the snows of yesteryear, have passed away, as do all things in this world.

The long, original Envoy to Rome, Lydgate's most direct judgment of the city in the *Fall of Princes*, is a powerful and complex attempt to assess what had been lost with the fall of ancient Rome, and why. Drawing on his learning, the poet first describes the ancient city's vices and its virtues, all of which, the good and the bad, have inevitably succumbed to the destruction of time. The second part of the envoy, however, identifies a deeper reason for pagan Rome's ruin, its separation from God, a division that can be healed only by Christian belief and practice.

Despite the melancholy that is common in the *ubi sunt* form, the poet's initial tone in the Envoy to Rome is less elegiac than accusatory, reminiscent of Saint Augustine's famous and thorough denunciation of pagan Rome in his early fifth-century *City of God*.[37] Lydgate, likewise, attacks the city by first reminding it of its "fals begynnyng," because of its "fals discencioun / Off slauhtre, moordre & outraious robbyng" (2.4460–66), a specific reference to the criminal acts of Romulus and Remus and their murderous fraternal strife (condemned in the *City of God* at 3.6 and likened to that of Cain and Abel at 15.5), which the English poet, generally following Laurent, has just narrated at length (2.3963–4263).[38] Later Roman leaders are hardly better, however, as seen in a list of crimes by various kinds of city officials: "the grete extorsioun" of consuls, the "oppressyng" of prefects, "the fals collusioun" of dictators, "the froward deceyvyng" of decemvirs, and "the fraudulent werkyng" of tribunes, all which "odious ravyne" time has "brouht onto ruyne" (2.4502–8). The general condemnation of ancient Rome that follows is even more explicitly Augustinian (2.4509–15): the city is blamed because of its lust for power ("thi dominacioun" and "the world al hool in thi subjeccioun"), its savagery ("the suerd of vengaunce all peeplis manacyng"), and its insatiable avarice ("ever gredi tencrece in thi getyng").[39]

The Envoy to Rome is not just a critique, however, and Lydgate, even more than Augustine, complicates his portrait of the ancient city by acknowledging that it also possessed elements of nobility, though the *ubi sunt* formula reminds us that these, too, have long since disappeared. Where now, the envoy asks, is the "lordshepe" of great Roman leaders like Julius Caesar and Octavian (2.4474–80), and where is "Tullius" (Cicero), whose rhetoric made him "cheeff lanterne off thi toun" (2.4488–89)? Where is "moral Senek or prudent sad Catoun," or Langland's great pagan hero, the "rihtful Trajan, most just in his demyng" (2.4490–93)?[40] The greatest Roman heroes, along with the city's wickedest criminals, all have come to naught.

Almost exactly halfway through the Envoy to Rome, Lydgate abandons his *ubi sunt* litany to give a more fundamental reason than the passage of time for the utter destruction of Rome and Romans: paganism. The ancient city, given to "goddis, goddessis falsli obeieng" (2.4519), is cut off from the Christian God and his salvation. Once again, the *Fall* is in accord here with the *City of God*. In the last chapter of his second book, Augustine exhorts Romans to reject "the degraded folly and malignant imposture of the [pagan] demons," saying that such "ungodliness" will bring them "to ruin and punishment." Instead, the saint urges them to accept "the true remission of sins" so that they become able to "take possession of the Heavenly Country" presided over by "the one true God" and forsake those "false and deceitful gods" who are nothing but "malignant fiends" (2.29). Lydgate's Envoy to Rome similarly begs the city to repent and renounce its sham religion: "Confesse thyn outrage, & lei thi boost a-doun / Alle false goddis pleynli diffieng" (2.4525–26). In the five stanzas that follow, the pagan deities are specifically denounced, one after another, from Saturn to the Gorgons, further evidence of Lydgate's knowledge of Roman culture (2.4530–62).

Lydgate concludes his attack on the pagan gods with the statement that "Crist Jesu may be thi medicyne" against "such raskaile to save the fro ruyne" (2.4563–64), borrowing the word "raskaile" from the denunciation of the pagan gods at the end of Chaucer's *Troilus and Criseyde*.[41] Like *Troilus* and Augustine, Lydgate not only damns Rome's false gods; he also promises the city a Christian remedy. In the second half of the envoy, each stanza continues to end with "ruyne," but now, instead of referring to Rome's fall, the word offers the cure for that dismal fate: the blood of Christ, who "hath maad thi ransoun to save the fro ruyne" (2.4529). The phrase "save the fro ruyne" ends all but one (the last) of the final nine stanzas of the envoy.

When Augustine urges Romans to reject their demonic gods and become Christians, he is addressing those who are still pagan, whereas Rome in Lydgate's day had been the seat of Christianity for a thousand years. Nevertheless, the English poet's language is equally passionate as he addresses the city ("O Rome, Rome") and begs it to put aside false pagan "cerimonies" and instead "Cri God merci, thi trespacis repentyng" (2.4579–82). The language of repentance, echoing a previous plea for Rome to "confesse" its outrages and false gods (2.4525–26), might seem to modern readers little more than an anachronistic rhetorical display. How can a culture that no longer exists repent of anything, let alone its long abolished religion? But ancient pagan Rome in the *Fall of Princes*, as in the *City of God*, is more than a particular place at a particular time with a particular system of belief; it also represents the ultimate futility of all worldly power. The final stanza of the Envoy to Rome makes this explicit, as Lydgate at last speaks directly to the princes whom Gloucester wanted advised by such envoys; in so doing, he draws the moral he believes the past always teaches: "O noble Pryncis, off hih discrecioun / Seeth in this world ther is non abidyng . . ." (2.4586–87); or as the Douay-Rheims Bible phrases the same idea, "For we have not here a lasting city" (Heb. 13:14). The ultimate lesson of Rome (or any earthly city) is that its glories, like its crimes, pass away, as Lydgate makes clear in the envoy's final couplet, which uses the word "ruin" for a final time to warn against trust in this world: "Lat this conceit ay in your thouhtis myne, / Bexaumple off Rome how al goth to ruyne" (2.4591–92). Despite Gloucester's hope for practical remedies, ancient Rome proves that there are none that can protect princes or other humans from the inexorable tragedy of unredeemed life in this world.

As Lydgate prepares to leave pagan Rome behind in the penultimate book of the *Fall of Princes*, he adds another original episode set in the city about the emperor Constantine, which both illustrates the repentance and conversion he had urged in the Envoy to Rome and provides an example of an ideal Roman leader.[42] This extended portrait demonstrates that even at a late stage in the *Fall*, the poet was actively amplifying his portrayal of Rome (8.1170–463).[43] Lydgate admits that the Constantine material is a "digressioun," since "Bochas" says little about him (8.1173–74). In fact, it is largely derived from the *Legenda aurea*, as are accounts of the emperor in the *Stacions of Rome* and *Confessio Amantis*, but whereas the *Stacions* emphasizes the divine grace bestowed on Constantine, and Gower shows that his pagan virtue was compromised after his conversion by the foolish gift of temporal power to the papacy, Lydgate salutes this former pagan as a model Christian ruler.[44] After his conversion in the *Fall*, the emperor acknowledges the pope's spiritual authority by going to him and, despite his own "roial excellence," making "his confessioun in open audience" (8.1343–44), just as he later helps build the papal church at the Lateran with his own hands (8.1394–400). Lydgate does not treat the emperor's reconsecration of the temple of Apollo as St. Peter's Basilica as an example of the continuity between pagan and Christian Rome (8.1273–74), as the Latin *Mirabilia* does with the Pantheon, but instead stresses the necessity of destroying the old religion to establish the new one, as in the Rome interpolation in the *Metrical Mandeville*. Lydgate's Constantine orders that Roman temples, with their "false goddis of silver & gold," be "tobroke upon ech partie" (8.1277–78).[45] At the same time, Lydgate's Constantine, unlike Gower's, for all his displays of Christian piety and devotion, does not compromise his royal authority (or poison the church) by giving his secular power to the pope, even though this so-called Donation is a significant moment in the *Legenda aurea*.⁴⁶ Constantine in the *Fall* is said to be "of Cristes feith thymperial champioun" (8.1440), and it is precisely by retaining his imperial power that he is able to be an effective Christian champion.⁴⁷ Constantine, almost alone in the *Fall of Princes*, suffers no fall: his rule is a political and spiritual success, the very opposite of a tragedy.

Roman Tragedies

Tragedies of Political Division

Lydgate's Envoy to Rome provides a Christian perspective for understanding the narratives of the downfall of individual Romans interspersed throughout the *Fall of Princes*. Repeatedly, these Roman tragedies are attributed to division: division between princes, or between princes and the state, or even division within the psyches of princes or other Roman men and women. Lydgate had already identified division as a characteristic Roman vice in his first work on the city, the *Serpent of Division*, which, as Nolan has shown, owes much to Gower's "thorough exegesis of division" in the prologue to the *Confessio Amantis*.⁴⁸ Like Gower, Lydgate in the *Serpent* finds the division between God and man in Eden to be the root of all subsequent divisions (thus the image of the serpent), a breach that is healed only by Christ's redemption. The *Confessio* contains some practical advice about avoiding political, as opposed to spiritual, division, such as ancient Rome's self-correcting civic governance, but Lydgate is more skeptical of such remedies than Gower.⁴⁹ The *Fall of Princes* presents only isolated examples of civic virtue but many more of conflict and rupture. In its penultimate book, Lydgate specifically reverts to the language of the *Serpent*, saying that Rome was a gloriously preeminent city until "discord, dyvisioun and envie" eclipsed its brightness "bi a false serpent brought in bi doubilnesse" (8.2542–48).⁵⁰

Roman division takes many forms in the *Fall*, but it is found throughout the city's ancient history. It has its origin in the "fraternal discord" of Romulus and Remus during Rome's founding (2.4110). Incapable of sharing power, the brothers resort to bird augury (another of Lydgate's additions concerning Roman customs). On the Aventine Hill, Romulus sees more birds than Remus does and so gets to rule and name the city after himself (2.4114–37), while Remus is soon killed. The divisions of some later Romans are between themselves and the city itself, for even those who have done the most for its welfare may suffer from its ill treatment. Coriolanus complains about "thyngratitude / Off the Romeyns," in spite of his unceasing efforts "ther comoun profit tawmente and encrese" (3.1895–900). The three noble Scipios (Africanus, Asiaticus, and Nasica), who served Rome well (5.1640–712, 1713–47, and 1776–845), all come into conflict with the city and are exiled or murdered.[51] Like Coriolanus, they were dedicated to Rome's "comoun proffit" (5.1677, 1725, 1815), but then suffered at the city's hands: "who that laboureth for a comounte / Leseth ofte his thank, be Scipiouns ye may see" (5.1746–47). Each of the five stanzas in Lydgate's original envoy on the Scipios ends with the word "comounte"—not to extol the Roman community or commune, as Gower often does, but to denounce its corruption and ingratitude. In contrast to the Scipios, "so worthi in knghthod," are all the treacherous "Romeyns, double & deceyvable" (5.1847–50).

No tragedy of political division in the *Fall* is more poignant than the fall of Pompey the Great. Pompey dies the victim of his civil war with Julius Caesar (6.2024–520), which is also the main subject of Lydgate's earlier *Serpent of Division*. Their conflict is told at length in the *Fall of Princes*, and, as in Laurent, Pompey is featured.[52] Lydgate introduces Pompey at the height of his glory, "wis & worthi & famous of prowesse" (6.2025), and stresses his good deeds, such as subduing Africa for the "comoun proffit" of Rome (6.2074) and ridding the sea of pirates (6.2096). The downfall of such a paragon is due solely to a lack of political unity: Rome is not big enough for two such dominant figures as Caesar and Pompey. In an original stanza (6.2220–26), which recalls the conflict between Romulus and Remus at Rome's founding, Lydgate insists on the inevitability of division between these two ambitious men: because neither "love nouther hih lordshippe" will tolerate a rival, they are incapable of "felashipe," for "ech wil put out othir."[53] The same heroic energy that allows Pompey to accomplish his great deeds prevents him from coexisting with Caesar (or Caesar with him), leading to their discord and to Pompey's ignominious death, vividly described by Lydgate, on a foreign shore: "Of fissh devoured, as he lay on quik sond" (6.2506).[54] Even Caesar weeps with "pite" when the head of his rival is brought to him, perhaps because of a presentiment of his own tragic fate (6.2486–92). The *Fall* portrays Pompey and Caesar as neither wholly selfish, as was Nero, nor wholly self-sacrificing, as was Regulus, but more like some of the protagonists of Greek and Renaissance tragedy whose inner struggles between serving the public good and self-aggrandizement brings about their destruction.[55]

Tragedies of the Powerless

The tragic ends of Coriolanus, the Scipios, and Pompey accord with the title of Lydgate's poem. They are indeed mighty princes of Rome who fell from high to low estate, and their fates support Lydgate's Augustinian view of the emptiness of worldly power, even when exercised well. But Lydgate does not restrict his attention to the downfall of the great. He gives equal importance to the ruins of Romans of lesser status, women especially, in three powerfully narrated stories developed from mere hints in book 2 of *Des cas des nobles hommes*. In that book, as part of an attack on the pride of princes, Laurent briefly mentions several ordinary Roman men from the city's early history who performed extraordinary deeds: Mucius Scaevola, Brutus, and Virginius.[56] Lydgate expands each of these passing references into an extended narrative and reverses Laurent's brief praise of Roman achievements into accounts of Roman tragedy and loss. Placed early in the *Fall*, even before the description of the founding of the city and before the Envoy to Rome, these stories set the tone for what is to come.

The first of Laurent's ordinary Roman heroes is Mucius Scaevola (2.918–66).[57] Most of Laurent's account praises Mucius for his courage in invading the camp of an army besieging Rome to assassinate its king, reminiscent of the brave squire in the *Mirabilia* who thwarts another siege by capturing that army's king. Mucius is not as successful as the squire, however. He kills the wrong man, and, realizing his mistake, punishes himself by putting the hand that did the deed into a fire until it is burned off. But Lydgate's expanded version undercuts Laurent's exemplum of bravery. Although he praises Mucius's "hih prowesse" (2.924) and "corage" (2.926) and says that his motive was "comoun profit" (2.926; cf. 2.956, 2.970), Lydgate emphasizes, in particular, the would-be Roman hero's futile incompetence. Unlike his French source, he concludes that however bold Mucius's act, it was done from "veray ignoraunce" (2.938). Moreover, the antiquarian information that Lydgate characteristically adds is bathetically anticlimactic: he tells us that Mucius's second name, Scaevola, means "withoute an hond," and that it was adopted by his descendants "for tencrece his fame" (2.962–65).[58] Surely, there is more than a touch of the ridiculous about such fame: the first of three ordinary Roman heroes is remembered for self-mutilation resulting from his own ineptitude.

The third Roman whom Laurent praises briefly in this section is Virginius, who kills his daughter Virginia to save her from being violated by the corrupt judge Apius. Lydgate expands a single short sentence in *Des cas des nobles hommes*, which does not even name Virginia, into fifty-five lines (2.1345–400).[59] Chaucer and Gower had told the story of Virginia in the previous century, as Lydgate surely knew, and that undoubtedly prompted him to add her to Laurent's brief mention of her father. In contrast to these earlier English versions, Lydgate's Virginia has none of the agency of the heroine of the *Physician's Tale*, nor does the poet question the harm caused by her father's strict Roman virtue, as the *Confessio* does. The episode in the *Fall of Princes* draws a simple opposition between good and evil: the "ontrewe, proud and luxurious" Apius (2.1349) in contrast to the "worthi knyht" Virginius (2.1356) and his "goodli douhter" (2.1359). As in the story of Mucius Scaevola, however, Lydgate stresses failure over success: the bad Apius loses his official position as decemvir in the city and kills himself, while the good Virginia loses her life, and the worthy Virginius his daughter. Lydgate concludes the episode with the added information that after the decemvirs were deposed, tribunes "in Rome gan succeede," who were able to distinguish "twen riht & wrong treuli," using Roman laws "justli to governe" (2.1398–400). But such optimism about the city's future righteousness is dashed by the numerous personal and public outrages that Lydgate attributes to Roman leaders, including tribunes, in the Envoy to Rome at the end of book 2 and in the rest of the *Fall*. This emphasis on Roman failure is reinforced when Lydgate tells about Apius again in book 3 with an added envoy on corrupt judges (3.3011–115). Despite its contribution to the negative depiction of Roman leaders in this section of the *Fall*, Lydgate's conventional treatment of Virginia tends to support the common view of the poet as a competent craftsman but little more. As if to recognize Virginia's prominence in the works of Chaucer and Gower, Lydgate expands his source by telling her story as well as her father's and adds new antiquarian information, but little more. The story of Lucretia that comes between those of Mucius and Virginia, however, reveals a very different poet, one who is more skillful and much bolder.

The First Tragedy of Lucretia in the *Fall*

The narrative of the chaste Roman wife Lucretia is the most sophisticated Roman tragedy in the *Fall of Princes*. Lydgate takes the occasion of Laurent's brief praise of her avenger, Brutus, to tell her story (though not his) at some length, after first saying that he won't. And then, in the next book, he tells Lucretia's story again, but in a quite different way. Lydgate thus well demonstrates his ability to put into practice the translation theory outlined at the beginning of the *Fall*. Fully aware of the previous versions of Lucretia's story by Chaucer (whom he names) and Gower (whom he does not), Lydgate dares to make it new. As in the prologue to book 1, the poet once again pays his respects to his patrons, Chaucer and Gloucester, while showing his literary independence with a subtle and searching analysis of Lucretia's conflicted, and perhaps unknowable, self. Drawing on contemporary, classical, and patristic sources, he imagines a Lucretia who is torn between honor and guilt and whose end is tragic because she can find no solution to this inner division in pagan Rome.

Past critical discussions of the Lucretia episodes in the *Fall of Princes*, while limited, accuse Lydgate of ineptitude. Much of this goes back to Pearsall, who, in his indispensable study of the poet, contends that Lydgate reluctantly added a long account of Lucretia in book 2 so as "to humour" Gloucester, before, unaccountably, telling her story again in book 3.[60] Although Nigel Mortimer, in his impressive book on the *Fall of Princes*, fully demonstrates how much Lydgate reshaped the Lucretia story, he also continues Pearsall's criticism when he charges that the insertion of an original account of her in book 2 has "unfortunate consequences" because it makes for an "awkward repetition" of her story later.[61] Yet what Pearsall and Mortimer find clumsy can also be read as a subtle instance of Lydgate's literary skill.

The pretext for the almost four-hundred-line Lucretia addition in book 2 (2.971–1344) is a single long sentence in *Des cas des nobles hommes* about Brutus (the second of Laurent's three ordinary Roman heroes), in which Lucretia appears simply as the prompt for his heroism. Laurent tells how in response to Lucretia's rape by the king's son, Tarquin, Brutus rallied the people against the royal dynasty.[62] Lydgate restates Laurent's information in three quick lines, with special emphasis on the abolition of the monarchy in the city: "As whilom Brutus for Lucrecis sake / Chaced Tarquyn for his transgressioun / And kynges alle out off Rome toun" (2.971–73). This historical explanation for the end of Rome's monarchy goes back to classical times, as in Livy's *Ab urbe condita*, although other ancient writers, especially Ovid in the *Fasti*, give a less political, more personal account of Lucretia's suffering and death.[63] Lydgate signals that he is aware of these competing traditions by immediately supplementing the political epitome in Laurent with a précis of the alternative, more personal treatment of her story, which contains echoes of Chaucer's Ovidian *Legend of Lucrece* (2.974–77).[64] This efficient juxtaposition of the two traditional interpretations of the Lucretia story clears a space for the poet's own new, more complex treatment of her tragedy.[65]

And yet, even as he calls attention to such variety in the telling of this story, Lydgate, at first, flatly refuses to add to it, asserting that because the great Chaucer has already told "a legende soverayne" about Lucretia, he himself "nedith nat rehersyn the processe" (1.978–80). It would, Lydgate goes on, be an act of "presumpcioun & veynglorie" if all he did was to follow "afftir his [Chaucer's] makyng"; after all, he says, his own rude language would be like the light of a distant star compared to that of the Chaucerian sun, making it "but veyn" to take something "seid be hym to write it newe ageyn" (2.992–1001).[66] Nevertheless, having declared the folly of repeating the tale of Lucretia because Chaucer has already told it so well, Lydgate promptly does just that, apparently for the good, if daring, reason that he believes he will be able to create not just a pale imitation but something that is truly "newe ageyn." To adapt the poet's image of good translation from the prologue to book 1, the old vessel of Chaucer's *Legend* must be broken to allow a fresh reconstruction of its elements.

Lydgate's confidence in his poetic abilities and a literary playfulness he learned from Chaucer are better explanations than sloppiness for the cheekiness with which he quickly abandons his vow to say no more about Lucretia. His abrupt change of plans, moreover, is announced in the very first word of the very next stanza: "*But* at Lucrece stynte I will a while" (2.1002–3, emphasis added). This ostentatiously metafictional maneuver (declaring you will not do what you then in fact do) does not surprise modern readers when encountered in Chaucer's poetry, but many consider Lydgate incapable of such subtlety. And yet, in this same stanza, Lydgate further plays with the concept of artistic agency by claiming that the responsibility for the Lucretia story he will now tell is not his, but rests with his patron, Gloucester. In another show of deference, he insists that he is only telling about Lucretia now because "my lord" ordered him "to translate / The doolful processe off hir pitous fate" (2.1007–8). Furthermore, he also seems to suggest that Gloucester requested that his version follow "the tracis of Collucyus, / Which wrot off her a declamacioun" (2.1009–10).[67] Lydgate's source for the first Lucretia story in the *Fall* is not either Chaucer's or Laurent's version, but, as announced here, the Latin prose *Declamatio Lucretiae* by the prominent fourteenth-century Italian humanist Coluccio Salutati.[68]

Whether the use of Salutati's text was really Gloucester's idea or Lydgate's (or a mutual decision), it makes a remarkable contribution to the poem. Not only the largest addition of Roman material in the entire *Fall of Princes*, Salutati's text is also precisely the "new thing" that Lydgate needed to go beyond what Chaucer (and Gower) had done and remake the story of Lucretia. Unlike the two traditional ways of presenting Lucretia's story, as political or personal, Salutati's *Declamatio* narrates neither Lucretia's rape and suicide nor the exile of Rome's kings, though it refers to both. Instead, the *Declamatio* is a formal prose debate between Lucretia and her husband, Collatinus: he tries to persuade her not to kill herself, and she explains why she must. Lydgate's intertextual interpolation of Salutati's relatively recent and somewhat exotic Italian humanist text is extraordinary for a poet so often portrayed as conventionally medieval.

The addition of Salutati's *Declamatio* is impressive in itself, and, as Mortimer has shown in detail, it is hardly a mechanical translation.[69] Lydgate expands the terse, factual introduction to the *Declamatio* with added detail and passionate language that demonizes Tarquin while sympathizing with Lucretia.[70] In the long dialogue that follows, Lydgate's version sharpens the contrast between the two speakers: whereas Lydgate's Collatinus is sweeter and more naive than his model, the English poet's Lucretia is more troubled and conflicted.

In the *Declamatio*, Collatinus addresses his wife formally, even after she has said she intends to kill herself. When he does call her by name, he usually says no more than "Lucretia," only once unbending enough to refer to her as "my Lucretia."[71] Lydgate, however, makes his Collatinus warmer from the start. He addresses her as "my dere Lucrece" (2.1058) and intensifies the single instance of "my Lucrece" in the Latin to "my trewe Lucrece" (2.1086). Salutati's Collatinus is logical rather than affectionate. As if he were Lucretia's lawyer rather than her husband, he defends her by citing exculpatory evidence—her quick reporting of the attack and her isolation during it.[72] Lydgate's more sentimental husband relies less on legal argument than on his own unshakeable belief in Lucretia's purity. Instead of saying that he and others believe her story, as in the *Declamatio*, Lydgate's husband swears that Lucretia is incapable of such wrongdoing and that it is "a maner *inpossible*, / And lik a thing which *never* yet was seyn" that her honor "was founde coruptible" (2.1107–10, emphasis added). Perhaps thinking of Gower's *Confessio*, in which division is the fundamental human sin, Lydgate makes Collatinus conceive of Lucretia as a woman of immutable stability and unity: she is "stedfast ay and indyvysible" and "ondepartid in vertu" (2.1111–12).[73]

The Lucretia of Salutati's *Declamatio* merits such praise for her integrity. Responding to her husband's pleas, she insists she did nothing wrong and must die only because of the wickedness done to her, being unable to endure the likelihood that others will never be certain that she did not choose dishonor over safety, which only her death can refute—though she also fears that Collatinus will reject her as the "whore of Tarquin" (*scortum Tarquini*) and even that she might be pregnant with Tarquin's child. Most of all, however, she is afraid that, given the power of Venus, Tarquin's violation might have so altered her chastity that, at some time in the future, "perhaps shameful acts will begin to please me" and cause her to welcome further adulteries.[74]

In refashioning Lucretia, Lydgate omits some of Salutati's more melodramatic details (the reference to herself as a whore and her possible pregnancy), and instead imagines a more psychologically divided and self-tortured character, whose greatest fear is not that she might someday begin to enjoy illicit sex but that she already has done so. In two stanzas that differ significantly from the corresponding passage in the *Declamatio*, Lydgate's Lucretia, in strained language that reveals her inner conflict, considers the possibly that she was, to however small a degree, a willing participant in her own rape. The possibility of such complicity forces her to question her own virtue, a self-doubt not found in Salutati's Lucretia or in the Lucretias of Chaucer and Gower, both of whom remove the issue of her active participation by having her fall unconscious before Tarquin's attack.[75]

In the *Fall of Princes*, Lucretia remains fully conscious during the act, and it is what she remembers having experienced that troubles her afterward. In an addition to the *Declamatio*, she begins with a general statement, citing what she calls a commonly held view on rape (however strange it may seem to us today) that the act may provoke in its victim "a false appetite," which, because of the frailty of the body, produces "delight" in spite of one's will:

> "Lust afforcid hath a fals appetit
> Of freelte includid in Nature;
> Maugre the will, ther folweth a delit,
> As summe folk seyn, in everi creature." (2.1275–78)[76]

Lucretia then moves from the general to the very personal and, challenging her husband's view of her unassailable purity and integrity, says that when she was attacked, she was incapable of not feeling some sexual response, though it was forced upon her:

> "Al-be I was ageyn my will oppressid,
> Ther was a maner constreyned lust in deede,
> Which for noun power myht nat be redressid." (2.1282–84)[77]

A model of marital chastity haunted by sexual feelings she neither sought nor welcomed, Lydgate's Lucretia raises psychological, moral, and even physiological questions only hinted at in the *Declamatio*.

Lydgate explores Lucretia's inner agony and self-questioning with great subtlety, suggesting something of the tortured protagonists in Greek tragedy who unwittingly commit crimes that later repel them, such as Oedipus or Agave in the *Bacchae*. Of course, Lydgate did not know Greek drama, except perhaps by reputation. In adding Lucretia's self-castigating words to Salutati's contemporary humanist dialogue, the English poet does seem to be looking back, however, but to a major patristic rather than a classical source—Augustine's *City of God*. Here, the resemblance goes beyond the generally similar critique of pagan Rome in both the Envoy to Rome and the *City of God*. Lucretia's psychological torment and pagan despair in the *Fall* seem specifically indebted, directly or indirectly, to Augustine's famous challenge to the traditional reputation of Lucretia as a noble Roman woman, which Augustine uses to defend Christian women, who had been raped during the recent sack of Rome, from pagan charges that they should have followed Lucretia's example and committed suicide (1.16–19). Augustine turns the tables on such accusations by arguing that the pagan heroine does not deserve imitation: if she was not guilty of adultery, as her admirers say she was not, then she must be guilty of murdering an innocent person, namely, herself.[78] His stark conclusion: "There is no possible way out: 'If she is an adulteress, why is she praised? If chaste, why was she put to death?'" (1.19).

In the course of his discussion of Lucretia, Augustine's restless curiosity about human motivation and sin produces ideas whose implications Lydgate will exploit in the *Fall*.[79] One is Augustine's general statement that a sexual attack may perhaps produce some bodily pleasure (*carnis aliqua voluptate*) in the victim, a position that parallels Lucretia's statement in the English poem that rape can create a "fals appetit" against one's will.[80] Augustine goes on to argue, however, that moral purity is "a virtue of the mind," not of the body, so that any physical pleasure that spontaneously occurs in response to another's lust does not affect the soul and therefore is no cause for guilt—and certainly not for self-murder (1.18). Augustine's contrast between physical and spiritual virtue has little meaning for the Lucretia portrayed in the *Declamatio* and the *Fall of Princes*, however. Given the intense shame culture of pagan Rome, she believes herself polluted despite her innocent intent.

Having established a general distinction between body and mind, Augustine examines the specific case of Lucretia. In a thought experiment that he says only she herself could confirm (*quod ipsa tantummodo nosse poterat*), he wonders whether during the attack Lucretia might have found herself so "enticed by her own desire" (*sua libidine inlecta*) that she feels that in some way she "consented" (*consensit*) to the act, resulting in guilt that must be atoned for by her death (1.19). Augustine's hypothesis, and it is only a hypothesis, that guilt over her own desire is a possible reason for Lucretia's suicide resembles the second passage quoted above from the *Fall*, Lucretia's admission that she herself experienced "a maner constreyned lust in deede": some form of pleasure, though one forced upon her during the assault. The similarity between the two passages in the *City of God* and in the *Fall*, one about "fals appetit" in general and the other about Lucretia's specific sexual response, suggests that Lydgate was familiar with Augustine's discussion of the Roman heroine. The important difference is that Lydgate does not show Lucretia "enticed by her own desire" in any way, as Augustine speculates the historical woman might have been. Lydgate's heroine never gives her consent to Tarquin. Thus although she might have experienced "lust," it was, as she says, something wholly "constreyned," in which she did not participate at all. Lucretia in the *Fall* feels guilty only because of the strictness of Roman standards of honor (her body has been polluted), though both Lydgate and Augustine judge her innocent because her will remained pure.

By portraying Lucretia as an ancient Roman in her understanding of what has happened to her, Lydgate shows us the limitations of paganism. The greatest tragedy in Lydgate's story of Lucretia is not her physical violation, horrible as that is, but that her pagan Roman beliefs demand her suicide. In the section we have been discussing, Augustine goes on to say that even if Lucretia had given sexual consent to Tarquin, she would not have had to kill herself "if she could have offered a profitable penitence to false gods" (1.19). The statement is clearly sarcastic. The *City of God* repeatedly demonstrates the fraudulence and ineffectuality of the pagan deities (as Lydgate does in the Envoy to Rome), in contrast to the power and mercy of the Christian God, who could absolve such a penitent. Unfortunately for Augustine's Lucretia, she lives in a culture whose exaggerated sense of honor requires public proof of innocence, in this case her own death.[81] Lydgate explores this dilemma by portraying his heroine as a divided and alienated figure who is not only cut off from her society by what one of its leaders has done to her, but who is also ignorant of the true source of divine consolation. When Lucretia says that she desires for "my gilt to make a recompence" (2.1293), the Christian vocabulary Lydgate employs reveals her plight. She may say that she seeks "an indulgence" for "my trespace" (2.1292) and may appeal to the "goddis &

goddessis callid off chastite" (2.1291), but the one deity she then names, Venus (2.1294), is, of course, the enemy of chastity. The pagan Lucretia has no way to obtain the Christian pardons so generously offered in the *Stacions of Rome*, though Lydgate makes us aware of her desperate need for them. Despite her loving husband and father, she has no hope of heaven, and can only look forward to the release of death. As is true for the ancient city in the Envoy to Rome at the end of book 2, her salvation is available only from the God of whom she knows nothing.

For all the respect Lydgate pays to Chaucer and Gloucester (the sincerity of which we have no reason to doubt), his interpolation about Lucretia from Salutati's *Declamatio* is a declaration of artistic independence and a demonstration of his literary skill. The version of her story so ostentatiously inserted into the *Fall of Princes* probes more deeply into Lucretia's moral psychology than Chaucer (or Gower) ever did, even as Lydgate refuses to deliver the practical optimism sought by his patron. Gloucester asked for lessons that would teach princes how to control Fortune, whereas the catastrophe that overwhelms Lucretia demonstrates how ungovernable by humans are forces like lust and violence.

Lydgate's Second Tragedy of Lucretia

The treatment of Lucretia in the *Fall of Princes*, a topic that Maura Nolan does not discuss, is nevertheless an example of what she calls Lydgate's ability, at times, to write like a "literary critic," by which she means "a poet who reads multiple versions of the stories he reproduces and attempts to do justice to them all, despite the contradictions and inconsistencies by which they are surrounded."[82] In book 2 of the *Fall*, as we have seen, Lydgate uses Laurent's passing reference to Lucretia as an opportunity to add brief summaries of the two ways, political and personal, in which Lucretia's story was traditionally told, which he then follows with an extended adaptation of Salutati's humanist *Declamatio*. But then, in the next book, book 3, at the point where Boccaccio and Laurent finally come to Lucretia as one part of their long accounts of the Tarquin dynasty, Lydgate tells her story again. Although he eliminates a great deal of Laurent's material about the Tarquins, Lydgate insists that he must follow his source and translate Lucretia's "compleynt," despite the fact that, "be biddying off my lord," he has already "rehersed" the "doolful declamacioun" of Salutati (here called Pierius) (3.974–87).[83]

This is much too much retelling of Lucretia's story for Pearsall, who goes so far as to pity the monk's royal patron: "To Gloucester, it must have been like trying to stop a steamroller."[84] Characteristically witty as this is, it seems to me to misrepresent what Lydgate has actually done. It is certainly possible to attribute Lydgate's second version of the Lucretia story to the poet's notorious prolixity—as if he were being paid by the line—or to a slavish fidelity to his source. But neither theory explains why, having quite sharply reduced so much material in the *Cas des nobles hommes* both before and after Lucretia's complaint, Lydgate chooses to translate her words at length. A more convincing explanation is that Lucretia is a prime instance of the poet's awareness of "multiple versions" of a story and his desire to do "justice to them all," despite their "contradictions and inconsistencies."

If we are willing to grant Lydgate this level of literary sophistication, then the appeal to him of Lucretia's complaint in book 3 (and the justification for his close translation of it) lies precisely in its radical difference in form and content from what he had written in book 2.[85] It allows the poet to create Lucretia anew and further deepen her complexity as a character. As to its form, instead of the dialogue between Lucretia and her husband in book 2, in book 3 we hear her voice alone, as she speaks at length to a silent Collatinus (3.1009–141). Moreover, what she says is not the same. Instead of the confident debater of the first episode, Lucretia is now, as in Laurent's original, a submissive wife, who addresses her husband as "my lord," promising him that she will behave "as humble subject with feithful obeisaunce / Under thi lordshipe and thi governaunce" (3.1011–15).[86] Requesting correction from Collatinus, she tells him near the end of her speech that if "it seeme in your opynyoun" that she is impure, she will accept the "just punycioun / And the peyne pacientli endure" (3.1135–38).

The meek Lucretia of book 3 may seem to easier to interpret than the tortured figure in book 2, but everything changes once she stops speaking:

> Hir tale told. Whan thei longe hadde musid
> On this compleynt in ther inward siht,
> Off trouthe echon thei heeld hir ful excusid,
> Made al beheste, with al ther fulle myght
> Tavenge hir wrong. And Lucrece anon riht
> Took a sharp knyff, or thei myhte adverte,
> And rooff hirsilff evene thoruh the herte. (3.1142–48)

Lydgate, with his usual expressions of modesty, had earlier insisted that he was unable to imitate his source's "eloquence" and could give only its "substaunce" (3.992–94). And yet the literary skill he exhibits here in exploiting the resources of poetry (his French source is prose) seems to resemble more a nimble sports car than Pearsall's runaway steamroller. Three short words in the first line of the stanza, ending with a strong caesura, mark the end of Lucretia's words and create a pause before what follows. The extended next sentence describes an apparently satisfactory resolution to her dilemma as, in indirect speech, her friends and family affirm Lucretia's innocence and promise forceful vengeance (note the parallel use of the intensifier "full").

Given their sympathetic response, Lucretia's self-destruction is shocking, even if we know from book 2 and other versions of her story that it must happen. The second half of the antepenultimate line, "And Lucrece anon riht," echoes in its abruptness the first half of the opening line of the stanza, and the phrase concludes with another strongly stressed half line of four simple but ominous words: "Took a sharp knyff." This is followed by a half line about her family's surprise and helplessness, and finally a brutal, highly visual last line as the violent deed is done: "And rooff hirsilff evene thoruh the herte." At this climactic moment, Lydgate's second account of Lucretia ends abruptly, omitting all of Laurent's extensive narration of the events that follow her death. Dramatic as this second episode is, however, the actual reasons for Lucretia's suicide in book 3 are more opaque than in book 2, which she announces from the first in her debate with Collatinus there. Her 133-line soliloquy in book 3 provides no clue as to why she decides to kill herself, the sudden willfulness of which act directly contradicts her repeated vows to obey Collatinus: "Lord and husbonde my bodi to governe" (3.1029). As readers of the *Fall* experience her tragedy for the second time, from a different perspective, Lydgate leaves us with a poignant sense of the final unknowableness of even the most vivid fictional characters.

Like great tragic drama, Lydgate's two stories of Lucretia, his most original and complex Roman narrative, deny his audience both the practical lessons that Gloucester sought and Chaucer's straightforward sympathy for oppressed women. The Lucretia episodes in the *Fall of Princes* offer instead the shock that comes from directly confronting the terror and pity of the human condition and our helplessness before its most wrenching tragedies, especially when suffered by those who lack the possibility of divine salvation. Lydgate's poem articulates an Augustinian view of ancient Rome as the paradigmatic earthly city, a stark contrast to the eternal City of God. While he constantly amplifies his source, adding information about both Rome and Romans, Lydgate reminds us that the city's magnificence (like its crimes) was as transient as all things of this world. But if Lydgate can sometimes be the moralizing monk, he is also an imaginative poet whose Roman episodes in the *Fall of Princes* attest to his literary ambition. He understands that stories from the ancient past are frequently in conflict, and that if they are to be represented truly, they must be retold and imagined anew. Lydgate's Lucretia is fashioned from multiple sources to create a fluid character whose psychological depths and inner divisions are unequalled in Middle English poetry about Romans. Even as Lydgate's last major work looks back to the patristic thought of Augustine, it also looks forward, however uncertainly, to the great English dramatic tragedies to come.

Contemporary critics have learned to distrust periodization in English literary history, and with good reason, but attitudes toward ancient Rome did change greatly from Middle English to Elizabethan poetry. The most obvious reason for this is England's break from the papacy. Spenser still laments the ancient city's material decline in his *Ruines of Rome* and traces Britain's historical connection with Rome in the *Faerie Queene*, but the false Duessa as Whore of Babylon also exemplifies the Roman Catholic Church. English Protestants no longer sought the saints of Rome, scorning the relics and pardons celebrated in the *Stacions of Rome*. Medieval accounts of the city's ancient pagan marvels in the *Mirabilia* and the interpolation on Rome in the *Metrical Mandeville* were also discredited, but for scholarly rather than religious reasons, as humanists, especially in Italy, increasingly demonstrated how faulty and incomplete their information was. In contrast to the fantasy Romes in the *Stacions* and the *Metrical* interpolation, the ancient city in Renaissance literature often appears more familiar and even contemporary. Shakespeare's Roman characters in *Julius Caesar* are not all that different from those in his English history plays. Alternatively, his *Rape of Lucrece* differs from Middle English versions of the story in its length and rhetorical complexity. Given the special importance of the Renaissance in English literary history, its more famous representations of ancient Rome may in large measure account for the critical neglect of the city's depictions in Middle English poetry. I have attempted here, however, to make the case for how much is to be gained from more careful attention to the subject. In recognizing Rome as a significant topic in Middle English poetry, readers are introduced to two anonymous but powerful descriptions of the ancient material city in the *Stacions* and the *Metrical* interpolation, for example, and can deepen their understanding of key elements in the works of major

Middle English poets, including Gower's ideas of governance, Chaucer's special interest in women and suspicion of male power, Langland's exploration of the relationship between truth and love, justice and mercy, and Lydgate's idea of tragedy and desire to make new the work of his great poetic predecessors. I hope more Middle English critical paths will lead to Rome in the future.

NOTES

INTRODUCTION

1. Stanbury, "*Man of Law's Tale*," 125.
2. I include "late antiquity" in the general term "antiquity." Bowersock, Brown, and Grabar define "late antiquity" as being "between around 250 and 800." *Late Antiquity*, ix.
3. Thus I do not discuss minor poems such as *Le bone Florence of Rome*, *Octavian*, or *The Seven Sages of Rome*, which in any case, despite their titles, are not seriously engaged with ancient Rome.
4. The classic study is Tatlock, *Legendary History of Britain*. Lavezzo says, "Conquering Rome, becoming its emperor, always serves in the *History of the Kings of Britain* as the ultimate imperial aim of Brutus's descendants from Belinus and Brennius to King Arthur himself." *Angels on the Edge*, 22.
5. Barron says that the *Brut* was "more widely diffused than any vernacular text other than the Wycliffite Bible" and "became the nearest equivalent to a national chronicle." "Prose Chronicles," 34. See also Eckhardt, "Presence of Rome."
6. Tinti, "Introduction," 1. See also Howe, "Rome," which says that "the Anglo-Saxons found an intellectual and spiritual *patria* that had Rome as its capital" (148).
7. On the popularity of pilgrimage to Rome among the Anglo-Saxons, see, for example, Ortenberg, "Archbishop Sigeric's Journey," 202–6; and Thacker, "Rome: The Pilgrims' City," 122–31. The quotation is from Krautheimer, *St. Peter's and Medieval Rome*, 25. See also Birch, *Pilgrimage to Rome*, 173.
8. See Ortenberg, "Archbishop Sigeric's Journey," 204–5; Birch, *Pilgrimage to Rome*, 140–41. Valenzani notes that medieval historians attributed the foundation of the *schola Anglorum* both to King Ine of Wessex and to King Offa of Mercia. "Hosting Foreigners," 84.
9. On the Hospital of Saint Thomas, see Harvey, *English in Rome*, chapter 3. Harvey's chapter 4 discusses a second English hospital (the hospice of Saint Chrysogonus, founded after 1390, in Trastevere), which was not as successful as Saint Thomas's and was finally amalgamated into it in 1464.
10. See, for example, Maddalo, *In figura Romae*, 1–10; and Woodward, *Rome: Time and Eternity*, 92.
11. For these population figures, see Watkin, *Roman Forum*, 107.
12. Walter Map quoted in Sumption, *Pilgrimage*, 221; Usk, *Chronicle of Adam Usk*, 161.
13. Quoted in Campanelli, "Monuments and Histories," 50n52.
14. Usk, *Chronicle of Adam Usk*, 189.
15. Petrarca, "Familiar Letter," 291–93.

16. Hildebert, "De Roma," 22 (poem 36, lines 1–2).
17. Hildebert, 26 (poem 38, line 11). My translation is a modification of that in Parks, *English Traveler to Italy*, 253.
18. Edwards, *Writing Rome*, xi.
19. Edwards, "Introduction," 3.

CHAPTER 1

1. Capgrave, *Solace of Pilgrimes*, 61.
2. The title *Stacions* is somewhat misleading. Although the English poem uses the word *station* as a generic term for church, its proper meaning is the specific church in Rome at which the pope (or his representative) celebrated a special Mass on a particular day, especially during Lent. Latin calendars of such masses, known as *Stationes*, were common in the Middle Ages and are sometimes found in the same manuscripts that contain examples of the Latin source of the *Stacions of Rome*. See Baldovin, *Urban Character of Christian Worship*.
3. Furnivall, *Political, Religious, and Love Poems*, xvii. Hulbert, "Some Medieval Advertisements," which is still the most useful commentary on the poem and its Latin source, describes both as "advertisements" for the city as "part of an organized propaganda to attract pilgrims to Rome" (404).
4. Duffy, "Dynamics of Pilgrimage," 175.
5. For a list of the manuscripts of the *Stacions*, see Boffey and Edwards, *New Index of Middle English Verse*, item 1172. They are also listed in my bibliography and described in n. 9 below. Of the nine extant texts of the *Stacions*, six are lengthy (ranging from about 550 to about 900 lines), one is a truncated collection of passages (Cotton Vespasian), and two are only brief fragments. For the dating of some of these manuscripts, see, for example, Doyle, "Shaping of the Vernon and Simeon," 1; James and Jenkins, *Descriptive Catalogue*, 421; Baugh, *Worcestershire Miscellany*, 41–42; Krochalis, "Newberry Stations of Rome," 132. The distinctions between versions of the *Stacions of Rome* are well set out in William Fahrenbach's paper "The Texts and Uses of *The Stacions of Rome*," a copy of which Fahrenbach kindly sent me.
6. Krochalis, "Newberry Stations of Rome," 132–33, assigns the dialect of the Newberry *Stacions* to the far west of the West Midlands, probably Shropshire. Sajavaara, "Relationship of the Vernon and Simeon," 439, identifies the dialect of Vernon and Simeon as northern Worcestershire, though Horobin, "Scribes of the Vernon," suggests that the Vernon was produced by lay scribes associated with Lichfield Cathedral. Thompson, "Looking Behind the Book," notes that scholars have proposed that the Cotton scribe was from "the general south-east, or south-east Midland, area" (171).
7. On Cotton as a household book, see Thompson, "Looking Behind the Book," 171–72. Krochalis, "Newberry Stations of Rome," 131, thinks that Lambeth and Cotton may have had lay readers. Baugh, *Worcestershire Miscellany*, says that Additional 37787, which contains a *Stacions* fragment, was probably written at Bordesley Abbey near Worcester (14), and that the Cotton and Cotton Vespasian manuscripts had connections with Carthusian houses and Newberry with Cistercian houses (42). Sajavaara, "Relationship of the Vernon and Simeon," 439, suggests that the scriptorium of Vernon and Simeon might be one of the Cistercian houses of north Worcestershire or Warwickshire.
8. None of the surviving versions has been identified as the original, in part because some of those assigned a later date (Cotton and Lambeth) contain

passages not in those dated earlier (Vernon and Simeon), passages that may have been either added by later scribes (not impossible, given the simplicity of the verse) or preserved from a fuller archetype.

9. Furnivall edited the 734-line main text of the Vernon version in *Stacions of Rome*, 1–29. Unless otherwise noted, this is the version of the *Stacions* I quote, cited parenthetically in the text by line number alone. Furnivall later edited the 78-line passage that begins Vernon in *Minor Poems of the Vernon MS*, 609–11; he called this a "prologue" even though the passage is not so designated in the manuscript. I thus cite this opening section as the Vernon Prologue parenthetically in the text by line number. Furnivall had earlier edited the Cotton version in *Political, Religious, and Love Poems*, 143–73, with variants from the Lambeth version for the first 553 lines (at which point Cotton concludes), continuing with the 359 lines that follow in Lambeth alone. I cite Furnivall's edition of Cotton and Lambeth parenthetically in the text by the name of the version followed by line numbers. The fifteenth-century Bicester manuscript is a 667-line version of the *Stacions* written on the back of a bursar's accounts roll from Bicester Priory and edited by Scattergood in "An Inedited MS." This edition is not a complete transcript, however; Scattergood provides only passages he says are not in Cotton/Lambeth or Vernon, though some of these are actually rewritten from other versions or appear in different places. The Wood fragment is edited in Keiser, "Verse Introductions," 314–15, and the Worcestershire fragment in Baugh, *Worcestershire Miscellany*, 106. There are also Middle English prose redactions, which, because they are not poetry, are not discussed in this study; see Aberystwyth, National Library of Wales, Porkington 10, fols. 132r–136v, edited by Furnivall in *Stacions of Rome*, 30–34; London, British Library, Additional 35298, fols. 65r–66v, edited in Hamer and Russell, *Supplementary Lives*, 75–83.

10. Brown, *Cult of the Saints*, 3. See also Brown's *Making of Late Antiquity*, esp. 12.

11. Geary, "Sacred Commodities," 176. See also Sumption, *Pilgrimage*, 48–49: "Ordinary men looked on the saints as individuals no less immediate, no less visible and tangible in death than they had been in life. It was essential to this view of things that the saint should be considered to inhabit the place where his relics were preserved, and in that place he should above all be venerated."

12. Brown, *Cult of the Saints*, 21.

13. Bartlett, *Why Can the Dead*, 626.

14. Snoek, *Medieval Piety*, 241.

15. Thacker argues that in fact Rome suffered less persecution than other places in the empire and that the Christian community there originally remembered only a limited number of martyrs. He concludes that most of the stories of the city's early martyrs were invented long after their supposed deaths: "For most of the early martyrs of Rome, the fabulous histories later ascribed to them suggest that their lives were *tabulae rasae* on which the romancers of the fourth and later centuries could project whatever they wished." "Rome of the Martyrs," 23.

16. Lanciani notes that Roman laws allowed honorable burial even for executed Christians. *Pagan and Christian Rome*, 119.

17. Sumption argues that the veneration of the relics of the Roman martyrs is attested as early as the second century (*Pilgrimage*, 22). Christie notes visits

to the catacombs in the third century and cites Prudentius on the busy traffic there in the early fifth century. *From Constantine to Charlemagne*, 157.
18. Sumption, *Pilgrimage*, 219–20; Christie, *From Constantine to Charlemagne*, 161. In the ninth century, Pashcal I was particularly active in such translations; see Goodson, "Relic Translations."
19. For the medieval story of the uniting of Saints Stephen and Lawrence, see Jacobus, *Golden Legend*, 2:42–43. The story is also illustrated in the late medieval murals still visible in the porch of S. Lorenzo in Rome.
20. Christie notes that whereas Jerusalem was the greatest of Christian pilgrimages, Rome was the closer alternative for most Westerners, and its possession of so many relics from the Holy Land gave it additional prestige. *From Constantine to Charlemagne*, 157.
21. The Vernon *Stacions* says that the Lateran even possessed Christ's foreskin (337–38), though several other places in Europe made the same claim. For a spirited survey of the foreskin controversy and a list of claimed sites, see Palazzo, "Veneration of the Sacred Foreskin(s)." There is debate about the location of the foreskin even among versions of the *Stacions*: Lambeth, 613, says it was at S. Maria Maggiore. Even in the Middle Ages, not everyone took this relic seriously.
22. "Objects that had been in contact with the saint during his or her lifetime, and objects that had been in contact with the saint's tomb, were treated as relics, and given the same reverence and credited with the same power as corporeal relics." Bartlett, *Why Can the Dead*, 239.
23. For the relics in the Lateran complex, especially those in the pope's private chapel, the Sancta Sanctorum, see Kessler and Zacharias, *Rome 1300*, chapters 1 and 2.
24. One example of such an early list of Roman holy sites, thought to date from the seventh century, with no mention of pardons, is that in William of Malmesbury's twelfth-century *Gesta regum Anglorum*, 1:613–21, 2:308–9. The famous eighth-century itinerary of Roman pilgrim routes from Codex Einsidlensis 326, edited in *Itineraria et alia geographica*, 330–43, also says nothing about pardons.
25. Parks, *English Traveler to Italy*, 592–93, notes that copies of the *Indulgentiae* became numerous in the fourteenth and fifteenth centuries, perhaps in response to the establishment of jubilee years at Rome beginning in 1300. Versions of the *Indulgentiae* survive in many Continental and English manuscripts and prints. For the most thorough surveys, see Miedema, *Römanischen Kirchen*, and her "Mirabilia Romae," which lists manuscripts in Latin and other languages of the *Indulgentiae* and of the *Mirabilia urbis Romae*, which is discussed in my next chapter. Manuscripts of the Latin *Indulgentiae* apparently produced in England include London, British Library, Cotton Julius D.viii; British Library, Cotton Titus A.xix; British Library, Cotton Titus D.xix; British Library, Harley 562; British Library, Harley 2321; Oxford, Bodleian Library, Digby 11; and Bodleian Library, Digby 196. For an account of the *Indulgentiae* based on examples in the British Library, see Hulbert, "Some Medieval Advertisements."
26. The catalogue form of the *Indulgentiae* means that its information was easily expanded, contracted, or rearranged from version to version. Huelsen, in *Chiese di Roma*, 137–56, provides an edition of an *Indulgentiae* text based on a mid-fourteenth-century manuscript (Rome, Biblioteca Apostolica Vaticana, Cod. Reg. lat. 520) with vari-

ants, large and small, from several other, mostly fourteenth-century, versions. I have used Huelsen's edition and compared it with other modern editions of the *Indulgentiae*, especially Schimmelpfennig, "Römische Ablassfälschungen," 637–58, based on a fourteenth-century manuscript, Stuttgart, Württembergische Landesbibliothek, Cod. hist. 2° 459; Valentini and Zucchetti, "Memoriale de mirabilibus," based on a late fourteenth- or early fifteenth-century manuscript from the monastery of Montserrat (MS 1); and the transcription of *Indulgentie ecclesiarum principalium alme urbis Rome*, a late fifteenth-century Roman print in the British Library (C.9.a.22), by Hulbert in "Some Medieval Advertisements," 405–9.

27. Schimmelpfennig, "Römische Ablassfälschungen," 655. The English translations of different Latin texts in the *Indulgentiae* are mine. In contrast to such terse accounts of minor churches is the description of the important basilica of S. Maria Maggiore from an early, and relatively concise printed text in the *Indulgentiae*, transcribed in Hulbert, "Some Medieval Advertisements," 407:

> Quarta ecclesia principalis est ad Sanctam Mariam Maiorem in qua sunt omni die quadraginta et octo anni indulgentiarum et totidem quadragene et similiter remissio tertie partis omnium peccatorum. Item hec sunt reliquie ecclesie predicte: Primo corpus beati Mathie apostoli, item corpus beati Hieronymi, item brachium beati Thome Cantuariensis archiepiscopi. Item nona die Maii est ibi remissio omnium peccatorum data a domino Pio Papa Secundo. Item in omnibus festivitatibus beate Marie virginis sunt ibi mille anni indulgentiarum. Item a festo assumptionis beate Marie virginis usque ad eius nativitatem sunt ibi duodecim milia anni indulgentiarum.

(The fourth principal church is Santa Maria Maggiore, in which every day there are forty-eight years of indulgence and the same number of *quadragene* and also the remission of one-third of all one's sins. Also these are the relics in the aforementioned church: First, the body of the Apostle Saint Matthew, also the body of Saint Jerome, also the arm of Saint Thomas, archbishop of Canterbury. Also on the ninth of May there is a remission of all one's sins granted by Pope Pius II. Also on every feast of the Blessed Virgin Mary there are one thousand years of indulgence. Also on the feast of the Assumption of the Blessed Virgin Mary until the feast of her birth there are twelve thousand years of indulgence.)

The term *quadragene* (often rendered as "Lents" in English) refers, as Comerford explains in *Book of Holy Indulgences*, "to the special penitential exercises of Lent. An Indulgence then, of, say, five years and five quarantines, means the remission of as much of the temporal punishment of sin as would be effected by the due performance of the canonical penance for five years, joined to the special penitential exercises of as many Lents" (8).

28. My discussion of indulgences draws especially on Swanson, *Indulgences*, and on the work of Shaffern, in particular his "Medieval Theology of Indulgences" (see also the other essays in Swanson, *Promissory Notes*), and his full-length study, *Penitents' Treasury*. A clear, earlier explanation of traditional Catholic doctrine on indulgence is found in the first section of Comerford, *Book of Holy Indulgences*.

29. Hulbert, in "Some Medieval Advertisements," cites a Syon Abbey sermon

on indulgences from London, British Library, Harley 2321, fols. 17ff., which offers "a very clear and systematic exposition of indulgences. There are two elements in deadly sin, it tells us: the offense to God and the pain which the sinner must suffer in hell on account of his sin. When a sinner is contrite and confessed, however, God forgives the sin and substitutes for pain in hell, temporal pain to be suffered in purgatory or on earth. Pardon (or indulgence) can take the place of this temporal pain. But one must understand that neither by confession nor by pardon alone is a man assoiled *a pena et a culpa*. By confession, one gets forgiveness of sin and is assoiled *a culpa*, but the debt of the pain remains. By pardon, he is released from this debt" (420).

30. Swanson, *Indulgences*, 11, says that the accumulated temporal punishments for sins would have exceeded what could be satisfied by penance during most lifetimes. Shaffern, *Penitents' Treasury*, 117–21, notes the diversity of views during the Middle Ages about the pains of purgatory; some, including Aquinas, thought they were hellish, whereas others, among them Dante, considered them relatively benign. For an account of purgatory and its representation in medieval English literature, see Matsuda, *Death and Purgatory*. See also Le Goff, *Birth of Purgatory*.

31. Shaffern, *Penitents' Treasury*, 35–53.

32. Shaffern offers a defense of the value and honesty of indulgences, drawing on recent scholarly work, that challenges persistent criticism, scholarly and popular, from the Middle Ages through the Reformation to the present day: "indulgences served both as modest incentives to good work and as measures of understanding of the basic teachings of the traditional Christian faith" (2).

33. Swanson, *Indulgences*, 19.

34. When Pope Boniface VIII originally conceived of the first Roman Jubilee in 1300, he may not have intended to offer a plenary indulgence to those who visited the city; he seems to have been forced to do so in response to popular expectation. Shaffern, *Penitents' Treasury*, 55. See also Sumption, *Pilgrimage*, 231: "In the autumn of 1299 a notion spontaneously arose that the year 1300 would be a year of Jubilee in which pilgrims to St. Peter's would win huge remission."

35. Matsuda, *Death and Purgatory*, notes that indulgences "inevitably fostered a kind of arithmetical thinking on the part of the laity, deceiving the sinner into believing that Purgatory could be measured in days and years which were in some way proportional to the length of penance on earth," even though "it was repeatedly pointed out that only God knows what term may be assigned to each sin and there was no way of knowing how penance on earth corresponds to that in Purgatory" (26–27). Swanson observes that the "mathematics of punishment were answered by a mathematics of commutation," though it is not clear who did the reckonings. *Indulgences*, 11.

36. In 1343, Pope Clement VI issued the bull *Unigenitus*, announcing the Jubilee of 1350 and setting out the scriptural basis for both jubilees and indulgences, as well as the concept of the Treasury of Merits. For the bull *Unigenitus*, see Shaffern, *Penitents' Treasury*, 79; Swanson, *Indulgences*, 16–17; and Webb, *Medieval European Pilgrimage*, 21. For the Treasury of Merits, see especially Shaffern, "Medieval Theology of Indulgences," and the other essays in Swanson, *Promissory Notes*.

37. Shaffern, "Medieval Theology of Indulgences," esp. 11 and 28–30; and Swanson, *Indulgences*, 27–30.
38. Swanson, *Indulgences*, 30.
39. For pardons attributed to Gregory and/or Sylvester in the Vernon *Stacions*, see, for example, lines 48, 172, 375, 443, 526, 539, and 660; for the pardons of other popes, see, for example, lines 27, 171, 173–74, 231, 405, 415, 431, 582, 593, 685, and 725.
40. Chaucer, *Sir Thopas*, 7.712–13.
41. Quoted from an early printed edition transcribed in Hulbert, "Some Medieval Advertisements," 408; compare Schimmelpfennig, "Römische Ablassfälschungen," 652; and London, British Library, Cotton Titus A.xix, fol. 14r, which Hulbert, 414, identifies as the only version of the *Indulgentiae* in the British Library whose structure is like that of the *Stacions* and that, though different in some ways, seems generally to resemble the manuscript that must have been the poem's immediate source.
42. The text and variants in Huelsen, *Chiese di Roma*, 150 (item 65) record versions of the *Indulgentiae* with the first part of the dialogue, but none with Peter's final plea for mercy, which is also not in Cotton Titus A.xix, fol. 13r, despite, as previously noted, other similarities between this text and the English *Stacions*.
43. Occasional lines such as "As I herde clerkes in Rome telle" (676) do not prove that the writer had been to the city. The reason for this particular phrase seems to be to make a rhyme with "welle" at the end of the previous line; it does not appear at this point in Lambeth (Lambeth, ca. line 829).
44. Robinson notes that large volumes such as the Vernon and Simeon "could not have been held in the reader's hand, but needed to be supported on a lectern or desk." "Vernon Manuscript," 15.
45. Stanbury, "*Man of Law's Tale*," 128. Swanson also speaks in his *Indulgences* of texts about Roman pardons allowing "an imaginative virtual pilgrimage" (240–41). In what follows, I extend and further explore these brief suggestions.
46. For the limited number of English pilgrims to Rome, see Parks, *English Traveler to Italy*, 346–48.
47. Rudy, *Virtual Pilgrimages*, 238–39.
48. See Swanson, *Indulgences*, 53–54.
49. Sumption, *Pilgrimage*, 241, 245; see also Webb, "Pardons and Pilgrims," 255.
50. As noted above, Hulbert could find only one example of a Latin *Indulgentiae* in the British Library—Cotton Titus A.xix—that does not first describe the principal churches of Rome ("Some Medieval Advertisements," 412). Nor does the version of the *Indulgentiae* edited by Valentini and Zucchetti, "Memoriale de mirabilibus," first describe the principal churches.
51. The corresponding passage in Schimmelpfennig, "Römische Ablassfälschungen," gives only the writing on the relic: "titulus Christi, scilicet, 'Iesus Nazarenus rex Iudeorum'" (653).
52. For accounts in the *Indulgentiae* of how the chains got to Rome, see Huelsen, *Chiese di Roma*, 153 (item 83) and 654 (item 1).
53. Cotton Titus A.xix, fol. 13r. The catacombs of Callisto are mentioned, without reference to the need for lighting, in Huelsen, *Chiese di Roma*, 142, and Schimmelpfennig, "Römische Ablassfälschungen," 653.
54. The passage is in Cotton, Lambeth, and Bicester, but not in Vernon.
55. A rare reference to contemporary pilgrims is the statement that because

Peter and Paul once dwelt at S. Pudenziana, the church offers pardon to "alle pilgrimes that come thore" (549), but such pilgrims are not described further.

56. Stanbury, "*Man of Law's Tale*," 125. Greenhalgh also writes that the "most popular collections of holy bones was [*sic*] at Rome" (*Survival of Roman Antiquities*, 187). See also Sumption, *Pilgrimage*, 220. Miedema gives an inventory of the relics in Roman churches in *Römanischen Kirchen*.

57. For the lower figure, see, for example, Huelsen, *Chiese di Roma*, 153 (item 85).

58. Swanson says that before 1300, papal pardons seem to have been restrained, the standard unit being one year and one Lent (*Indulgences*, 30); the later Middle Ages, however, saw a "massive inflation in indulgences" (18), though many of the more extravagant numbers, as in the *Stacions*, do not seem to have had any official sanction.

59. Similar numbers occur in copies of the Latin *Indulgentiae*, without the doubling in Lent; see Huelsen, *Chiese di Roma*, 139; Schimmelpfennig, "Römische Ablassfälschungen," 650; and Hulbert, "Some Medieval Advertisements," 407.

60. For the mathematical and economic metaphors used with indulgences, see Shaffern, "Medieval Theology of Indulgences," 21–26.

61. Cotton, 366–71, also repeats the claim found in some Latin *Indulgentiae* that a plenary indulgence could be obtained by passing through four particular doors at the Lateran.

62. For this debate, see Shaffern, "Learned Discussions of Indulgences."

63. This last example is not in the Lambeth version of the *Stacions*, but both it and Cotton, in a passage not in Vernon, claim that attendance at S. Giovanni a Porta Latina on the saint's feast day earned a personal pardon of five hundred years and meant that "a sowle fro purgatorye wynne thou may" (Cotton, 270–71).

64. This apparent claim that one could free a friend from hell ("he loseth hym") is not in Vernon or Lambeth, although the fragmentary *Stacions* in British Library, Cotton Vespasian D. ix, fol. 184r, makes the much more orthodox claim that at this church one might bring a soul from purgatory to paradise, as does the Latin *Indulgentiae* in Cotton Titus A.xix, fol. 13r.

65. The end of line 729 in the Vernon manuscript reads "miht my," but Furnivall is certainly right to reverse these two words in his edition to preserve the rhyme.

66. The purification of the soul is announced in the Vernon Prologue, which declares that "at Rome" each man may discover how to "clene his soule of synne" (29–31).

67. The story of Constantine's baptism is referred to briefly in some, but not all, Latin *Indulgentiae*, such as Schimmelpfennig, "Römische Ablassfälschungen," 651–52, and Cotton Titus A.xix, fol. 13v.

68. The use of "Mahoun" does not, of course, mean that Constantine was an actual Muslim, only that he was not a Christian.

69. The *Stacions* also notes that Constantine went on to build other churches in Rome.

70. See the prayer that concludes the Vernon *Stacions of Rome*, whose final word is also "benisoun," in which the narrator asks not for any specific Roman pardon but rather that all his readers receive a "part" of the general redemption of the world brought about when God became man:

> Nou God that was in Bedlem bore
> To save the world that was forlore,
> Graunt us part of this pardoun,
> And therto his benisoun. Amen.
>   (731–34)

71. See Watson, "Visions of Inclusion."
72. The numbering of the Psalms follows the Catholic Vulgate.

CHAPTER 2

1. Gregorovius, in his magisterial if somewhat dated *History of the City of Rome*, says, "The author was an investigator and the forerunner of Flavius Blondus [Flavio Biondo]; and to him belongs the credit of the first attempt to reconstruct the ruined city and to trace the plan of its historic monuments" (4:665). Richardson's *New Topographical Dictionary* calls the *Mirabilia* "one of the more extraordinary productions of the twelfth-century revival of interest in antiquity" and notes that its author knew the Rome of his own day very well (xxi–xxii).
2. The date of the *Mirabilia* and its authorship by Benedict were first proposed by Duchesne, "Auteur des *Mirabilia*." The date 1143 has been accepted by most later scholars and Benedict's authorship by many, though not all. See, for example, Hyde, "Medieval Descriptions of Cities," 320; Benson, "Political *Renovatio*," 352; Accame and dell'Oro, *Mirabilia urbis Romae*, 15; and Kinney, "Fact and Fiction," 235–36. The creator of the *Mirabilia*, as often in medieval writing, is both a compiler of previous materials and an original author, though I usually use the latter term for convenience.
3. See, for example, Bloch, "New Fascination," 632; Kinney, "*Mirabilia urbis Romae*," 210–14; Nardella, *Fascino di Roma*, 57; and Accame and dell'Oro, *Mirabilia urbis Romae*, esp. 28–30. Hyde, "Medieval Descriptions of Cities," says that the *Mirabilia* contains a "considerable amount of undigested earlier material" (320).
4. Iain Higgins uses the term "multitext" in reference to an even more plastic medieval work, *Mandeville's Travels*, arguing that "inter- and intra-textual multiplicity is the overwhelming fact about medieval writing" (*Writing East*, viii). In her "Topography as Historiography," Jennifer Summit has many interesting things to say about the *Mirabilia*, but the only text she cites is the 1986 revision of Francis Nichols's 1889 English translation, without any acknowledgment that Nichols's text is a composite, blending the twelfth-century original with several quite different later redactions. The original edition of the Nichols translation more clearly indicates which passages are from which versions.
5. For a catalogue of the many manuscripts and early printed editions of the versions of the *Mirabilia* in several European languages, see Miedema, "*Mirabilia Romae*."
6. Quotations from the *Mirabilia* are from the text edited by Valentini and Zucchetti in *Codice topografico*, 3:3–65. The editors title their edition "La più antica redazione dei *Mirabilia*," and, as Kinney notes, it is a likely approximation of the *Mirabilia* "urtext," or what I call the original *Mirabilia* ("Fact and Fiction," 235). I also use the translation by Nichols in *The Marvels of Rome*, 2nd ed., with some modifications. Both Valentini and Zucchetti's Latin *Mirabilia* and Nichols's translation are hereafter cited parenthetically in the text, the first by page and line number and the second by "Nichols" and page number.
7. The original *Mirabilia* may have had thirty-one chapters; in their edition of the oldest version, Valentini and Zucchetti, in "Più antica redazione," 31n2, say that their chapter 13 is interpolated from a later version.
8. Scholars have generally accepted this tripartite division, even though the

sections are not marked as such in medieval manuscripts and none is entirely consistent.

9. Miedema, "Medieval Images," 205; Miedema, *Mirabilia urbis Romae*," 722. For Kinney's opposing view, see his "Fact and Fiction," esp. 251.

10. Kinney, "Fact and Fiction," 246.

11. Almost a century ago, Hulbert observed that whereas medieval texts on Rome like the *Mirabilia* do not interest students of classical antiquity because "they have no topographical value," they nevertheless "have importance for those interested in the medieval mind." "Some Medieval Advertisements," 403.

12. Freud, *Civilization and Its Discontents*, 17. See Bernfeld, "Freud and Archeology."

13. See also 17, lines 1 and 5; 18, line 7; 20, line 1. Because this is an account of ancient structures, some of the bridges listed were no longer functional in the Middle Ages.

14. The *Mirabilia* also makes no effort to record more incremental changes in the city's structures over time. Thus Rome's walls are listed without mention of their many rebuildings over the centuries, though the separate description in the *Mirabilia* of the walls across the Tiber and around the Vatican might be intended to suggest that they were later Christian additions (17, lines 1–4; Nichols, 4–5).

15. What the Middle Ages thought of as the tomb of Remus is the white stone pyramid built by Caius Cestius as a tomb for himself in about 15 B.C., which still stands near the Ostia railroad station and the Protestant cemetery.

16. Brentano, *Rome Before Avignon*, 79–80; Osborne, *Master Gregorius*, 9; see also Nardella, *Fascino di Roma*, 58–60.

17. Brentano, *Rome Before Avignon*, 76–79.

18. Miedema, "*Mirabilia urbis Romae*," 722.

19. Summit, "Topography as Historiography," 227.

20. Kinney, "Fact and Fiction," 248–49, mentions the debate in the late antique *Passion of St. Sebastian* over whether this astrological marvel should be destroyed.

21. Valentini and Zucchetti, in a note to this passage in their edition of the oldest version of the *Mirabilia*, say that the story of Romulus's statue may have been a gloss that was later inserted into the text. "Più antica redazione," 21n10.

22. Accame and dell'Oro note the frequency with which versions of this verse appear in medieval poetry. *Mirabilia urbis Romae*, 72.

23. Hildebert, "De Roma," 22 (poem 36, lines 1–2).

24. This incident is based on the legend of Marcus Curtius.

25. The Latin *Graphia* text was edited by Valentini and Zucchetti in *Codice topografico*, 3:67–110 (hereafter cited by page number followed by line number); some of its material is included in Nichols's translation *The Marvels of Rome* and in Gardiner's revised edition.

26. The third and most popular recension of Martinus's *Chronicon pontificum* is prefaced with descriptions of four ancient realms, the last being Rome. The most recent edition of this third version is *Chronicon pontificum et imperatorum*, edited by Ludwig Weiland, 377–475, which is the version I cite hereafter by page and line number. On Martinus, see Embree, *Chronicles of Rome*, 2–4; and Ikas, "Martinus Polonus' Chronicle."

27. The third version appears as "Tertia classis," in Urlichs, *Codex urbis Romae*, 126–33.

28. Urlichs, "Tertia classis," 132n, translated in part in Nichols, *Marvels of Rome*, 38. Urlichs's third version

includes the warning bells with his description of the Capitol, unlike the *Mirabilia* and *Graphia*, which describe them as part of their account of the Pantheon, though both say the marvel was in fact located on the Capitol.

29. Urlichs, "Quarta classis," 136, translated in Nichols, *Marvels of Rome*, 28–29. The Colosseum is mentioned only in passing in the original *Mirabilia*, the *Graphia*, and Martinus's *Chronicle*. The Temple of the Sun in the fourth version bears some general resemblance to the astrological Olovitreum in the original *Mirabilia*, mentioned previously, which was eventually destroyed by Saint Sebastian (63, line 6–64, line 2; Nichols, 45).

30. These texts are Cambridge University Library, Gg.4.25, fols. 68r–71v; British Library, Cotton Faustina A.viii, fols. 147r–150v; British Library, Cotton Titus A.xix, fols. 11v–12v; British Library, Harley 562, fols. 1r–5r; and British Library, Harley 2321, fols. 115r–118v. I found no examples of the Hybrid among the five manuscripts of the *Mirabilia* in the Bodleian Library, but I have been unable to check one copy of the *Mirabilia*, Manchester, John Rylands University Library, 71.

31. Both Harley manuscripts seem to have had associations with the important Brigittine monastery of Syon Abbey, founded by Henry V opposite the royal palace of Richmond. This is especially true of Harley 2321, as shown by Powell in "Preaching at Syon Abbey," 233, 252. The case for Harley 562 as a Syon manuscript is less clear, but in its text of the *Mirabilia*, it does add a reference to Brigittine fathers at the church of S. Cecilia in Trastevere (fol. 1v).

32. What I call the Bicester *Mirabilia* is found in the Bicester Priory bursar's accounts roll for 17–18 Edward III, Michaelmas to Michaelmas (PRO SC 6/956/5) and is edited by Scattergood in "Unpublished Middle English Poem"; this edition (slightly modernized) is hereafter cited parenthetically in the text by line number.

33. Scattergood, "Unpublished Middle English Poem," reads "how" at line 31, as in the manuscript, but I have emended this to the more logical "yow."

34. Although Scattergood attributes many details in the Bicester *Mirabilia* to the *Graphia aureae urbis Romae* (the second version of the *Mirabilia*), the Bicester prehistory of Rome somewhat suggests those in the Harley Hybrid texts, which themselves owe much to Martinus's *Chronicon pontificum*, other elements of which are also in Bicester (Scattergood, "Unpublished Middle English Poem," 279). In its list of the gates of Rome, for example, the Bicester *Mirabilia* mentions that a saint was murdered near the gate named "Appya" (lines 55–56), a detail not in the *Graphia* (80, lines 5–6) but found in Harley 2321, fol. 115v. Even this manuscript is far from an exact match, however. Bicester's information that another gate ("Numentana") leads to the church of S. Agnese (lines 63–64) is not in Harley 2321, but it is in Martinus, *Chronicon pontificum* (400, lines 32–33). The Bicester *Mirabilia* does not continue long enough to contain the two most significant elements of the Hybrid: the description of the Capitol, from Urlichs's third version, and the Colosseum as Temple of the Sun, from his fourth.

35. "Ylia" (line 18) is a Virgilian name used for the Vestal Rhea Silvia to emphasize her Trojan roots, and she is said to have begotten Romulus in *Aeneid* 6.778. Martinus, *Chronicon pontificum*, calls the woman "filia Rea" (399, line 33) and proceeds to tell the non-Virgilian story of Mars's rape of

Rhea and how her twins, Romulus and Remus, were left by the Tiber to die, only to be found and nursed by either a wolf or humans. Elements of this story are included in Harley 562 but not in Harley 2321. In Harley 562, Rhea is called "Ita" (fol. 1r), which might help to explain the name here.

36. A reference to Rome's founding 453 years after the fall of Troy (similar to the 454 years in Martinus's *Chronicon pontificum* [398, line 31, and 400, line 16]) is in Harley 2321, fol. 115r, but not in Harley 562.

37. Scattergood suggests, with no strong evidence, that the Bicester *Mirabilia* "seems to have been conceived as a longer and more ambitious work," while speculating, more persuasively, that it "probably owes its inclusion in the MS. to the fact that it is similar in subject matter to *The Stations of Rome*." "Unpublished Middle English Poem," 279, 278.

38. The Mandeville text occupies fols. 77v–95v of Coventry City Record Office, PA 325, and it was edited as *The Metrical Version of Mandeville's Travels* by M. C. Seymour, hereafter cited parenthetically in the text by line number. Seymour dates the writing of the poem to between circa 1375 and circa 1460, saying that "an informed guess" of between 1400 and 1425 "might not be wildly misleading" (xvi). The full Coventry manuscript, of which the *Metrical Mandeville's Travels* is perhaps the least well known item, contains the *Siege of Jerusalem*, several minor poems by Chaucer, six poems by Hoccleve, including the *Regiment of Princes*, and Lydgate's *Siege of Thebes* and *Danse Macabre*. For a description of the manuscript and its contents, see Doyle in Doyle and Pace, "New Chaucer Manuscript," 22–26, which notes that the manuscript "underwent early alteration as well as subsequent losses" (23); Seymour speculates that more leaves of the manuscript were lost than now survive (*Metrical Version*, xxi, xxii). There are brief discussions of the *Metrical Mandeville* as a whole in Moseley, "Metamorphoses," esp. 14–16, and in Higgins, *Writing East*, passim. But the only comments on the Rome interpolation itself that I am aware of are those in the notes to Seymour's edition, 80–91.

39. Higgins, *Writing East*, 44. Seymour says, "Compared with the tentative approach of other English abridgements of *Mandeville's Travels*, the Metrical Version appears a bold and successful enterprise executed to a careful design" (*Metrical Version*, xix). The verse of the *Metrical Version* has been disparaged by most of the few who have examined it. Seymour calls it "unrelievedly pedestrian," though he also says its author is "an experienced and fluent writer" (xviii; see also xx). Higgins refers to its "pedestrian verse" (*Writing East*, 284n65), and Moseley says, "The poet has no outstanding ability" ("Metamorphoses," 14). It is true that the Rome interpolation, like the rest of the *Metrical Mandeville*, has tags and limp lines, but it also contains couplets and longer passages that are brisk, effective, and clever, as we shall see.

40. For the argument that the work might be based on a Latin version of *Mandeville's Travels*, see Seymour, *Metrical Version*, xi–xvi.

41. Other lines directly addressing readers in the Rome interpolation alone include 67, 73, 75, 79 ("Lesteneth and ye shalle weten"), 105, 119, 128 ("the kinges that wee erst of spoken"), 138, 163, 167, 194 ("And I shal rekene or I goo hens"), 213, 222, 228, 273, 294, 296, 301, 336, 349, 366, 385, 440, 457–58 ("I wolde you reherce with good wille /

And I had space to abide theretille"), 460, 461, and 462.
42. The phrase "reflective passages" is from Higgins, *Writing East*, 127. See also Seymour, *Metrical Version*, 79–80, and his commentary. Moseley says that the *Metrical Version* adapted *Mandeville Travels* for a "popular audience" and that the poet "either did not understand or did not respect the serious side of the book" ("Metamorphoses," 16). Thus the English poet conflates the discussions of Greek Christianity and Islam in standard versions of *Mandeville's Travels* and reduces them both.
43. Forms of the words *marvel* and *wonder* appear throughout the work.
44. Seymour, the editor of the *Metrical Version*, is aware that most of the Rome interpolation is derived from the *Mirabilia* tradition, but he admits to being "not clear" about which recession the author used and assumes that the prehistory of Rome is from an unidentified chronicle (80–81). He, like others, is unaware of the Latin Hybrid as a distinct version of the *Mirabilia* and of the prehistories in the Harley manuscripts.
45. The contrasting stories of the founding of Rome (by Aeneas or by Romulus), which Virgil combines more deftly in the *Aeneid*, both appear in Martinus's *Chronicon pontificum*. Martinus's phrasing, in explaining that Romulus and Remus had Trojan ancestors (*Ab hiis ergo duobus, scilicet Romolo et Remo, de Enea Troiano descendentibus* [399, lines 43–44]), might have suggested the idea that Aeneas was the twins' father, though Martinus elsewhere is clear that they were born centuries after the fall of the city (400, lines 16ff).
46. The precise number of these mural fortifications is somewhat different in Harley 2321, fol. 115v. The "barbicans" seem to represent what are called *propugnacula* in Harley 2321, fol. 116r, a word not in the original *Mirabilia* but found in the *Graphia* (80, line 2).
47. Some of these stories are included in other manuscripts of the Hybrid *Mirabilia*, however. The Hybrid texts in both Cambridge University, Gg.4.25 and British Library, Cotton Faustina A.viii include stories from the *Mirabilia* tradition about philosophers commemorated by gigantic marble horsemen, about Agrippa's building of the Pantheon, and about Octavian's vision. The Hybrid text in British Library, Cotton Titus A.xix also includes Octavian's vision, and Harley 562 tells of Octavian's vision and the story behind the gigantic marble horsemen. The absence of such narratives in the Rome interpolation is especially notable because the rest of the *Metrical Mandeville* shows a taste for such fabulous stories, including the legend of the woman turned into a dragon on the island of Lango (668–745) and the "wondir grete mervelle" of the spearhawk (1547–612).
48. Harley 2321, fol. 116v. Neither Harley nor the interpolation names the emperor.
49. See, for example, Comparetti, *Vergil in the Middle Ages*.
50. The sole surviving manuscript of the *Metrical Version* calls attention to this event with a rare red *nota* sign in the margin.
51. The *Metrical* manuscript identifies the palace as Remus's, clearly a mistake for Romulus and corrected in Seymour's edition, since Remus was long dead. Remus is also the name used in Harley 2321, fol. 116v, but the Latin text does not call the statue a god or say that the whole palace was destroyed.
52. This section follows quite closely the Latin text of the English Hybrid in Harley 2321, fols. 117r–118r, with the

exception of the few significant changes discussed in the rest of this chapter.

53. Although the original *Mirabilia*, followed by other versions, clearly states that the warning system was located on the Capitol, it describes it as part of its explanation of how Rome was alerted to the Persian rebellion that Agrippa, the builder of the Pantheon, suppressed.

54. For the variant description of the Capitol in Urlichs's third version, see Urlichs, "Tertia classis," 132n. Some versions of the Hybrid, like Urlichs's third version, describe the warning system in their accounts of both the Capitol and the Pantheon. Harley 2321, fol. 117v, and the *Metrical* interpolation describe it only in their accounts of the Capitol.

55. Because Seymour was not aware of the English Hybrid version of the *Mirabilia*, he concluded that the description of the warning bells here meant that the poet was describing the Pantheon, as in the original *Mirabilia*, rather than the Capitol, even though his edition correctly records that the *Metrical Mandeville* manuscript reads *pito* at line 318.

56. See the *Mirabilia* in Valentini and Zucchetti, "Più antica redazione," 51, lines 5–6; Nichols 38, and the variant description in Urlichs's third version, 132n, which is used in the Hybrid *Mirabilia*, though the version in Titus A.xix, fol. 12r, reads *gemmis* instead. Other ornamentation, but not precious stones, is mentioned in the *Graphia* (89, line 5) and in Martinus's *Chronicon pontificum* (401, line 16).

57. See, for example, Evans, *Magic Jewels*.

58. No such central image of Rome is mentioned with the warning bells in the original *Mirabilia*. The account of the bells in the variant description of the Capitol in Urlichs's third version, "Tertia classis," 132n, says that the image of the rebellious province immediately *vertebat se contra illam* (turned away from it), without specifying what the "it" referred to. Harley 2321, fol. 117v, and other versions of the English Hybrid, however, say that it was a large statue of the city of Rome (*ymaginem urbis Rome*).

59. That hostility is seen elsewhere in the *Metrical Mandeville*, long after the Rome interpolation, when "mamettis" are said to be inhabited by "wickid spirites" who cause pagans to sacrifice their children and cut their own bodies (1951–73).

60. The twelfth-century *Mirabilia* says that ceremonies were performed in this detached solar temple in honor of a statue of the sun that stood on the top of the Colosseum (58, lines 2–3; Nichols, 42). The *Graphia* (90, lines 20–23) and Martinus (401, lines 27–29) add that the statue had a golden crown ornamented with jewels and that its head and hand are now at the Lateran.

61. Quotations of the fourth version are from Urlichs, "Quarta classis," 136, translated by Nichols, *Marvels of Rome*, 28–29. The description of the Colosseum is on fol. 118r of Harley 2321, which generally follows the fourth version, with some rephrasing.

62. This Phoebus may be a confused reference to the monumental golden statue of Nero, which, after his death, was refigured as a statue of the sun and placed in front of the Colosseum.

63. Urlichs, "Quarta classis," 136; Nichols, *Marvels of Rome*, 28.

64. Urlichs, "Quarta classis," 136; Nichols, *Marvels of Rome*, 29. The original *Mirabilia*, as already noted, briefly mentions the destruction of another building by Saint Sebastian, the Olovitreum, a temple containing an *astronomia* with the signs of the zodiac (63, line 6–64, line 2; Nichols, 45).

65. Both the English interpolation and Harley 2321, unlike other copies of the English Hybrid, conclude with the description of the Colosseum. Like Harley 2321 but unlike Urlichs's fourth version, the poem says that it was a temple of the moon as well as of the sun (388), does not call it beautiful, and adds that it was painted with rich colors (392).
66. Langland, *Vision of Piers Plowman*, 15.595.
67. Harley 2321, fol. 118r, and Urlichs, "Quarta classis," 136, call him an idol at this point.
68. Whereas Urlichs's fourth version, "Quarta classis," 136, and other Hybrid manuscripts state that the pope destroyed other palaces (*alia palatia*), the poem, following Harley 2321, fol. 118r, says that he destroyed "othir templis" (418), with no mention of palaces.
69. This last passage is not in Harley 2321, though the story of the Pantheon occurs, often in quite a different form, in other versions of the Hybrid.
70. Camille, *Gothic Idol*, notes that "to want to destroy a false image, one has to believe in its evil efficacy" (xxvii).
71. The Hybrid's view is based on Urlichs's fourth version, "Quarta classis," 136.
72. Jacks, *Antiquarian and the Myth of Antiquity*, refers to "the multitude of pilgrims who came to Rome in pious devotion but, once there, found themselves lured by the spectacle of ancient ruins and intrigued by the anecdotes that circulated about Rome's nefarious emperors" (51). The monuments of Rome continued to be objects of fear and anxiety, as well as awe, into modern times. The Colosseum at night is where Henry James's Daisy Miller catches the fever that kills her, just as the catacombs in Hawthorne's *The Marble Faun* are populated less with saints than with specters.
73. This, of course, is the antithesis of the gentle architectural transition from pagan to Christian that Summit, in "Topography as Historiography," argues occurs in the original *Mirabilia*.
74. Chaucer, *Troilus and Criseyde*, 5.1849–69.
75. Seymour's edition of the *Metrical Version* emends line 437 to "foure [score] and sixti and seven there be," but the manuscript reads "hundrid."
76. Compare, for example, Vernon *Stacions of Rome*, lines 285–93, in Furnivall's edition.

CHAPTER 3

1. All quotations from Gower's *Confessio Amantis*, with some modification in punctuation, are from Peck's three-volume edition, cited parenthetically in the text by book and line number. Peck's commentary on the text is cited in the notes by volume and page number.
2. See Peck, *Kingship and Common Profit*; Simpson, *Sciences and the Self*, esp. chapter 7; Ferster, *Fictions of Advice*, chapter 7; and Minnis, "John Gower, *Sapiens*."
3. Wetherbee, "Rome, Troy, and Culture," 23–25.
4. Genius claims that his source is a historical chronicle (1.759), and the story is told in Josephus Flavius's *Antiquitatum Judaicarum*, though Gower probably knew it in a later version that has not been positively identified. See Peck's comment at 1:312.
5. Porter, "Gower's Ethical Microcosm," 147; Peck, *Kingship and Common Profit*, 41.
6. See Peck, *Kingship and Common Profit*, 41–45.
7. On the general topic of such rhymes in the *Confessio*, see Zarins, "Rich Words."
8. See especially Porter, "Gower's Ethical Microcosm"; and Peck's notes to book

7 in vol. 3 of the *Confessio Amantis*. For an English version of Latini's *Tresor*, see Latini, *Book of the Treasure*.

9. See, for example, Olsson, *John Gower and the Structures*, 191–98; Simpson, *Sciences and the Self*, esp. 204–5; Peck, *Kingship and Common Profit*, esp. 140. See also Runacres, "Art and Ethics," 115; and Scanlon, *Narrative, Authority, and Power*, 249.

10. Nolan, *John Lydgate*, 219.

11. Nolan finds a Roman theme, though only a mini-theme, in three linked episodes within book 7, the purpose of which "is to describe Rome as a culturally distinct and historically distant entity—which then functions in exemplary terms as a model for princes by virtue of its very difference from the present" (223). This is well said, but my claim in this chapter is broader still: that Rome is a model of civic governance throughout the *Confessio* and that even book 7 is addressed to estates other than princes.

12. The Roman tales, as I calculate them, are Julius and the Poor Knight (7.2061–114), the Roman Triumph (7.2355–411), the Emperor and the Masons (7.2412–31), Caesar's Answer (7.2449–86), the Emperor Maximin (7.2765–82), Gaius Fabricius (7.2783–832), Carmidotirus (7.2845–88), Pompey and the King of Armenia (7.3215–66), Tarquin, Aruns, and the Rape of Lucretia (7.4593–5123), and Virginia (7.5131–306). In addition, there are briefer mentions of the pity of Constantine and Trajan (7.3137–62), the cruelty of Leoncius (7.3267–87), and the pity of Emperor Antonius (7.4181–88).

13. For example, there is almost no acknowledgment that the story of Virginia took place during the republic. See Scanlon, *Narrative, Authority, and Power*, 293–95.

14. See Middleton, "Idea of Public Poetry," on the concept of the common good in late medieval English poetry.

15. The fourth story in this sequence on justice (and the third set in ancient Rome) is about the overscrupulous Carmidotirus.

16. Among the illustrations of largesse, four are Roman, one is Chaldean, one is Carthaginian, one is Greek, and one is biblical.

17. See Peck, *Kingship and Common Profit*, 145.

18. Gower also tells a story in the section on pity about a "king of Rome," Lucius, who brings relief to his people by rejecting the flattery of his steward and replacing vicious councilors with virtuous ones (7.3945–4026).

19. Nolan, *John Lydgate*, 220–28, has the best account of Gower's triumph as an illustration of Roman plain speaking and self-knowledge. She identifies Gower's source as Higden's *Polychronicon* (217–19).

20. Simpson, *Sciences and the Self*, 204, argues that self-knowledge, which is explicit here, is implicit in the structure of the whole poem. The mention of justice in these lines is another example of Gower's intermingling of the different virtues of kingship in book 7.

21. Runacres, "Art and Ethics," 123. Nolan says that Gower, following Higden's *Polychronicon*, "links the two exempla—the triumph and the masons—because they concern Romans and together suggest a particular quality of Romanness (a willingness to be confronted by unpleasant truths) he wishes to hold up as an example to present-day kings." *John Lydgate*, 223.

22. The section also contains another, very brief negative Roman example: the lust of Antonius, the son of the emperor Severus (7.4574–84).

23. In fact, such deference by Roman emperors was limited to Vestal Virgins, but Gower either did not know this or deliberately expanded the practice. This section also tells of Phyrinus, "the faireste / Of Rome and ek the comelieste" (5.6373–74), who deals with the temptations women arouse in him by deliberately defacing his beauty; thus "his maidehiede he boghte" (5.6384).

24. Gower's double narrative of the Tarquins is, according to Peck, much enlarged from Ovid, *Fasti* 2.687–852, as is his narrative of Virginius and Virginia from Livy, 3.44–50, or from a French medieval translation of Livy. See Peck's edition, 3:480, 483.

25. The mention of pity in this story of chastity is another example of how the five different points of policy often overlap in the *Confessio*.

26. Simpson, *Sciences and the Self*, 213, notes the similarity between Aruns's attack on Lucretia in her own house and his similar "invasion" of the Gabines.

27. Aruns is later called a "tirannysshe knyht" (7.4889; cf. 7.4899 and 7.4959) and is said to be practicing "slih tresoun" (7.4936) as he plans his assault on Lucretia.

28. Bertolet, "From Revenge to Reform," stresses the political focus of Gower's version of this story, which he says is more classical than medieval in emphasizing Aruns as a tyrant (and Brutus as a reformer) instead of Lucretia as a tragic victim.

29. For another negative reading of Virginius, though in the context of fathers and daughters rather than Roman principles, see Bullón-Fernández, *Fathers and Daughters*, 145–57.

30. Strohm, *Social Chaucer*, esp. chapter 6; and Wallace, *Chaucerian Polity*, esp. chapter 2. See also Galloway, "Gower's Quarrel with Chaucer."

31. Compare Ovid, *Fasti* 2.849–52.

32. Gower's Latin marginal summary of this story reports no such extended discussion but says only that the Tarquins were sent into exile "by the clamoring of all Rome." See the translation by Andrew Galloway in Peck's edition of the *Confessio*, 3:481.

33. For the marginal summary, see Peck's edition, 3:483.

34. In his note to lines 2.3187ff., Peck (2:351) follows Macaulay's edition of the *Confessio* in *English Works of John Gower*, 1:492, in identifying the source of the tale as the Life of Sylvester in the *Legenda aurea*.

35. Pearsall says, "Gower's special achievement is to embody, in Constantine's soliloquy and in the description of the workings of his mind and heart, the very substance of human charity and pity." "Chaucer's Narrative Art," 478.

36. See Olsson, "Natural Law"; Olsson, *John Gower and the Structures*, 102–6; and Peck, *Kingship and Common Profit*, 76; see also, more generally, Minnis, "'Moral Gower.'"

37. See Michael Livingston's edition of this poem in Gower, *Minor Latin Works*, 89–132. Constantine is mentioned briefly in the poem (lines 337–57) as an example of one whose pity in choosing to risk his own life to save innocent children earns him God's pity in return and a cure in body and soul. Livingston's note to these lines cites Grady, "Lancastrian Gower," 568–69, to support the observation that the Constantine of this poem is a simpler and more wholly positive figure than he is in the *Confessio*.

38. Nicholson, *Love and Ethics*, 174–75, argues that Constantine's leprosy in the *Confessio*, instead of being a punishment for persecuting Christians as in the *Legenda aurea*, is an indication of his empty spiritual state.

39. See Cooper, "'Peised Evene in the Balance'": "Constantine, initially a pagan, learns first the rule of himself, then the right rule of his people, then the law of God: the three are replicas of each other, though the first two are available to all the virtuous, just as Constantine learns to act well before his conversion" (125).
40. No mention of Constantine's damaging transfer of temporal power to the pope appears in the brief account of the emperor in Gower's "In Praise of Peace" or in the Constantine episode in the *Stacions of Rome*.
41. For the thematic links between Gower's tales of Constance and Constantine, see Bullón-Fernández, *Fathers and Daughters*, esp. 86–87, 97–100.
42. Constance's father is also portrayed in the *Confessio* as continuing to care about his daughter after her departure. He is said to be "nevere glad" and performs much charity ("ful gret almesse") on her behalf (2.1465–72); when Constance finally reveals herself to him after returning to the city, he is overcome with such joy that there "was nevere fader half so blithe" (2.1521).
43. Bullón-Fernández, *Fathers and Daughters*, 91–93, also notes that the pope is relegated to a spiritual role here.
44. Scanlon, *Narrative, Authority, and Power*, 248–67, traces an anticlerical critique in the *Confessio* that begins in the prologue and culminates in the tales of Boniface and Constantine and Sylvester.

CHAPTER 4

1. I am, of course, echoing the title of Mann's important study, *Feminizing Chaucer*, though Mann does not address the topic of Rome and women. See also Hansen, *Chaucer and the Fictions of Gender*, for a trenchant warning against anachronistic and superficial attempts by contemporary scholars to enlist Chaucer in the ranks of twentieth-century feminism.
2. Galloway argues that Chaucer "frequently uses a feminine perspective for establishing a critique of masculine or pagan or clerical social assumptions," though he differs from what I argue in this chapter when he adds that "Chaucer takes care to avoid any closer identification with the women through whose eyes he looks, beyond the purposes of an ideological critique that profits his own and his generally male audience's authority more than that of the women he describes." "Chaucer's *Legend of Lucrece*," 825.
3. Hirsh says that "Rome as a place figures with particular emphasis" in only two tales (the *Second Nun's Tale* and the *Physician's Tale*) ("Chaucer's Roman Tales," 45); whereas Fichte, "Rome and Its Anti-Pole," discusses, as his full title indicates, a different pair of tales: those of the Man of Law and the Second Nun. Chaucer refers to Rome only sporadically in his early poems, and his first extensive mention of the city comes in his prose translation of Boethius's *Consolation of Philosophy*.
4. Patterson, *Chaucer and the Subject of History*, 236.
5. All citations of Chaucer are from the *Riverside Chaucer* and are noted parenthetically in the text by fragment and line number (*Canterbury Tales*), book and line number (*Troilus and Criseyde*), or line number alone (all other poems); all citations of the *Legend of Good Women* (cited by line number) are to version F.
6. McCall says in *Chaucer Among the Gods*, "Rome is not mentioned once and has absolutely no role" (107). I agree with the first but not the second part of this statement.

7. In "Did Chaucer Visit Rome," Hirsh suggests, without much proof, that Chaucer may have visited Rome and knew the church of Saint Cecilia in Trastevere, but the *Second Nun's Tale* offers no clear evidence of such first-hand knowledge.
8. See, for example, the study of Chaucer's Trojan interiors in Smyser, "Domestic Background."
9. On Criseyde's vulnerability as a woman in Troy, see the pioneering, if somewhat unbalanced, essay by Aers, "Criseyde: Woman in Medieval Society." For the importance of friendship between men and women in Trojan high society, see Lambert, "*Troilus*, Books I–III."
10. Edwards, *Chaucer and Boccaccio*, 75–103.
11. The introduction to the *Man of Law's Tale* links the two poets when it declares that Chaucer "hath toold of loveris up and doun / Mo than Ovide made of mencioun / In his Epistles [*Heroides*]" (2.53–55). For the influence of Ovid on Chaucer, see especially Fyler, *Chaucer and Ovid*; and Calabrese, *Chaucer's Ovidian Arts*.
12. Simpson, "Chaucer as a European Writer," 62.
13. Douglas, "The Proloug of the First Buik of Eneados," in *Poetical Works*, 2:17, line 21. Although the Virgilian Douglas is critical of such sympathy for Dido, he otherwise admires Chaucer.
14. Fyler, "Explanatory Notes to *The House of Fame*," 980, note to lines 240–382.
15. For Chaucer's sympathy for Dido and blame of Aeneas, see, for example, Edwards, *Chaucer and Boccaccio*, 77–83; and Simpson, "Chaucer as a European Writer," 69–70.
16. Although Anthony becomes the enemy of Rome for his love affair with Cleopatra, he, like the city's other leaders, treats his own countrywomen badly, having deserted his wife like a latter-day Aeneas: "He lafte hire falsly" (593).
17. Hirsh notes, without specific reference to women, that authority misused in such tales as those of the Knight and the Clerk "pale in comparison" with "the corruption of legitimate civic authority" in the Roman tales. "Chaucer's Roman Tales," 47.
18. The *Legend of Lucrece* is the third narrative in the *Legend of Good Women* about a woman whose suicide is caused by men associated with Rome, following those of Cleopatra and Dido, discussed above.
19. Ovid, *Fasti* 2.811–12 (Frazier's translation somewhat modified).
20. Percival notes that the "lexical pattern" of Chaucer's description of Tarquin's passion renders it not only irrational and illicit but also nakedly sexual and devoid of love or courtly refinement. *Chaucer's Legendary Good Women*, 271–73.
21. Ovid, *Fasti* 2.779.
22. For previous discussions that have noted the darkness of Chaucer's version, see, for example, Frank, *Chaucer and "The Legend,"* 106; Minnis, *Shorter Poems*, 364; and Mann, *Feminizing Chaucer*, 35–36.
23. Compare Ovid, *Fasti* 2.851–52. The episode in the *Fasti* is more political throughout, for its purpose is to describe the origin of the Roman holiday known as the *Regifugium* (celebrating the expulsion of Rome's monarchy) and the beginnings of the republic.
24. Block, "Originality, Controlling Purpose," 589, notes that Constance's farewell speech in Chaucer is developed from just a hint in Trevet.
25. Even more ineffective than Hector in *Troilus and Criseyde*, who, although he cannot prevent the trading of Criseyde

to the Greeks, does at least offer her his protection while she is in Troy.

26. Gower describes the "contienance" she makes with her dying eyes, "in thonkinge as it were," and her continuing to gaze at Brutus "whil sche to loke mai suffise" (7.5088–92). Ovid says that Lucretia moves her lightless eyes and by the stirring of her hair seems to approve of Brutus's words (*Fasti* 2.845–46).

27. For defenses of Virginius, see, for example, Bartholomew, *Fortuna and Natura*, 53; and Gray, *Oxford Companion to Chaucer*, 380.

28. Schildgen notes that the men and women in Chaucer's "polemically Christian tales" (those of the Second Nun, Prioress, and Man of Law) are "feminized" in that they choose powerlessness, like women and children. *Pagans, Tartars, Moslems, and Jews*, 111.

29. Neither feminine pathos nor feminine valor in Chaucer's Roman tales has been studied as a separate topic. For Chaucerian pathos in general, see Gray, "Chaucer and 'Pite.'"

30. For discussions of the pathos of these two tales, see, for example, Baker, "Chaucer's Experiments"; and Mann, *Feminizing Chaucer*, 112–14. See also Gray, *Oxford Companion to Chaucer*, 379–81, on Chaucer's efforts to increase the pathos and horror of the *Physician's Tale*.

31. Lynch calls Lucretia "the best of Chaucer's 'good women,' the least subject to qualification" (*Chaucer's Philosophical Visions*, 131), though Percival believes that Chaucer follows Ovid in gently mocking her as "too good to be true" (*Chaucer's Legendary Good Women*, 278).

32. Kean stresses Chaucer's emphasis on Virginia's virtues and how his additions to the tale make her an embodiment of the nobility of humankind. *Chaucer and the Making of English Poetry*, 179–82.

33. Frank says that the *Second Nun's Tale* is closer to the heroic than to the pathetic. *Chaucer and "The Legend,"* 97.

34. Kolve notes that the later parts of the tale adopt "the language of military alliance and victory, then of juridical debate." "Chaucer's *Second Nun's Tale*," 151.

35. See Damon, "*Seinte Cecile*."

36. Those who have called attention to elements of the saint's life in the *Man of Law's Tale* include Paull, "Influence of the Saint's Legend"; Block, "Originality, Controlling Purpose," 589; Jordan, "Heteroglossia," 90; and Spearing, "Narrative Voice," 738.

37. For a discussion of the *Legend of Lucrece* as a saint's life, see esp. Minnis, *Shorter Poems*, 406–14.

38. Middleton argues that Chaucer adds to his source in the *Roman de la Rose* "a strong interest in Virginia as a virgin martyr." "*Physician's Tale* and Love's Martyrs," 11.

39. Lucretia's agency is made more emphatic by Chaucer than in the more perfunctory account in his source in Ovid, *Fasti* 2.831: "celato fixit sua pectora ferro" (she stabbed her breast with the steel she had hidden).

40. For the importance of Virginia's informed verbal consent to her death, see especially Farber, "Creation of Consent." For contrary arguments that Virginia has no free will here, see Fletcher, "Sentencing of Virginia," esp. 306; and Hirsh, "Modern Times," esp. 390.

41. In Livy, Apius is said to have been one of the decemvir in charge of Rome, and his misuse of his office for sexual gratification ends that system, just as Tarquin's crime ends the monarchy. Gower does not mention the decemvir, but he talks about a "comun conseil" that deposes Apius and uses the "lawe"

to hold others responsible as a warning to those "that scholden afterward governe" (7.5294–306). For the "depoliticisation" of the story of Virginia, first by Jean de Meun in the *Roman de la Rose* and then, even more thoroughly, by Chaucer in the *Physician's Tale*, see Delany, "Politics and the Paralysis."

42. For a characteristically learned and original essay on Chaucer's relationship to the long tradition of Christian writers who wrote about Lucretia, see Galloway, "Chaucer's *Legend of Lucrece*." In *Fall of Women*, Schmitz argues that Chaucer historicizes Lucretia to defend her against a narrow Christian understanding of her virtue (76–88); see also Saunders, "Classical Paradigms of Rape."

43. For the disjunction between the classical world and the Christian world in the *Legend*, see, further, Boffey and Edwards, "*Legend of Good Women*," esp. 124–25.

44. I disagree with Bartholomew, who argues that both Virginia and Virginius achieve a spiritual triumph. *Fortuna and Natura*, 56–57.

45. Winstead, *Virgin Martyrs*, 83. See also Ames, *God's Plenty*: "Cecilia forces the action at every stage, accompanying it with theory and plan" (171); and Martin, *Chaucer's Women*: "Cecilia is a militantly active heroine" (150).

46. Beichner, "Confrontation, Contempt of Court," 204. Helen Cooper says that "Cecilia herself is a woman of intellect and authority" and "she can run rings round [Almachius] intellectually." *Canterbury Tales*, 365.

47. Pope Paschal I in the ninth century claimed to have rediscovered her uncorrupted corpse in the Roman catacombs and had it translated to the church within the city walls that he had built on what was believed to be the site of her house. See my "Statues, Bodies, and Souls," esp. 276.

48. See Keiser, "Spiritual Heroism."

49. Mann argues that the rudderless boat is at the heart of tale, revealing Constance's courage in throwing herself into the "flux of events." *Feminizing Chaucer*, 110.

50. The *Man of Law's Tale* says that Maurice "lyved cristenly" and to "Cristes chirche he dide greet honour," but no details are given, and the reader is directed instead to "olde Romyn geestes" (2.1121–27). The historical Maurice seems to have been rather unsavory, though whitewashed by medieval writers; see Schlauch, "Historical Precursors," esp. 402–7.

51. Schildgen says that the golden age of Christianity in the *Second Nun's Tale* is distanced from the corruption and decline of the present church. *Pagans, Tartars, Moslems, and Jews*, 120.

CHAPTER 5

1. Unless otherwise noted, all references are to the B-text of *Piers Plowman* and are from Schmidt's edition of Langland, *Vision of Piers Plowman*, cited parenthetically in the text by passus and line number. See also the same editor's Langland, *Piers Plowman: A Parallel-Text Edition*. For the C-text, I use Pearsall's edition of Langland, *New Annotated Edition of the C-Text*.

2. See, for example, Mann, "'He Knew Nat Catoun.'"

3. For this Latin spelling of the name Trajan, see Wenzel, "Langland's *Troianus*."

4. The only scholar of whom I am aware who has called attention to the Romanness of Trajan and Gregory, however briefly, is Grady; see his powerful and sophisticated "Trouble with Trajan," 17.

5. Salter, *Fourteenth-Century English Poetry*, 111; cf. Zeeman, "*Piers Plowman*," 228–29.

6. Galloway, "Making History Legal," 17. Grady says that, in contrast to personifications and to "transhistorical figures like Christ, Trajan is the only 'real' historical person to appear" ("Trouble with Trajan," 25). Pope Gregory in the Trajan episode is also a historical person, of course, but he does not speak in his own voice.
7. Wittig notes that W. W. Skeat attributed these lines to Lewte; he suggests that other possible speakers in addition to Trajan could be the dreamer, Scripture, or the poet himself ("'Piers Plowman' B," 255n143). In the C-text, the corresponding lines are later attributed to Rechelesnesse at C 13.129. On the textuality of first-person speakers in medieval literature, see Spearing, *Textual Subjectivity* and *Medieval Autographies*.
8. See Schmidt's comment in *Vision of Piers Plowman*, 451; see also Schmidt's edition *Piers Plowman: A Parallel-Text Edition*, which says, with even less certainty, that "the speaker is likely to be Trajan" (2:604).
9. See, for example, Rudd, *Managing Language in "Piers Plowman,"* 178–79; Simpson, *"Piers Plowman": An Introduction*, 112; Steiner, *Reading "Piers Plowman,"* 127–30; and Zeeman, *"Piers Plowman,"* 229n58.
10. See Langland, *Piers Plowman: The B Version*; Kane and Donaldson amend their edition of the text with added first-person pronouns to make lines 141–43a also the direct speech of Trajan. The only support for this, as they record in their notes, is Crowley's 1550 print. I follow instead Schmidt's edition and the readings of the manuscripts.
11. For Spearing, see note 7 above. Schmidt, in both his editions—*Vision of Piers Plowman* and *Piers Plowman: A Parallel-Text Edition*—attributes B 11.153–69 to Trajan himself. In the latter edition, Schmidt says the lines are "spoken by Trajan about himself in the 3rd person as an example" (2:604), though why such a direct and autobiographical speaker would suddenly refer to himself in this way is not explained. Pearsall, in his edition of the C-text, notes that in the comparable passage in the C-text, the "speaker is not immediately identifiable" (Langland, *New Annotated Edition of the C-Text*, 220) but that 13.129 suggests it is Rechelesnesse.
12. For the history of the legend, see Whatley, "Uses of Hagiography"; for the Whitby life of Gregory, see 27–28. Another early life of Gregory, which was more widely known in the Middle Ages than the Whitby one, was written in the late ninth century by John the Deacon; see Whatley, 28–31.
13. Whatley, 26.
14. John of Salisbury, *Policraticus*, 79–80. See Whatley, "Uses of Hagiography," 32–34.
15. See Dante, *Divine Comedy: Purgatorio* and *Divine Comedy: Paradiso*, both edited and translated by Singleton.
16. See Whatley, "Uses of Hagiography," 43–50.
17. For Jacobus's life of Gregory, see *Golden Legend*, 1:171–84; for the Trajan/Gregory episode, 178–79.
18. Jacobus follows this long narrative with a briefer one about Trajan and a different widow, a story that was sometimes conflated in the Middle Ages with the first (*Golden Legend*, 1:178). This second story tells how Trajan's son's careless riding kills the son of the other widow. When she complains to the emperor, he hands over his son to replace hers.
19. The emperor is also the primary figure in the accounts of John of Salisbury and Dante.

20. I know of no other medieval text in which Trajan, after escaping from hell, speaks about his earthly life.
21. Obviously, Gregory desires Trajan's release from hell, which happens, but neither the *Legenda* nor *Piers Plowman* shows Gregory explicitly praying for his release (although the *Legenda* reports that some say he did) or offering a Mass on the emperor's behalf. In the *Legenda*, but not in *Piers*, God tells Gregory never to petition on behalf of a damned soul again, implying that he has done so in some fashion.
22. Aers challenges Trajan's Pelagian boast that he is responsible for his own salvation. *Salvation and Sin*, 122–31.
23. I am not willing to go as far as Aers in his latest and fullest argument, in *Beyond Reformation*, for Langland's questioning of the efficacy of the traditional church.
24. Chambers, "Long Will, Dante."
25. Dunning, "Langland and the Salvation"; Harwood, "'Clergye' and the Action." For a discussion of the different views of Chambers and Dunning, see Wittig, "'Piers Plowman' B."
26. Grady, "Trouble with Trajan," esp. 20–22. The Adams quotation is from "Langland's Theology," 96.
27. Adams, "Piers's Pardon." Compare, more generally, Coleman, *"Piers Plowman" and the Moderni.*
28. Adams, "Piers's Pardon," 377, 390.
29. Burrow, "Thinking in Poetry"; Simpson, *"Piers Plowman": An Introduction*, 111–12; Steiner, *Reading "Piers Plowman*," 124–39; and Minnis, "Looking for a Sign."
30. Jacobus, *Golden Legend*, 1:179.
31. See the discussion of these views in Wittig, "'Piers Plowman' B," 252; and in Grady, "Trouble with Trajan," 18–19.
32. Higden, *Polychronicon*, 5:4–7 (book 4, chapter 13).
33. The lack of punctuation marking spoken words in medieval manuscripts forces modern editors to make their own decisions about what speech is direct and what indirect, although the distinction undoubtedly seemed less clear-cut to Middle English poets and readers than it does to us.
34. See, for example, the texts of the *Indulgentiae* in Huelsen, *Chiese di Roma*, 137–56.
35. The Vernon *Stacions* edited by Furnivall in *Stacions of Rome* says, for example, that at the church of S. Maria Maggiore, in addition to other pardons, "Therto grauntcd Seint Gregori / An hundred yer to pardoun / And therto Godes benysoun" (lines 526–28), and that at S. Pudenziana there was "Foryivenesse of al thi synne / . . . Seint Gregori telleth thus" (537–39). These claims are anachronistic because such papal indulgences for all were a late medieval practice that occurred long after Gregory's time, as discussed in chapter 1.
36. Furnivall, *Stacions of Rome*, in *Political, Religious, and Love Poems*, lines 898–902.
37. Valentini and Zucchetti, "Più antica redazione," 3:56, lines 1–5. A later Latin version of the *Mirabilia* includes the incident of Trajan's giving justice to a widow in its description of the Arch of Pity, although only some manuscripts actually name the emperor as Trajan. This story, without Trajan's name, occurs in what Urlichs calls the third version of the *Mirabilia*, which he dates to the fourteenth century. See his "Tertia classis," 129. The story is found in several manuscripts of the *Mirabilia* produced in England that postdate *Piers Plowman*, some of which name Trajan and some of which do not.

38. After B 11.158, which is revised as C 12.91–92, the C-text omits lines B 11.159–69.
39. The same combination of love and truth is made at B 11.161, as already noted. This convergence is not so apparent in the C-text, which omits B 11.159–69 and whose version of B 11.170 (C 12.93), where its text resumes, replaces "love" with "leutee."
40. Coghill, "Pardon of Piers Plowman," 147.
41. Alford, "Design of the Poem," 34.

CHAPTER 6

1. Nigel Mortimer gives the line count and says that the *Fall of Princes* "is perhaps the longest poem in the English language" (*Lydgate's "Fall of Princes,"* 1). Meyer-Lee calls the *Fall* "the greatest work of his later career" (*Poets and Power*, 78). Widely popular, the *Fall of Princes* survives in more than thirty-five manuscripts, in addition to excerpts in some forty other manuscripts; it was first printed in 1494 and was reprinted three times in the next sixty years. See Edwards, "Influence of Lydgate's *Fall*"; and Pearsall, *John Lydgate (1371–1449)*, 69–72.
2. Unless otherwise noted, all references to the *Fall of Princes* are from Bergen's four-volume edition, hereafter cited parenthetically in the text by book and line number (but see n. 13 below). In addition to modernizing other spellings noted at the beginning of the book, I have changed Bergen's i's to j's where appropriate.
3. The preeminent Lydgate scholar of our time, Derek Pearsall, has often directed his considerable wit against what he takes to be the dogged, wearying conventionality of the *Fall*, while expressing admiration for individual elements of the poem. In his major, pioneering study of the poet, *John Lydgate*, he says that an anthology could be compiled from the *Fall* that "would represent it as Lydgate's most considerable achievement" (250).
4. See Mortimer, *Lydgate's "Fall of Princes,"* 3–11, for the early literary reputation of the *Fall*.
5. Nolan, "'Now Wo, Now Gladnesse.'" The complexity that Nolan celebrates is seen as incoherence by other critics. See, for example, Norton-Smith, *John Lydgate: Poems*: "The poet's insights into the concept of Fortune and human motivation are inconsistent and eclectic. They are scarcely combined into an intelligible pattern" (127). For Nolan's discussion of the *Serpent of Division*, see her *John Lydgate*, 33–70.
6. Strohm, "Lydgate and the Rise of *Pollecie*"; Scanlon, *Narrative, Authority, and Power*, 344–49.
7. The presence of Rome in various books of the *Fall of Princes* is noted in Schirmer's summary of the poem (*John Lydgate*, 216, 218, 220, 222). Ebin and Mortimer also mention it. See Ebin, *John Lydgate*, 70; Mortimer, *Lydgate's "Fall of Princes,"* 79.
8. Schirmer notes a central contradiction in the *Fall*, most clearly expressed in the debate of Fortune and Poverty at 3.204–707, between history as "a fatalist drama of the fickleness of Fortune" versus "a manifestation in this world of divine justice" (*John Lydgate*, 213). Nolan argues that the tension between misfortune as a punishment for sin and as the result of chance was already present in Lydgate's sources, and she calls attention to the *Fall*'s "distinctly mixed aesthetic, one that renders history in deeply ambivalent fashion, as both sexual and moral, providential and continent, tragic and elegiac all at once" ("'Now Wo, Now Gladnesse,'" 532). In *John Lydgate*, Nolan says that Lydgate's "fundamen-

tally incompatible visions of historical causation and the role of human agency" (63) are present in his first Roman work, the prose *Serpent of Division*, in which his attempt to synthesize Gower's "economy of sin and punishment" with "a Chaucerian drama of contingencies in which catastrophe proceeds not from sin but from chance" results in a "fundamental philosophical conflict between these two notions of causality" (35). Galloway cites Nolan and especially Mortimer as recognizing Lydgate's "multiple vision of historical causality" in the *Fall*, which Mortimer links to classical writers such as Seneca and Lucan ("John Lydgate and the Origins," 471).

9. Simpson, *Reform and Cultural Revolution*, 244–45.
10. For selections from *De casibus* in English, see Boccaccio, *Fates of Illustrious Men*. For the full Latin text, see Boccaccio, *De casibus virorum illustrium*. On the two versions of Laurent's *Cas des nobles hommes*, see Gathercole, "Two Old French Translations," and her "Manuscripts." See also her essays "Boccaccio in French" and "Fifteenth-Century Translation."
11. For the limited circulation of Boccaccio's *De casibus* in England and Lydgate's lack of knowledge of it, see Edwards, "Influence of Lydgate's *Fall*," 425–28; and Hammond, *English Verse*, 154.
12. Hammond says that "Laurent also diverges and amplifies wherever excuse for divergence offers; the mention by Boccaccio of a place, a custom, a person, sends Laurent off on a detour" (*English Verse*, 151–52). For brief comments on scholarly discussions of the differences between the texts of Boccaccio and Laurent, see Mortimer, *Lydgate's "Fall of Princes*," 16–17, 34–35.
13. There is no modern critical edition of the entire text of Laurent's *Cas des nobles hommes et femmes*, though book 1 has been edited and introduced by Gathercole in *Premierfait's "Des cas."* For Laurent's text and its difference from Lydgate's *Fall*, I have depended largely on the selections and notes in the first and fourth volumes of Henry Bergen's edition of the *Fall of Princes*, which, unless otherwise noted, is the edition I cite in subsequent notes, by volume and page number.
14. The accounts of these marvels, which are somewhat different from those in the *Mirabilia*, probably came from texts that Lydgate was more likely to have known. For example, the statue of Romulus appears in Higden's *Polychronicon*, 1:214, and the astrological temple appears in Martinus Polonius's *Chronicon pontificum* (402, lines 13–14). Alexander Neckam describes the warning bells in his *De naturis rerum* (see Graf, *Roma nella memoria*, 151n15; and Comparetti, *Vergil in the Middle Ages*, 293–98). Neckam, like Lydgate but unlike the *Mirabilia*, attributes the marvel to Virgil.
15. Lydgate explicitly attributes his information on Roman crowns to the second-century Roman grammarian Aulus Gellius (4.239). Bergen agrees that Gellius, who wrote *Attic Nights*, is probably the source (4:206). Wakelin says that manuscript marginalia indicate Aulus Gellius as the source by giving seven rough excerpts from his work. *Humanism, Reading, and English Literature*, 41.
16. See Bergen's edition, 4:206.
17. The information about the three estates apparently comes from Isidore of Seville. Bergen (4:206) cites Hammond's attribution to Isidore, whose account is found in his *Etymologies* 18.2 (see Barney's translation, 360). Schirmer (*John Lydgate*, 86) says that

the triumphal procession in Lydgate's *Serpent* follows the *Polychronicon*, though the grandiose triumph in the *Fall* is from an unknown source (218). Other details about triumphs that are new to the *Fall*'s version include the conqueror's bearing a red standard (4.547–48) and a new form of the Greek phrase "know yourself," which was whispered in the conqueror's ear (4.568).

18. There are limits to Lydgate's geographical knowledge, however, which is understandable in one who never saw the city. He says that Manlius was thrown from the Capitol into the Tiber (4.489–90), which is not humanly possible.

19. Lydgate's addition of these lines is noted in Bergen's edition, 4:206.

20. Pearsall says that the prologue is "full of vigour" (*John Lydgate*, 227). But he also says that in it, Lydgate is "significantly little interested in poetic theory and is quite content," like Boccaccio, Laurent, and Chaucer's monk before him, "to prefix his catalogue of tragedies with the simplest and most conventional definition of their nature and purpose" (233). I offer a different view.

21. A transcription of Laurent's prologue is found in Bergen's edition, 1:lii–iv, and in Gathercole's edition of book 1 of *Des cas des nobles hommes*, 88–90. The most thorough discussion of Lydgate's view of translation in the prologue to book 1 appears in Scanlon, *Narrative, Authority, and Power*, 327–35. Laurent's specific reason for the image of the potter is to refer to the extensive changes he made in the second version of his own translation of Boccaccio's *De casibus* in 1409, though he also allows the same license to those revising the works of others.

22. Only after emphasizing the innovative capacities of these "expert maistres" does Lydgate go back to Laurent's more limited claims about having the "licence" to change a thing "fro good to bettir" (1.19–20).

23. The metaphor of clean corn from old chaff is a blend of Chaucer's proverb at the beginning of the *Parliament of Fowles* (lines 22–23), about the new corn of literature coming from old fields, and his advice to readers at the end of *Nun's Priest's Tale* to take the fruit and leave the chaff (7.3443). All Chaucer quotations are from the *Riverside Chaucer*.

24. Or at least such a metamorphosis will occur, according to Lydgate, if a writer, by a combination of "subtil witt," "labour," and the "colours" of rhetoric, is able to "make olde thynges for to seeme newe" (1.26–28). Scanlon is unusual in recognizing how radical such claims are, noting that these "give the translator an almost unlimited latitude for innovation." *Narrative, Authority, and Power*, 330.

25. Laurent's original is in Bergen's edition, 1:liii, and Gathercole's edition of Laurent's *Cas des nobles hommes*, 89.

26. For a general discussion of Lydgate's literary ambition, see Flannery, *John Lydgate and the Poetics*: "One of this study's chief contentions is that Lydgate's view of his role as a poet is far more ambitious—and less anxious—than previously thought" (9).

27. For Lydgate's self-aggrandizing modesty toward Chaucer and Gloucester in the prologue to book 1, see Meyer-Lee, *Poets and Power*, 79–81.

28. Mortimer says that in including Petrarch, Lydgate is thinking of his *De remediis utriusque fortunae*. Lydgate's *"Fall of Princes,"* 42–44.

29. The following stanza concludes the catalogue with a mention of unspecified "ful many a fressh dite, / Compleyntis, baladis, roundelis, virelaies" (1.352–53).

30. The transition from Chaucer to Gloucester is deftly made. After referring to several writers of tragedy he has just mentioned, including Chaucer, Lydgate says that in olden times princes valued such writers and took pleasure in their "wise bookis" (1.358–64). For the relationship between Gloucester and Lydgate, see especially Hammond, "Poet and Patron."
31. Lydgate's self-assertion is never blatant and again coexists with statements of his subservience, such as that his translation needs the support of Gloucester's "magnificence"; because the poet lacks "eloquence," he will submit "mi reud language to my lordis grace" (1.435–41).
32. For the medieval popularity of the envoys in the *Fall of Princes*, see Edwards, "Influence of Lydgate's *Fall*," 431–32. Pearsall says that they contain "much of the best writing in the *Fall*." *John Lydgate*, 244.
33. Edwards notes the frequent copying of this envoy. "Influence of Lydgate's *Fall*," 431.
34. Pearsall, *John Lydgate*, 248. Schirmer refers to "its melancholic beauty." *John Lydgate*, 215.
35. Nolan points out that "Lydgate has ambitions that exceed the mandate he receives from Humphrey." "'Now Wo, Now Gladnesse,'" 532.
36. Mortimer, *Lydgate's "Fall of Princes,"* 153; for a full discussion of tragedy in the *Fall*, see Mortimer's chapter 5. For the *Monk's Tale* quotation, see 7.1975–77.
37. The depth of Lydgate's knowledge of the *City of God* is uncertain, but as an educated cleric, he certainly would have known this influential work. I suggest below that the poet borrows from the *City of God* for his portrait of Lucretia. Pearsall notes that Augustine's works were well represented in the library of Lydgate's monastery at Bury (*John Lydgate*, 32). English quotations from the *City of God* are from the translation by Henry Bettenson, hereafter cited parenthetically in the text by book and chapter number. They have been checked against Bombart, Kalb, and Divjak's Latin edition of *De civitate Dei*, which I also occasionally quote.
38. Compare, for example, the parallel mention of Rome's "slauhtre, moordre & false robberie" at 2.4073.
39. The *City of God* makes these same accusations, as at the end of the preface to book 1: "a city which aims at domination, which holds nations in enslavement, but is itself dominated by that very lust of domination." See also, for example, 3.14, 5.19. The crimes of Roman leaders highlighted at the beginning of the envoy appear throughout later books of the *Fall*, including a long narrative about the "vicious tiraunt Nero" (as he is called in a rubric between 7.592 and 593), of whom Lydgate declares in a concluding envoy, "Yif that I myhte, I wolde race his name / Out of this book" (7.782–83). Nero is soon followed by the lives of three other bad emperors (7.810–1103).
40. Other ancient Romans are praised elsewhere in the *Fall*, as they are, more grudgingly, in the *City of God*. Both works extol Marcus Regulus, in particular, for willingly choosing execution by Carthage in order to benefit the city. In an extended narrative of Regulus (5.444–840), which closely follows Laurent until its conclusion (see Bergen's edition, 4:228–29), Lydgate calls him "worthi & trewe" (5.447) and says there "was no bettir kniht" (5.456), which is also the judgment of Augustine (*City of God*, 1.24). Regulus's choice to put the welfare of Rome over his own self-interest (and life) is reminiscent of the civic virtue and dedication to the "common proffit"

(some version of the phrase occurs six times within the story of Regulus: 5.449, 564, 622, 689, 698, 706) so often praised by Gower in the *Confessio Amantis.*

41. Chaucer, *Troilus and Criseyde,* 5.1853.
42. Rome appears less often and more briefly hereafter because, with the establishment of Constantinople in the East, it is no longer a princely capital. The final book of the *Fall* moves on from ancient Rome and deals only briefly with medieval European history, when outsiders like Charlemagne (9.944–45) and Charles of Anjou (9.1898–915) had to come to the aid of the papacy. Brief accounts are also given of some of the worst holders of the chair of Saint Peter, including Pope John XII (9.1060–120) and Gower's and Dante's special object of contempt, Boniface VIII (9.2077–125).
43. Mortimer notes that the story of Constantine is one of the two longest additions to *Fall* (Lydgate's "Fall of Princes," 107). The other is the story of Theodosius later in book 8. Although Lydgate says that Theodosius was a co-ruler of Rome and destroyed many idols there (8.1805–11), most of his narrative takes place outside the city, including his pious repentance before Bishop Ambrose at Milan for his cruelty in battle (8.2029–93). See note 47 below. For a discussion of Lydgate's treatment of Theodosius, which he may have based on that in Augustine's *City of God,* see Mortimer, *Lydgate's "Fall of Princes,"* 103–8.
44. For comparisons of Gower's and Lydgate's accounts of Constantine, see Scanlon, *Narrative, Authority, and Power,* 335–36; and Mortimer, *Lydgate's "Fall of Princes,"* 109–13. Lydgate stresses Constantine's supposed British heritage at the beginning and end of the episode (8.1177–78, 8.1450–56).
45. Mortimer compares Lydgate's Constantine as a successful Christian emperor to Augustine's Constantine in the *City of God,* 5.25. *Lydgate's "Fall of Princes,"* 108.
46. Lydgate's Constantine acts as Gower would have had him do by separating the authority of church and state. Although one of Constantine's decrees in the *Fall* gives the pope "reule and juredicicoun" over all priests, he himself retains jurisdiction over "temporal lordis" (8.1310–16); the comparison draws an explicit distinction between papal and royal power.
47. Two emperors who follow Constantine in the *Fall,* and whose stories are expanded by Lydgate, reinforce his portrait of Constantine by providing negative and positive models of a Christian ruler. Julian, who immediately follows him, is Constantine's antithesis, a hypocritical apostate who reverts to the "goddis infernal" (8.1542) and the persecution of martyrs (8.1557). Augustine also contrasts Constantine and Julian in the *City of God,* 5.21. Later in the *Fall,* Theodosius is described as a penitent emperor, who regains power after meekly acknowledging his sins and praying to be rescued from his enemies (8.1916–53). Lydgate offers Theodosius as an "exaumple" to "vertuous princis" (8.2094) because, while retaining imperial power, he recognizes God as the ultimate source of his rule and obeys ecclesiastical authority in things spiritual.
48. Nolan, *John Lydgate,* 43–52, quoted at 44.
49. Nolan notes that Rome "occupies an anomalous place" in Gower's conception of a progressively fragmented world (ibid., 47). His great Roman hero Julius Caesar appears in the *Confessio* as a healer of division, in contrast to his violent conflicts with Pompey in

the *Serpent of Division* and the *Fall of Princes*.
50. Earlier in this book, Lydgate says that Carthage, like Rome, was destroyed by "dyvisioun," as was, more recently, France (8.2453–57).
51. The perverse ingratitude of the citizens toward Scipio Africanus is underlined by eight appearances in his episode of the words "unkynde" or "unkyndnesse," which are apparently original with Lydgate, including the opening line of his epitaph addressed to Rome: "O peeple unkynde, unkynde ageyn resoun" (5.1696). See Bergen's edition, 4:236.
52. See Hammond, *English Verse*, 176; and Mortimer, *Lydgate's "Fall of Princes,"* 173.
53. For the originality of this stanza, see Bergen's edition, 4:260.
54. In reference to Lydgate's tragic heroes, including Pompey and Caesar, Scanlon says that the poet frequently shows "that the pride which leads to a protagonist's downfall is nearly indistinguishable from the self-assertion that constitutes his heroism." *Narrative, Authority, and Power*, 346.
55. Scanlon says that Caesar's pity for the dead Pompey is an example of the "moral doubleness" that looks forward to the final soliloquies of Macbeth and Richard II (ibid., 348). The envoy that follows the narrative in the *Fall* is flatly censorious, however, condemning both Pompey and Caesar in Augustinian terms for their "veyn ambicioun," heedlessness of "wrong or riht" (the refrain), and "avarice" (6.2521–48).
56. Laurent's text is in Bergen's edition, 4:174–75.
57. The three sentences Laurent gives to Mucius Scaevola make his the longest of the three examples of ordinary heroism in the *Cas des nobles hommes*. See Bergen's edition, 4:174.
58. This information is perhaps taken from Livy, whom Lydgate, unlike Laurent, cites at 2.932 (Bergen's edition, 4:174).
59. See Bergen's edition, 4:175.
60. Pearsall, *John Lydgate*, 244–45; in a later article, "Lydgate as Innovator," Pearsall restates his criticism (11–12).
61. Mortimer, *Lydgate's "Fall of Princes,"* 62.
62. Bergen's edition, 4:174–75. Boccaccio does not mention Lucretia at all here, and Laurent does so only in passing.
63. The Lucretia story was retold many times from classical times to the Middle Ages. See Mortimer, *Lydgate's "Fall of Princes,"* 63–66, and Donaldson, *Rapes of Lucretia*, 5–12.
64. The specific parallels with Chaucer's version are "wifli trouthe," "yonge Tarquyn," "oppresse," and "routhe" (2.974–76); compare Chaucer, *Legend of Good Women*, F 1686, 1698, 1868, 1861.
65. In "'Now Wo, Now Gladnesse,'" Nolan says that throughout his poetic career Lydgate's "favorite *modus operandi* was to place his writing in the middle of a contradictory set of source texts while refusing to choose one or the other as the final authority" (549; see also 536).
66. Not cancelling this refusal to narrate has been judged especially clumsy of Lydgate because he does go on to tell Lucretia's story. See Pearsall, *John Lydgate*, 245; Mortimer, *Lydgate's "Fall of Princes,"* 61–62.
67. The loose syntax between stanzas at 2.1008–9 makes it possible to interpret the passage as meaning either that Gloucester ordered him to translate the story of Lucretia as written by "Collucyus" (Coluccio Salutati) or that Gloucester ordered him to translate the story of Lucretia but that Lydgate chose that version. The ambiguity may be intentional. Most critics, however, attribute the insertion of Salutati to

Gloucester. See, for example, Hammond, "Lydgate and Coluccio Salutati"; Pearsall, *John Lydgate*, 245; Mortimer, *Lydgate's "Fall of Princes,"* 61–62; and Wakelin, *Humanism, Reading, and English Literature*, 34.

68. On Salutati, see especially Witt, *Coluccio Salutati*. References to the *Declamatio* are to the Latin/English texts transcribed and translated by Jed in an appendix to her *Chaste Thinking*, 143–52; I cite the Latin first and then Jed's English translation, both by page number.

69. On this point, see Mortimer, *Lydgate's "Fall of Princes,"* 70–75. Even if one does not accept Mortimer's argument that Lydgate's prime motive is to make the *Declamatio* more acceptable to Gloucester, he convincingly establishes that the poet refashions his source with care.

70. Mortimer says that Lydgate thus abandons Salutati's "emotional neutrality." *Lydgate's "Fall of Princes,"* 70.

71. For the single example of "my Lucretia" (*mea Lucretia*), see Jed, *Chaste Thinking*, 145 (Latin), 149 (English). Collatinus's formality extends to referring to himself in the third person: "do not wish to make your husband a widow." Jed, 145–46 (Latin), 149 (English).

72. "Who does not know that you could not resist him? You were sleeping, unguarded and nude, as one fearing nothing from such a youth, armed for murder, prepared for adultery." Jed, 146 (Latin), 150 (English).

73. This is much stronger than any comparable passage in Salutati. At this point in Salutati's text, Collatinus is arguing that Lucretia is morally superior to the daughters and daughters-in-law of the king, who have been discovered reveling in Rome (Jed, 145 [Latin], 149 [English]), a comparison Lydgate does not use. A rare expression in the *Declamatio* of Collatinus's faith in Lucretia's mental purity, as well as in her noble actions, occurs in the middle of his speech: "But you kept your mind most chaste during the violence of copulation" (*Sed mentem intra concubitus violentiam pudicissimam conservasti*). Jed, 146 (Latin), 150 (English). Compare *Fall of Princes*, 2.1164–67.

74. Jed, *Chaste Thinking*, 147–48 (Latin), 151 (English). Galloway puts it well in "Chaucer's *Legend of Lucrece*," when he says that Lucretia in the *Declamatio* describes "in fine and lurid detail the danger of future lustful and adulterous emotions which might now overtake her" (814).

75. Sylvester says that "Lucretia's conscious decision to submit to the rape in the source texts appears to have suggested to Chaucer and Gower an acquiescence that could be constructed as having led to enjoyment, and so, in their texts, Lucretia faints rather than actively submit to her rapist." "Reading Narratives of Rape," 133.

76. The most accurate reading of these difficult lines seems to me to be that of Saunders, "Classical Paradigms of Rape": "Lucretia argues finally that although the body may be forced into intercourse unwillingly, it may, despite the intent of the mind, experience an instinctive reaction of pleasure" (252).

77. Lydgate is more explicit than Salutati about the sexual feelings that Lucretia may have experienced during the rape itself and gives more attention to them, though Salutati's text may have suggested this new development. Donaldson goes too far, in my view, in claiming that Lucretia in the *Declamatio* "confesses that, despite everything, she could not prevent herself from feeling a furtive enjoyment in the rape" (*Rapes of Lucretia*, 36). This better describes what Lydgate, not Salutati, has written. Mortimer more accurately

says that in the *Fall* the "issue of Lucretia's sexual arousal during the rape is subtly different from Salutati's concern that she might survive to discover [in the future] sexual pleasure in a polluted body." *Lydgate's "Fall of Princes,"* 72.

78. Donaldson notes that many Christian writers before Augustine had praised Lucretia's suicide, as Dante did later (*Rapes of Lucretia*, 25–26). Although Augustine's argument has been attacked as misogynist, sometimes sharply so, this is to ignore his ultimate purpose: not to censure the long-dead Lucretia, but to use her to defend female fellow believers accused of sexual dishonor. On this point, see, Donaldson, *Rapes of Lucretia*, 29–30; and Percival, *Chaucer's Legendary Good Women*, 270.

79. Lydgate might have been prompted to think of Augustine by Chaucer's puzzling claim in the *Legend of Lucrece* that "the grete Austyn hath gret compassioun / Of this Lucresse" (F 1690–91), about which there has been much critical discussion.

80. Augustine says that it may be believed that such an act "perhaps could not have taken place without some physical pleasure" (*quod fieri fortasse sine carnis aliqua voluptate non potuit*). *City of God* 1.16.

81. See O'Daly, *Augustine's "City of God,"* 78. Galloway, "Chaucer's Legend of Lucrece," says that after Augustine, Lucretia became "a central figure for defining the secular ethics and ideology of Rome, especially its zeal for honor and fame" (813–14). Mortimer, *Lydgate's "Fall of Princes,"* observes that Augustine "sees the legend [of Lucretia] as a weak link in the belief of pagan shame-cultures that death is preferable to personal dishonour" (66); he also says that in the *Fall*, 2.1044–48, "the pressure of the pagan shame ethic here aligns the Lydgatian version of the story within the Augustinian tradition of the legend" (70). Christians, of course, were supposed to be freed from the pagan Roman cult of honor as they were from the dictates of the Jewish law.

82. Nolan, "'Now Wo, Now Gladnesse,'" 531. Nolan adds that "these moments of contradiction do not occur very often."

83. For the reduction of the Tarquin material, see Bergen's edition, 4:186–87.

84. Pearsall, *John Lydgate*, 245; in his "Lydgate as Innovator," Pearsall intensifies the image to "like trying to reverse the direction of a driverless steamroller" (12).

85. Pearsall implies that the Lucretia episode in book 3 is identical to that in book 2. "Lydgate as Innovator," 12.

86. For the beginning of Lucretia's complaint in Laurent's *Cas des nobles hommes*, see Bergen's edition of the *Fall of Princes*, 4:187.

BIBLIOGRAPHY

Editions of the *Indulgentiae ecclesiarum urbis Romae*, the *Mirabilia urbis Romae*, and the *Stacions of Rome* are listed under the names of their editors.

MANUSCRIPTS
Indulgentiae ecclesiarum urbis Romae
London, British Library, Cotton Titus
    A.xix, fols. 12v–15v
Metrical Version of Mandeville's Travels
    Coventry, Coventry City Record
    Office, PA 325
Mirabilia urbis Romae (English Hybrid in Latin)
    Cambridge, Cambridge University Library, Gg.4.25, fols. 68r–71v
    London, British Library, Cotton Faustina A.viii, fols. 147r–150v
    London, British Library, Cotton Titus A.xix, fols. 11v–12v
    London, British Library, Harley 562, fols. 1r–5r
    London, British Library, Harley 2321, fols. 115r–118v
Stacions of Rome
    Chicago, Newberry Library, MS-32, roll (Newberry)
    London, British Library, Additional 22283, fols. 123r–124v (Simeon)
    London, British Library, Additional 37787, fol. 18r, fragment
    London, British Library, Cotton Caligula A.ii, fols. 83r–86v (Cotton)
    London, British Library, Cotton Vespasian D.ix, fols. 183r–188r (Cotton Vespasian)
    London, Lambeth Library, MS 306, fols. 152v–165r (Lambeth)
    London, Public Records Office, SC 6/956/5, roll (Bicester)
    Oxford, Bodleian Library, Eng. poet. A.i, fols. 314r–315v (Vernon)
    Oxford, Bodleian Library, Wood empt. 25, fol. iiir, fragment

PRINTED PRIMARY SOURCES
Augustine. *Concerning the City of God Against the Pagans*. Translated by Henry Bettenson. Rev. ed. London: Penguin, 2003.
——. *De civitate Dei*. Edited by Bernhard Dombart, Alfons Kalb, and Johannes Divjak. 5th ed. 2 vols. 1928–29. Reprint, Darmstadt: Wissenschaftliche Buchgesellschaft, 1981.
Baugh, Nita Scudder, ed. *A Worcestershire Miscellany: Compiled by John Norwood, c. 1400*, 106. Philadelphia, 1956. (*The Stacions of Rome*, fragment, 106.)
Bede the Venerable. *Bede's Ecclesiastical History of the English People*. Edited

and translated by Bertram Colgrave and R. A. B. Mynors. 1969. Reprint, Oxford: Clarendon Press, 1972.

Boccaccio, Giovanni. *De casibus virorum illustrium*. Edited by Pier Giorgio Ricci and Vittorio Zaccaria. Vol. 9 of *Tutte le opere di Giovanni Boccaccio*, edited by Vittore Branca. Milan: Mondadori, 1983.

———. *The Fates of Illustrious Men*. Translated by Louis Brewer Hall. New York: Ungar, 1965.

Byron, George Gordon. *Childe Harold's Pilgrimage*. In *The Poetical Works of Lord Byron*, 179–252. 1904. Reprint, London: Oxford University Press, 1960.

Capgrave, John. *Ye Solace of Pilgrimes*. Edited by C. A. Mills. London: Oxford University Press, 1911.

Chaucer, Geoffrey. *The Riverside Chaucer*. Edited by Larry D. Benson. 3rd ed. Boston: Houghton Mifflin, 1987.

Dante Alighieri. *The Divine Comedy: Paradiso*. Edited and translated by Charles S. Singleton. Princeton: Princeton University Press, 1975.

———. *The Divine Comedy: Purgatorio*. Edited and translated by Charles S. Singleton. Princeton: Princeton University Press, 1973.

Douglas, Gavin. *The Poetical Works of Gavin Douglas*. Vol. 2. Edited by John Small. Edinburgh: William Paterson, 1874.

"Einsiedeln Itinerary." In *Itineraria et alia geographica: Notitia ecclesiarum urbis Romae*, 330–43. Corpus Christianorum, Series Latina, 175. Turnhout: Brepols, 1965.

Furnivall, Frederick J., ed. *The Minor Poems of the Vernon MS*. Early English Text Society, Original Series, 117. London: Kegan Paul, 1901. (*The Stacions of Rome*, Vernon Prologue, 609–11.)

———, ed. *Political, Religious, and Love Poems*. Early English Text Society, Original Series, 15. 2nd ed. London: Kegan Paul, 1903. (Cotton and Lambeth *Stacions of Rome*, 143–73.)

———, ed. *The Stacions of Rome*. Early English Text Society, Original Series, 25. London: Trübner, 1867. (Vernon *Stacions*, 1–29; prose *Stacions*, 30–34.)

Gower, John. *Confessio Amantis*. Edited by Russell A. Peck, with Latin translations by Andrew Galloway. 3 vols. Kalamazoo: Medieval Institute Publications, 2000–2004.

———. *The English Works of John Gower*. Edited by G. C. Macaulay. 2 vols. Early English Text Society, Extra Series, 81–82. 1900–1901. Reprint, London: Oxford University Press, 1957.

———. "In Praise of Peace." Edited by Michael Livingston. In *The Minor Latin Works*, edited by R. F. Yeager, 89–133. Kalamazoo: Medieval Institute Publications, 2005.

Gregorius, Master. *Narracio de mirabilibus urbis Rome*. Edited by R. B. C. Huygens. Leiden: Brill, 1970.

Hamer, Richard, and Vida Russell, eds. *Supplementary Lives in Some Manuscripts of the Gilte Legende*. Early English Text Society, Original Series, 315. Oxford: Oxford University Press, 2000. (Prose *Stacions of Rome*, 75–83.)

Higden, Ralph. *Polychronicon*. With English translation by John Trevisa. Vol. 1. Edited by Churchill Babington. Rolls Series. London: Longman, 1865.

———. *Polychronicon*. With English translation by John Trevisa. Vol. 5. Edited by Joseph Rawson Lumby. Rolls Series. London: Longman, 1874.

Hildebert of Lavardin. "De Roma." In *Carmina minora*, edited by A. Brian Scott, 22–24 (poem 36), 25–27 (poem 38). Leipzig: B. G. Teubner, 1969.

Huelsen, Christian, ed. *Le chiese di Roma nel Medio Evo*. Florence: Olschki, 1927. (*Indulgentiae ecclesiarum urbis Romae*, 137–56.)

Isidore of Seville. *The Etymologies*. Translated by Stephen Barney. Cambridge: Cambridge University Press, 2006.

Jacobus de Voragine. *The Golden Legend: Readings on the Saints*. Translated by William Granger Ryan. 2 vols. Princeton: Princeton University Press, 1993.

John of Salisbury. *Policraticus*. Edited and translated by Cary J. Nederman. Cambridge: Cambridge University Press, 1990.

Keiser, George R. "Verse Introductions to Middle English Medical Treatises." *English Studies* 84, no. 4 (2003): 301–17. (*Stacions of Rome*, fragment, 314–15.)

Langland, William. *Piers Plowman: A New Annotated Edition of the C-Text*. Edited by Derek Pearsall. 2nd ed. Exeter: University of Exeter Press, 2008.

———. *Piers Plowman: A Parallel-Text Edition of the A, B, C, and Z Versions*. Edited by A. V. C. Schmidt. 2nd ed. 2 vols. Kalamazoo: Medieval Institute Publications, 2011.

———. *Piers Plowman: The B Version*. Edited by George Kane and E. Talbot Donaldson. Rev. ed. London: Athlone Press, 1988.

———. *The Vision of Piers Plowman*. Edited by A. V. C. Schmidt. 2nd ed. London: Everyman, 1995.

Latini, Brunetto. *The Book of the Treasure (Li livres dou tresor)*. Translated by Paul Barrette and Spurgeon Baldwin. New York: Garland, 1993.

Laurent de Premierfait. *Laurent de Premierfait's "Des cas des nobles hommes et femmes": Book I*. Edited by Patricia May Gathercole. Chapel Hill: University of North Carolina Press, 1968.

Lydgate, John. *Lydgate's "Fall of Princes."* Edited by Henry Bergen. 4 vols. Early English Text Society, Extra Series, 121–24. 1924–27. Reprint, London: Oxford University Press, 1967.

Martinus Polonus. *Chronicon pontificum et imperatorum*. Edited by Ludwig Weiland. In *Monumenta Germaniae Historia*, Scriptorum 22, 377–475. 1872. Reprint, New York: Kraus, 1963.

The Metrical Version of Mandeville's Travels. Edited by M. C. Seymour. Early English Text Society, Original Series, 269. London: Oxford University Press, 1973.

Nichols, Francis Morgan, trans. *The Marvels of Rome*. London: Ellis and Elvey, 1889. 2nd ed., with additions by Eileen Gardiner. New York: Italica Press, 1986. Citations are to the 1986 edition.

Ovid. *Fasti*. Edited and translated by James George Frazier. 2nd ed., rev. by G. P. Goold. Cambridge: Harvard University Press, 1989.

Petrarca, Francesco. "Familiar Letter, VI.2." In *Rerum familiarium: Libri I–VIII*, translated by Aldo S. Bernardo, 290–95. Albany: SUNY Press, 1975.

Salutati, Coluccio. *Declamatio Lucretiae*. Edited and translated by Stephanie H. Jed. In Jed, *Chaste Thinking: The Rape of Lucretia and the Birth of Humanism*, 143–52. Bloomington: Indiana University Press, 1989.

Scattergood, V. J., ed. "An Inedited MS of *The Stacions of Rome*." *English Philological Studies* 11 (1968): 51–54. (Bicester *Stacions*.)

———, ed. "An Unpublished Middle English Poem." *Archiv für das Studium der Neueren Sprachen und Literaturen* 203 (1967): 277–82. (Bicester *Mirabilia urbis Romae*.)

Schimmelpfennig, Bernhard, ed. "Römische Ablassfälschungen aus der Mitte des 14. Jahrhunderts." In *Fälschungen im Mittelalter: Internationaler Kongress der Monumenta Germaniae Historica, München, 16–18 September 1986*, 637–58. Hannover: Hahnsche, 1988. (*Indulgentiae ecclesiarum urbis Romae*.)

Urlichs, Carl Ludwig, ed. "Quarta classis." In *Codex urbis Romae topographicus*, 134–38. Wurzburg: Stahel, 1871. (*Mirabilia urbis Romae*, fourth version.)

———, ed. "Tertia classis." In *Codex urbis Romae topographicus*, 126–33. Wurzburg: Stahel, 1871. (*Mirabilia urbis Romae*, third version.)

Usk, Adam. *The Chronicle of Adam Usk: 1377–1421*. Edited and translated by C. Given-Wilson. Oxford: Clarendon Press, 1997.

Valentini, Roberto, and Giuseppe Zucchetti, eds. *Graphia aureae urbis Romae*. In *Codice topografico della città di Roma*, 4 vols., 3:67–110. Rome: Tipografia del Senato, 1940–53.

———, eds. "Memoriale de mirabilibus et indulgentiis quae in urbe Romana existunt." In *Codice topografico della città di Roma*, 4 vols., 4:75–88. Rome: Tipografia del Senato, 1940–53. (*Indulgentiae ecclesiarum urbis Romae*.)

———, eds. "La più antica redazione dei Mirabilia." In *Codice topografico della città di Roma*, 4 vols., 3:3–65. Rome: Tipografia del Senato, 1940–53. (*Mirabilia urbis Romae*.)

Virgil. *Aeneidos liber sextus*. Edited by R. G. Austin. Oxford: Clarendon Press, 1977.

William of Malmesbury. *Gesta regum Anglorum: The History of the English Kings*. Edited and translated by R. A. B. Mynors, R. M. Thomson, and M. Winterbottom. 2 vols. Oxford: Clarendon Press, 1998–99.

CRITICISM

Accame, Maria, and Emy dell'Oro, eds. *I mirabilia urbis Romae*. Rome: Tored, 2004.

Adams, Robert. "Langland's Theology." In *A Companion to "Piers Plowman,"* edited by John A. Alford, 87–114. Berkeley: University of California Press, 1988.

———. "Piers's Pardon and Langland's Semi-Pelagianism." *Traditio* 39 (1983): 367–418.

Aers, David. *Beyond Reformation? An Essay on William Langland's "Piers Plowman" and the End of Constantinian Christianity*. Notre Dame: University of Notre Dame Press, 2015.

———. "Criseyde: Woman in Medieval Society." *Chaucer Review* 13 (1979): 177–200.

———. *Salvation and Sin: Augustine, Langland, and Fourteenth-Century Theology*. Notre Dame: University of Notre Dame Press, 2009.

Alford, John A. "The Design of the Poem." In *A Companion to "Piers Plowman,"* edited by John A. Alford, 29–65. Berkeley: University of California Press, 1988.

Ames, Ruth M. *God's Plenty: Chaucer's Christian Humanism*. Chicago: Loyola University Press, 1984.

Astell, Ann W. *Chaucer and the Universe of Learning*. Ithaca: Cornell University Press, 1996.

Baker, Denise N. "Chaucer's Experiments with the 'Thrifty Tale': The Narratives of the Man of Law, the Clerk, and the Physician." *Mediaevalia* 14 (1988): 115–26.

Baldovin, John F. *The Urban Character of Christian Worship: The Origins, Development, and Meaning of Stational Liturgy*. Orientalia Christiana Analecta 228. Rome: Pontificium Institutum Studiorum Orientalium, 1987.

Barron, W. R. J. "Prose Chronicles." In *The Arthur of the English: The Arthurian Legend in Medieval English Life and Literature*, edited by W. R. J. Barron, 32–38. Cardiff: University of Wales Press, 1999.

Bartholomew, Barbara. *Fortuna and Natura: A Reading of Three Chaucer Narratives*. The Hague: Mouton, 1966.

Bartlett, Robert. *Why Can the Dead Do Such Great Things? Saints and Worshippers from the Martyrs to the Reformation*. Princeton: Princeton University Press, 2013.

Beichner, Paul E. "Confrontation, Contempt of Court, and Chaucer's Cecilia." *Chaucer Review* 8 (1974): 198–204.

Benson, C. David. *The History of Troy in Middle English Literature*. Cambridge: D. S. Brewer, 1980.

———. "Statues, Bodies, and Souls: St. Cecilia and Some Medieval Attitudes Toward Ancient Rome." In *Medieval Women and Their Objects*, edited by Jenny Adams and Nancy Mason Bradbury, 267–87. Ann Arbor: University of Michigan Press, 2017.

Benson, Robert L. "Political *Renovatio*: Two Models from Roman Antiquity." In *Renaissance and Renewal in the Twelfth Century*, edited by Robert L. Benson and Giles Constable, with Carol D. Lanham, 339–86. Cambridge: Harvard University Press, 1982.

Bernfeld, Suzanne Cassirer. "Freud and Archeology." *American Imago* 8 (1951): 107–28.

Bertolet, Craig. "From Revenge to Reform: The Changing Face of 'Lucrece' and Its Meaning in Gower's *Confessio Amantis*." *Philological Quarterly* 70 (1991): 403–21.

Birch, Debra J. *Pilgrimage to Rome in the Middle Ages*. 1998. Reprint, Woodbridge: Boydell Press, 2000.

Bloch, Herbert. "The New Fascination with Ancient Rome." In *Renaissance and Renewal in the Twelfth Century*, edited by Robert L. Benson and Giles Constable, with Carol D. Lanham, 615–36. Cambridge: Harvard University Press, 1982.

Block, Edward A. "Originality, Controlling Purpose, and Craftsmanship in Chaucer's *Man of Law's Tale*." *PMLA* 68 (1953): 572–616.

Boffey, Julia, and A. S. G. Edwards. "The *Legend of Good Women*." In *The Cambridge Companion to Chaucer*, 2nd ed., edited by Piero Boitani and Jill Mann, 112–26. Cambridge: Cambridge University Press, 2003.

———, eds. *A New Index of Middle English Verse*. London: British Library, 2005.

Bowersock, G. W., Peter Brown, and Oleg Grabar, eds. *Late Antiquity: A Guide to the Postclassical World*. Cambridge: Harvard University Press, 1999.

Brentano, Robert. *Rome Before Avignon: A Social History of Thirteenth-Century Rome*. New York: Basic Books, 1974.

Brown, Peter. *The Cult of the Saints: Its Rise and Function in Latin Christianity*. Chicago: University of Chicago Press, 1981.

———. *The Making of Late Antiquity*. Cambridge: Harvard University Press, 1978.

Bullón-Fernández, María. *Fathers and Daughters in Gower's "Confessio Amantis."* Cambridge: D. S. Brewer, 2000.

Burrow, J. A. "Thinking in Poetry: Three Medieval Examples." *New Compass: A Critical Review* 4 (2004). Accessed 14 July 2018. http://people.auc.ca/disanto/dec2004/burrow.html.

Calabrese, Michael A. *Chaucer's Ovidian Arts of Love*. Gainesville: University Press of Florida, 1994.

Caldwell, Dorigen. "Introduction: Continuities of Place." In *Rome: Continuing Encounters Between Past and Present*, edited by Dorigen Caldwell and Lesley Caldwell, 1–16. Farnham: Ashgate, 2011.

Camille, Michael. *The Gothic Idol: Ideology and Image-Making in Medieval Art*. Cambridge: Cambridge University Press, 1989.

Campanelli, Maurizio. "Monuments and Histories: Ideas and Images of

Antiquity in Some Descriptions of Rome." In *Rome Across Time and Space: Cultural Transmission and the Exchange of Ideas, c. 500–1400*, edited by Claudia Bolgia, Rosamond McKitterick, and John Osborne, 35–51. Cambridge: Cambridge University Press, 2011.

Chambers, R. W. "Long Will, Dante, and the Righteous Heathen." *Essays and Studies* 9 (1924): 50–69.

Christie, Neil. *From Constantine to Charlemagne: An Archaeology of Italy, AD 300–800*. Aldershot: Ashgate, 2006.

Coghill, Nevill. "The Pardon of Piers Plowman." *Proceedings of the British Academy* 30 (1946, for 1944): 303–57. Reprinted in *The Collected Papers of Nevill Coghill*, edited by Douglas Gray, 137–98. Brighton: Harvester Press, 1988.

Coleman, Janet. *"Piers Plowman" and the Moderni*. Rome: Edizioni di Storia e Letteratura, 1981.

Comerford, Michael. *The Book of Holy Indulgences*. Dublin: James Duffy and Sons, 1876.

Comparetti, Domenico. *Vergil in the Middle Ages*. Translated by E. F. M. Benecke. 2nd ed. 1908. Reprint, London: Allen and Unwin, 1966.

Cooper, Helen. *The Canterbury Tales*. Oxford Guides to Chaucer. 2nd ed. Oxford: Oxford University Press, 1996.

———. "'Peised Evene in the Balance': A Thematic and Rhetorical Topos in the *Confessio Amantis*." *Mediaevalia* 16 (1993): 113–39.

Damon, John. "*Seinte Cecile* and *Cristes Owene Knyghtes*: Violence, Resignation, and Resistance in the *Second Nun's Tale*." In *Crossing Boundaries: Issues of Cultural and Individual Identity in the Middle Ages and the Renaissance*, edited by Sally McKee, 41–56. Turnhout: Brepols, 1999.

Delany, Shelia. "Politics and the Paralysis of the Poetic Imagination in the *Physician's Tale*." *Studies in the Age of Chaucer* 3 (1981): 47–60.

Donaldson, Ian. *The Rapes of Lucretia: A Myth and Its Transformations*. Oxford: Clarendon Press, 1982.

Doyle, A. I. "The Shaping of the Vernon and Simeon Manuscript." In *Studies in The Vernon Manuscript*, edited by Derek Pearsall, 1–13. Cambridge: Brewer, 1990.

Doyle, A. I., and George B. Pace. "A New Chaucer Manuscript." *PMLA* 83 (1968): 22–34.

Duchesne, Louis. "L'auteur des *Mirabilia*." *Mélanges d'Archéologie et d'Histoire de l'École Française de Rome* 24 (1904): 479–89.

Duffy, Eamon. "Dynamics of Pilgrimage in Late Medieval England." In *Pilgrimage: The English Experience from Becket to Bunyan*, edited by Colin Morris and Peter Roberts, 164–77. Cambridge: Cambridge University Press, 2002.

Dunning, T. P. "Langland and the Salvation of the Heathen." *Medium Aevum* 12 (1943): 45–54.

Dyer, Joseph. "Roman Processions of the Major Litany (*Litaniae maiores*) from the Sixth to the Twelfth Century." In *Roma Felix—Formation and Reflections of Medieval Rome*, edited by Éamonn Ó Carragáin and Carol Neuman de Vegvar, 112–37. Aldershot: Ashgate, 2007.

Ebin, Lois A. *John Lydgate*. Boston: Twayne, 1985.

Eckhardt, Caroline D. "The Presence of Rome in the Middle English Chronicles of the Fourteenth Century." *Journal of English and Germanic Philology* 90 (1991): 187–207.

Edwards, A. S. G. "The Influence of Lydgate's *Fall of Princes*, c. 1440–1559: A Survey." *Medieval Studies* 39 (1977): 424–39.

Edwards, Catharine. "Introduction: Shadows and Fragments." In *Roman Presences:*

Receptions of Rome in European Culture, 1789–1945, edited by Catharine Edwards, 1–18. Cambridge: Cambridge University Press, 1999.

———. *Writing Rome: Textual Approaches to the City*. Cambridge: Cambridge University Press, 1996.

Edwards, Robert R. *Chaucer and Boccaccio: Antiquity and Modernity*. New York: Palgrave, 2002.

Embree, Dan, ed. *The Chronicles of Rome: An Edition of the Middle English "Chronicle of Popes and Emperors" and "The Lollard Chronicle."* Woodbridge: Boydell, 1999.

Epstein, Robert. "London, Southwark, Westminster: Gower's Urban Contexts." In *A Companion to Gower*, edited by Siân Echard, 43–60. Cambridge: Brewer, 2004.

Evans, Joan. *Magic Jewels of the Middle Ages and the Renaissance*. Oxford: Oxford University Press, 1922.

Fahrenbach, William. "The Texts and Uses of *The Stacions of Rome*." Paper presented at the Illinois Medieval Association Conference, February 15–16, 2013, Newberry Library, Chicago.

Famiglietti, Richard C. "Laurent de Premierfait: The Career of a Humanist in Early Fifteenth-Century Paris." In *Un traducteur et un humaniste de l'époque de Charles VI: Laurent de Premierfait*, edited by Carla Bozzolo, 31–51. Paris: Sorbonne, 2004.

Farber, Lianna. "The Creation of Consent in the *Physician's Tale*." *Chaucer Review* 39 (2004): 151–64.

Farnham, Willard. *The Medieval Heritage of Elizabethan Tragedy*. Berkeley: University of California Press, 1936.

Favro, Diane. "The IconiCity of Ancient Rome." *Urban History* 33 (2006): 20–38.

Ferster, Judith. *Fictions of Advice: The Literature and Politics of Counsel in Late Medieval England*. Philadelphia: University of Pennsylvania Press, 1996.

Fichte, Joerg O. "Rome and Its Anti-Pole in the *Man of Law's* and the *Second Nun's Tale*: Cristendom and Hethenesse." *Anglia* 122 (2004): 225–49.

Flannery, Mary C. *John Lydgate and the Poetics of Fame*. Cambridge: Brewer, 2012.

Fletcher, Angus. "The Sentencing of Virginia in the *Physician's Tale*." *Chaucer Review* 34 (2000): 300–308.

Frank, Robert Worth, Jr. *Chaucer and "The Legend of Good Women."* Cambridge: Harvard University Press, 1972.

Freud, Sigmund. *Civilization and Its Discontents*. Translated by James Strachey. New York: W. W. Norton, 1962.

Fyler, John M. *Chaucer and Ovid*. New Haven: Yale University Press, 1979.

———. "Explanatory Notes to *The House of Fame*." In *The Riverside Chaucer*, edited by Larry D. Benson, 3rd ed., 977–90. Boston: Houghton Mifflin, 1987.

Galloway, Andrew. "Chaucer's *Legend of Lucrece* and the Critique of Ideology in Fourteenth-Century England." *ELH* 60 (1993): 813–32.

———. "Gower's Quarrel with Chaucer, and the Origins of Bourgeois Didacticism in Fourteenth-Century London Poetry." In *Calliope's Classroom: Studies in Didactic Poetry from Antiquity to the Renaissance*, edited by Annette Harder, Alasdair A. MacDonald, and Gerrit J. Reinink, 245–67. Dudley, Mass.: Peeters, 2007.

———. "John Lydgate and the Origins of Vernacular Humanism." *Journal of English and Germanic Philology* 107 (2008): 445–71.

———. "The Literature of 1388 and the Politics of Pity in Gower's *Confessio Amantis*." In *The Letter of the Law: Legal Practice and Literary Production in Medieval England, edited by Emily Steiner and Candace Barrington, 67–104. Ithaca: Cornell University Press, 2002.

———. "Making History Legal: *Piers Plowman* and the Rebels of Fourteenth-Century England." In *William Langland's "Piers Plowman": A Book of Essays*, edited by Kathleen M. Hewett-Smith, 7–39. New York: Routledge, 2001.

Gathercole, Patricia May. "Boccaccio in French." *Studi sul Boccaccio* 5 (1969): 275–97.

———. "Fifteenth-Century Translation: The Development of Laurent de Premierfait." *Modern Language Quarterly* 21 (1960): 365–70.

———. "The Manuscripts of Laurent de Premierfait's Works." *Modern Language Quarterly* 19 (1958): 262–70.

———. "Two Old French Translations of Boccaccio's *De casibus virorum illustrium*." *Modern Language Quarterly* 17 (1956): 304–9.

Geary, Patrick. "Sacred Commodities: The Circulation of Medieval Relics." In *The Social Life of Things: Commodities in Cultural Perspective*, edited by Arjun Appadurai, 169–91. Cambridge: Cambridge University Press, 1986.

Goodson, Caroline. "The Relic Translations of Pascal I: Transforming City and Cult." In *Roman Bodies*, edited by Andrew Hopkins and Maria Wyke, 123–41. London: British School at Rome, 2005.

Grady, Frank. "The Lancastrian Gower and the Limits of Exemplarity." *Speculum* 70 (1995): 552–75.

———. "The Trouble with Trajan." In *Representing Righteous Heathens in Late Medieval England*, 17–44, 138–46. New York: Palgrave, 2005.

Graf, Arturo. *Roma nella memoria e nelle immaginazioni del Medio Evo*. 2 vols. 1923. Reprint, Turin: Arnaldo Forni, 1987.

Gray, Douglas. "Chaucer and 'Pite.'" In *J. R. R. Tolkien, Scholar and Storyteller: Essays in Memoriam*, edited by Mary Salu and Robert T. Farrell, 173–203. Ithaca: Cornell University Press, 1979.

———. *The Oxford Companion to Chaucer*. Oxford: Oxford University Press, 2003.

Green, Richard Firth. *A Crisis of Truth: Literature and Law in Ricardian England*. Philadelphia: University of Pennsylvania Press, 1999.

Greenhalgh, Michael. *The Survival of Roman Antiquities in the Middle Ages*. London: Duckworth, 1989.

Gregorovius, Ferdinand. *History of the City of Rome in the Middle Ages*. Translated by Mrs. Gustavus W. (Annie) Hamilton. 4th ed. 8 vols. 1905–12. Reprint, New York: AMS Press, 1967.

Hammond, Eleanor Prescott, ed. *English Verse Between Chaucer and Surrey*. Durham: Duke University Press, 1927.

———. "Lydgate and Coluccio Salutati." *Modern Philology* 25 (1927): 49–57.

———. "Poet and Patron in the *Fall of Princes*: Lydgate and Humphrey of Gloucester." *Anglia* 38 (1914): 121–36.

Hansen, Elaine Tuttle. *Chaucer and the Fictions of Gender*. Berkeley: University of California Press, 1992.

Harvey, Margaret. *The English in Rome, 1362–1420: Portrait of an Expatriate Community*. Cambridge: Cambridge University Press, 1999.

Harwood, Britton J. "'Clergye' and the Action of the Third Vision in *Piers Plowman*." *Modern Philology* 70 (1973): 279–90.

Hedeman, Anne D. *Translating the Past: Laurent de Premierfait and Boccaccio's "De casibus."* Los Angeles: Getty Museum, 2008.

Higgins, Iain Macleod. *Writing East: The "Travels" of Sir John Mandeville*. Philadelphia: University of Pennsylvania Press, 1997.

Hirsh, John C. "Chaucer's Roman Tales." *Chaucer Review* 31 (1996): 45–57.

———. "Did Chaucer Visit Rome?" *English Language Notes* 37 (2000): 1–8.

———. "Modern Times: The Discourse of the *Physician's Tale*." *Chaucer Review* 27 (1993): 387–95.

Horobin, Simon. "The Scribes of the Vernon Manuscript." In *The Making of the Vernon Manuscript*, edited by Wendy Scase, 27–47. Turnhout: Brepols, 2013.

Howe, Nicholas. "Rome: Capital of Anglo-Saxon England." *Journal of Medieval and Early Modern Studies* 34 (2004): 147–72.

Hulbert, J. R. "Some Medieval Advertisements of Rome." *Modern Philology* 20 (1923): 403–24.

Hyde, J. K. "Medieval Descriptions of Cities." *Bulletin of the John Rylands Library* 48 (1965–66): 308–40.

Ikas, Wolfgang-Valentin. "Martinus Polonus' *Chronicle of the Popes and Emperors*: A Medieval Best-Seller and Its Neglected Influence on Medieval English Chroniclers." *English Historical Review* 116 (2001): 327–41.

Jacks, Philip. *The Antiquarian and the Myth of Antiquity: The Origins of Rome in Renaissance Thought*. Cambridge: Cambridge University Press, 1993.

James, M. R., and Claude Jenkins. *A Descriptive Catalogue of the Manuscripts in the Library of Lambeth Palace*. Part 3. Cambridge: Cambridge University Press, 1932.

Jed, Stephanie H. *Chaste Thinking: The Rape of Lucretia and the Birth of Humanism*. Bloomington: Indiana University Press, 1989.

Jordan, Robert M. "Heteroglossia and Chaucer's *Man of Law's Tale*." In *Bakhtin and Medieval Voices*, edited by Thomas J. Farrell, 81–93, 203–4. Gainesville: University Press of Florida, 1995.

Kean, P. M. *Chaucer and the Making of English Poetry: The Art of Narrative*. London: Routledge, 1972.

Keiser, George R. "The Spiritual Heroism of Chaucer's Custance." In *Chaucer's Religious Tales*, edited by C. David Benson and Elizabeth Robertson, 121–36. Cambridge: Brewer, 1990.

Kelly, Henry Ansgar. "The Evolution of *The Monk's Tale*: Tragical to Farcical." *Studies in the Age of Chaucer* 22 (2000): 407–14.

Kennedy, Duncan F. "A Sense of Place: Rome, History, and Empire Revisited." In *Roman Presences: Receptions of Rome in European Culture, 1789–1945*, edited by Catharine Edwards, 19–34. Cambridge: Cambridge University Press, 1999.

Kessler, Herbert L., and Johanna Zacharias. *Rome 1300: On the Path of the Pilgrim*. New Haven: Yale University Press, 2000.

Kinney, Dale. "Fact and Fiction in the *Mirabilia urbis Romae*." In *Roma Felix—Formation and Reflections of Medieval Rome*, edited by Éamonn Ó Carragáin and Carol Neuman de Vegvar, 235–52. Aldershot: Ashgate, 2007.

———. "*Mirabilia urbis Romae*." In *The Classics in the Middle Ages*, edited by Aldo S. Barnardo and Saul Levin, 207–21. Medieval and Renaissance Texts and Studies. Binghamton, N.Y.: Center for Medieval and Early Renaissance Studies, 1990.

Kolve, V. A. "Chaucer's *Second Nun's Tale* and the Iconography of Saint Cecilia." In *New Perspectives in Chaucer Criticism*, edited by Donald M. Rose, 137–74. Norman: Pilgrim Books, 1981.

Krautheimer, Richard. *Rome: Profile of a City, 312–1308*. 1980. Reprint, Princeton: Princeton University Press, 1983.

———. *St. Peter's and Medieval Rome*. Rome: Unione Internazionale Degli Istituti di Archeologia, Storia e Storia dell'Arte in Roma, 1985.

Krochalis, Jeanne. "The Newberry Stations of Rome." In *Tributes to Kathleen L. Scott: Medieval Manuscripts; Readers, Makers, and Illuminators*, edited by Marlene Villalobos Hennessy, 129–37. London: Harvey Miller, 2009.

Lambert, Mark. "*Troilus*, Books I–III: A Criseydan Reading." In *Essays on "Troilus and Criseyde*,*"* edited by Mary Salu, 105–25, 139–40. Cambridge: Brewer, 1979.

Lanciani, Rodolfo. *Pagan and Christian Rome*. Boston: Houghton Mifflin, 1892.

Lavezzo, Kathy. *Angels on the Edge of the World: Geography, Literature, and English Community, 1000–1534*. Ithaca: Cornell University Press, 2006.

Le Goff, Jacques. *The Birth of Purgatory*. Translated by Arthur Goldhammer. Chicago: University of Chicago Press, 1984.

Lerer, Seth. *Chaucer and His Readers: Imagining the Author in Late-Medieval England*. Princeton: Princeton University Press, 1993.

Lynch, Kathryn L. *Chaucer's Philosophical Visions*. Cambridge: Brewer, 2000.

Maddalo, Silvia. *In figura Romae: Immagini di Roma nel libro mediovale*. Rome: Viella, 1990.

Mann, Jill. *Feminizing Chaucer*. Cambridge: Brewer, 2002.

———. "'He Knew Nat Catoun': Medieval School-Texts and Middle English Literature." In *The Text in the Community: Essays on Medieval Works, Manuscripts, Authors, and Readers*, edited by Jill Mann and Maura Nolan, 41–74. Notre Dame: University of Notre Dame Press, 2006.

Martin, Priscilla. *Chaucer's Women: Nuns, Wives, and Amazons*. London: Macmillan, 1990.

Matsuda, Takami. *Death and Purgatory in Middle English Didactic Poetry*. Cambridge: Brewer, 1997.

McCall, John P. *Chaucer Among the Gods: The Poetics of Classical Myth*. University Park: Pennsylvania State University Press, 1979.

Meyer-Lee, Robert J. "Lydgate's Laureate Pose." In *John Lydgate: Poetry, Culture, and Lancastrian England*, edited by Larry Scanlon and James Simpson, 36–60. Notre Dame: University of Notre Dame Press, 2006.

———. *Poets and Power from Chaucer to Wyatt*. Cambridge: Cambridge University Press, 2007.

Middleton, Anne. "The Idea of Public Poetry in the Reign of Richard II." *Speculum* 53 (1978): 94–114.

———. "The *Physician's Tale* and Love's Martyrs: 'Ensamples Mo Than Ten' as a Method in the *Canterbury Tales*." *Chaucer Review* 8 (1973): 9–32.

Miedema, Nine Robijntje. "Medieval Images of the Eternal City: Rome Seen Through the *Mirabilia Romae*." In *The Power of Imagery: Essays on Rome, Italy, and Imagination*, edited by Peter van Kessel, 203–21. Rome: Apeiron, 1992.

———. *Die "Mirabilia Romae."* Tübingen: Niemeyer, 1996.

———. "*Mirabilia urbis Romae*." In *Medieval Italy: An Encyclopedia*, edited by Christopher Kleinhenz, 722–23. New York: Routledge, 2004.

———. *Die römanischen Kirchen im Spätmittelalter nach den "Indulgentiae ecclesiarum urbis Romae."* Tübingen: Niemeyer, 2001.

Minnis, A. J. "John Gower, *Sapiens* in Ethics and Politics." *Medium Aevum* 49 (1980): 207–29.

———. "Looking for a Sign: The Quest for Nominalism in Chaucer and Langland." In *Essays on Ricardian Literature in Honour of J. A. Burrow*, edited by A. J. Minnis, Charlotte C. Morse, and Thorlac Turville-Petre, 142–78. Oxford: Clarendon Press, 1997.

———. "'Moral Gower' and Medieval Literary Theory." In *Gower's "Confessio Amantis": Responses and Reassessments*, edited by A. J. Minnis, 50–78. Cambridge: Brewer, 1983.

———. *The Shorter Poems*. Oxford Guides to Chaucer. Oxford: Clarendon Press, 1995.

Mortimer, Nigel. *John Lydgate's "Fall of Princes": Narrative Tragedy in Its Literary and Political Contexts*. Oxford: Clarendon Press, 2005.

Moseley, C. W. R. D. "The Metamorphoses of Sir John Mandeville." *Yearbook of English Studies* 4 (1974): 5–25.

Nardella, Cristina. *Il fascino di Roma nel Medioevo: Le "Meraviglie di Roma" di Maestro Gregorio*. Rev. ed. Rome: Viella, 1997.

Nicholson, Peter. *Love and Ethics in Gower's "Confessio Amantis."* Ann Arbor: University of Michigan Press, 2005.

Nolan, Maura. *John Lydgate and the Making of Public Culture*. Cambridge: Cambridge University Press, 2005.

———. "'Now Wo, Now Gladnesse': Ovidianism in the *Fall of Princes*." *ELH* 71 (2004): 531–58.

Norton-Smith, John, ed. *John Lydgate: Poems*. Oxford: Clarendon Press, 1966.

O'Daly, Gerard. *Augustine's "City of God": A Reader's Guide*. Oxford: Oxford University Press, 1999.

Olsson, Kurt. *John Gower and the Structures of Conversion: A Reading of the "Confessio Amantis."* Cambridge: Brewer, 1992.

———. "Natural Law and John Gower's *Confessio Amantis*." *Medievalia et Humanistica*, new ser., 11 (1982): 229–61.

Ortenberg, Veronica. "Archbishop Sigeric's Journey to Rome in 990." *Anglo-Saxon England* 19 (1990): 197–246.

Osborne, John, trans. and ed. *Master Gregorius: The Marvels of Rome*. Toronto: Pontifical Institute of Medieval Studies, 1987.

Palazzo, Robert P. "The Veneration of the Sacred Foreskin(s) of Baby Jesus—A Documented Analysis." In *Multicultural Europe and Cultural Exchange in the Middle Ages and Renaissance*, edited by James P. Helfers, 155–76. Arizona Studies in the Middle Ages and the Renaissance 12. Turnhout: Brepols, 2005.

Parks, George B. *The English Traveler to Italy*. Stanford: Stanford University Press, 1954.

Patterson, Annabel. "Introduction." In *Roman Images: Selected Papers from the English Institute, 1982*, edited by Annabel Patterson, vii–ix. Baltimore: Johns Hopkins University Press, 1984.

Patterson, Lee. *Chaucer and the Subject of History*. Madison: University of Wisconsin Press, 1991.

Paull, Michael R. "The Influence of the Saint's Legend Genre in the *Man of Law's Tale*." *Chaucer Review* 5 (1971): 179–94.

Pearsall, Derek. "Chaucer's Narrative Art." *PMLA* 81 (1966): 475–84.

———. "The Gower Tradition." In *Gower's "Confessio Amantis": Responses and Reassessments*, edited by A. J. Minnis, 179–97. Cambridge: Brewer, 1983.

———. *John Lydgate*. Charlottesville: University Press of Virginia, 1970.

———. *John Lydgate (1371–1449): A Bio-Bibliography*. Victoria: English Literary Studies, University of Victoria, 1997.

———. "Lydgate as Innovator." *Modern Language Quarterly* 53 (1992): 5–22.

Peck, Russell A. *Kingship and Common Profit in Gower's "Confessio Amantis."* Carbondale: Southern Illinois University Press, 1978.

Percival, Florence. *Chaucer's Legendary Good Women*. Cambridge: Cambridge University Press, 1998.

Petrina, Alessandra. *Cultural Politics in Fifteenth-Century England: The Case of Humphrey, Duke of Gloucester*. Leiden: Brill, 2004.

Porter, Elizabeth. "Gower's Ethical Microcosm and Political Macrocosm." In *Gower's "Confessio Amantis": Responses and Reassessments*, edited by A. J. Minnis, 135–62. Cambridge: Brewer, 1983.

Powell, Susan. "Preaching at Syon Abbey." *Leeds Studies in English*, new ser., 31 (2000): 229–67.

Richardson, Lawrence, Jr. *A New Topographical Dictionary of Ancient Rome*. Baltimore: Johns Hopkins University Press, 1992.

Robinson, P. R. "The Vernon Manuscript as a 'Coucher Book.'" In *Studies in the Vernon Manuscript*, edited by Derek Pearsall, 15–28. Cambridge: Brewer, 1990.

Rudd, Gillian. *Managing Language in "Piers Plowman."* Cambridge: Brewer 1994.

Rudy, Kathryn M. *Virtual Pilgrimages in the Convent: Imagining Jerusalem in the Late Middle Ages*. Turnhout: Brepols, 2011.

Runacres, Charles. "Art and Ethics in the 'Exempla' of 'Confessio Amantis.'" In *Gower's "Confessio Amantis": Responses and Reassessments*, edited by A. J. Minnis, 106–34. Cambridge: Brewer, 1983.

Sajavaara, Kari. "The Relationship of the Vernon and Simeon Manuscripts." *Neuphilologische Mitteilungen* 68 (1967): 428–39.

Salter, Elizabeth. *Fourteenth-Century English Poetry: Contexts and Readings*. Oxford: Clarendon Press, 1983.

Saunders, Corinne J. "Classical Paradigms of Rape in the Middle Ages: Chaucer's Lucretia and Philomela." In *Rape in Antiquity*, edited by Susan Deacy and Karen F. Pierce, 243–66. London: Duckworth, 1997.

Scanlon, Larry. *Narrative, Authority, and Power: The Medieval Exemplum and the Chaucerian Tradition*. New York: Cambridge University Press, 1994.

Schildgen, Brenda Dean. *Pagans, Tartars, Moslems, and Jews in Chaucer's "Canterbury Tales."* Gainesville: University Press of Florida, 2001.

Schirmer, Walter F. *John Lydgate: A Study in the Culture of the XVth Century*. Translated by Ann E. Keep. Berkeley: University of California Press, 1961.

Schlauch, Margaret. "Historical Precursors of Chaucer's Constance." *Philological Quarterly* 29 (1950): 402–12.

Schmitz, Götz. *The Fall of Women in Early English Narrative Verse*. Cambridge: Cambridge University Press, 1990.

Shaffern, Robert W. "Learned Discussions of Indulgences for the Dead in the Middle Ages." *Church History* 61 (1992): 367–81.

———. "The Medieval Theology of Indulgences." In *Promissory Notes on the Treasury of Merits: Indulgences in Late Medieval Europe*, edited by R. N. Swanson, 11–36. Leiden: Brill, 2006.

———. *The Penitents' Treasury: Indulgences in Latin Christendom, 1175–375*. Scranton: University of Scranton Press, 2007.

Simpson, James. "Chaucer as a European Writer." In *The Yale Companion to Chaucer*, edited by Seth Lerer, 55–86. New Haven: Yale University Press, 2006.

———. *"Piers Plowman": An Introduction*. 2nd ed. Exeter: University of Exeter Press, 2007.

———. *Reform and Cultural Revolution, 1350–1547*. Oxford English Literary History. Oxford: Oxford University Press, 2002.

———. *Sciences and the Self in Medieval Poetry: Alan of Lille's Anticlaudianus and John Gower's "Confessio Amantis."* Cambridge: Cambridge University Press, 1995.

Smyser, H. M. "The Domestic Background of *Troilus and Criseyde*." *Speculum* 31 (1956): 297–315.

Snoek, G. J. C. *Medieval Piety from Relics to the Eucharist: A Process of Mutual Interaction*. Leiden: Brill, 1995.

Spearing, A. C. *Medieval Autographies: The "I" of the Text*. Notre Dame: University of Notre Dame Press, 2012.

———. "Narrative Voice: The Case of Chaucer's *Man of Law's Tale*." *New Literary History* 32 (2001): 715–46.

———. *Textual Subjectivity: The Encoding of Subjectivity in Medieval Narratives and Lyrics*. Oxford: Oxford University Press, 2005.

Stanbury, Sarah. "The *Man of Law's Tale* and Rome." *Exemplaria* 22 (2010): 119–37.

Steiner, Emily. *Reading "Piers Plowman."* Cambridge: Cambridge University Press, 2013.

Strohm, Paul. "Lydgate and the Rise of *Pollecie* in the *Mirror* Tradition." In *Politique: Languages of Statecraft Between Chaucer and Shakespeare*, 87–132, 256–67. Notre Dame: University of Notre Dame Press, 2005.

———. *Social Chaucer*. Cambridge: Harvard University Press, 1989.

Summit, Jennifer. "Topography as Historiography: Petrarch, Chaucer, and the Making of Medieval Rome." *Journal of Medieval and Early Modern Studies* 30 (2000): 211–46.

Sumption, Jonathan. *Pilgrimage: An Image of Mediaeval Religion*. Totowa, N.J.: Rowman and Littlefield, 1975.

Swanson, R. N. *Indulgences in Late Medieval England: Passports to Paradise?* Cambridge: Cambridge University Press, 2007.

———, ed. *Promissory Notes on the Treasury of Merits: Indulgences in Late Medieval Europe*. Leiden: Brill, 2006.

Sylvester, Louise. "Reading Narratives of Rape: The Story of Lucretia in Chaucer, Gower, and Christine de Pizan." *Leeds Studies in English*, new ser., 31 (2000): 115–44.

Tatlock, J. S. P. *The Legendary History of Britain: Geoffrey of Monmouth's "Historia Regum Britanniae" and Its Early Vernacular Versions*. Berkeley: University of California Press, 1950.

Thacker, Alan. "Rome of the Martyrs: Saints, Cults, and Relics, Fourth to Seventh Centuries." In *Roma Felix—Formation and Reflections of Medieval Rome*, edited by Éamonn Ó Carragáin and Carol Neuman de Vegvar, 13–49. Aldershot: Ashgate, 2007.

———. "Rome: The Pilgrims' City in the Seventh Century." In *England and Rome in the Early Middle Ages: Pilgrimage, Art, and Politics*, edited by Francesca Tinti, 89–139. Turnhout: Brepols, 2014.

Thompson, John J. "Looking Behind the Book: MS Cotton Caligula A.ii, Part 1, and the Experience of Its Texts." In *Romance Reading on the Book: Essays on Medieval Narrative Presented to Maldwyn Mills*, edited by Jennifer Fellows, Rosalind Field, Gillian Rogers, and Judith Weiss, 171–87. Cardiff: University of Wales Press, 1996.

Tinti, Francesca. "Introduction: Anglo-Saxon England and Rome." In *England and Rome in the Early Middle Ages: Pilgrimage, Art, and Politics*, edited by Francesca Tinti, 1–15. Turnhout: Brepols, 2014.

Twyman, Susan. *Papal Ceremonial at Rome in the Twelfth Century*. Henry Bradshaw Society, Subsidia 4. London: Boydell, 2002.

Valenzani, Riccardo Santangeli. "Hosting Foreigners in Early Medieval Rome: From *Xenodochia* to *Scholae Peregrinorum*." In *England and Rome in the Early Middle Ages: Pilgrimage, Art, and Politics*, edited by Francesca Tinti, 69–88. Turnhout: Brepols, 2014.

Wakelin, Daniel. *Humanism, Reading, and English Literature, 1430–1530*. Oxford: Oxford University Press, 2007.

Wallace, David. *Chaucerian Polity: Absolutist Lineages and Associational Forms in England and Italy*. Stanford: Stanford University Press, 1997.

Watkin, David. *The Roman Forum*. Cambridge: Harvard University Press, 2009.

Watson, Nicholas. "Visions of Inclusion: Universal Salvation and Vernacular Theology in Pre-Reformation England." *Journal of Medieval and Early Modern Studies* 27 (1997): 145–87.

Webb, Diana. *Medieval European Pilgrimage, c. 700–c. 1500*. New York: Palgrave, 2002.

———. "Pardons and Pilgrims." In *Promissory Notes on the Treasury of Merits: Indulgences in Late Medieval Europe*, edited by R. N. Swanson, 241–75. Leiden: Brill, 2006.

Wenzel, Siegfried. "Langland's *Troianus*." *Yearbook of Langland Studies* 10 (1996): 181–85.

Wetherbee, Winthrop. "Rome, Troy, and Culture in the *Confessio Amantis*." In *On John Gower: Essays at the Millennium*, edited by R. F. Yeager, 20–42. Kalamazoo: Medieval Institute Publications, 2007.

Whatley, Gordon. "The Uses of Hagiography: The Legend of Pope Gregory and the Emperor Trajan in the Middle Ages." *Viator* 15 (1984): 25–63.

Wickham, Chris. *Medieval Rome: Stability and Crisis of a City, 900–1150*. Oxford: Oxford University Press, 2015.

Winstead, Karen A. *Virgin Martyrs: Legends of Sainthood in Late Medieval England*. Ithaca: Cornell University Press, 1997.

Witt, Ronald G. *Coluccio Salutati and His Public Letters*. Geneva: Librairie Droz, 1976.

Wittig, Joseph S. "'Piers Plowman' B, Passus IX–XII: Elements in the Design of the Inward Journey." *Traditio* 28 (1972): 211–80.

Woodward, Anthony. *Rome: Time and Eternity*. Upton-upon-Severn: Images Publishing, 1995.

Zarins, Kim. "Rich Words: Gower's *Rime Riche* in Dramatic Action." In *John Gower, Trilingual Poet: Language, Translation, and Tradition*, edited by Elisabeth Dutton, with John Hines and R. F. Yeager, 239–53. Cambridge: Brewer, 2010.

Zeeman, Nicolette. *"Piers Plowman" and the Medieval Discourse of Desire*. Cambridge: Cambridge University Press, 2006.

INDEX

Names of Roman churches are in Italian except for the Lateran and Saint Peter's.

Adams, Robert, 109–10
Aeneas, 5
    See also *House of Fame* (Chaucer); *Legend of Dido* (Chaucer); *Metrical Mirabilia*; *Mirabilia* (Bicester)
Aers, 165n9, 169nn22–23
Agrippa. See *Mirabilia Urbis Romae* (Bicester)
Alford, John, 117
Ames, Ruth M., 167n45
Anglo-Saxons and Rome, 4
Apius. See *Canterbury Tales* (Chaucer): *Physician's Tale*; *Confessio Amantis* (Gower); *Fall of Princes* (Lydgate);
Aruns, son of King Tarquin. See *Confessio Amantis* (Gower)
Augustine. See *City of God* (Augustine)
Augustus (Emperor Octavain), 15, 122
    See also *Fall of Princes* (Lydgate); *Legend of Good Women* (Chaucer): *Legend of Cleopatra*; *Mirabilia Urbis Romae*

Bartlett, Robert, 150n22
Bede, Venerable, 4
Beichner, Paul, 95–96
Benôit de Sainte-Maure, 50
Bertolet, Craig, 163n28
Bible, 67, 69, 95, 101, 105
    Apocalypse 21:19–21, 50
    2 Corinthians 3:2, 91
    Epistle of James 2:26, 116
    Genesis, 52
    Hebrews 13:14, 130

    John 14:6, 117
    John 19:28, 21
    1 John 4:8, 118
    Matthew 22:21, 101
Bicester. See *Mirabilia* (Bicester)
Boccaccio, Giovanni. See *Fall of Princes* (Lydgate)
Bone Florence, Le, 147n3
Boniface, Pope, 28
Boniface IV, Pope, 38, 52
Boniface VIII, Pope, 152n34
    See also *Confessio Amantis* (Gower)
Book of Margery Kempe, (Kempe), 3, 4, 21
Book of the Duchess (Chaucer), 90
Bowersock, Brown, and Grabar, *Late Antiquity*, 147n2
Bracciolini, Poggio, 5
Brecht, Bertolt, 71
Brentano, Robert, 7, 38
Brown, Peter, 7, 15–16
Brut (Layamon), prose, 4
Brutus, Lucius Junius, cousin of Lucretia, 117
    See also *Confessio Amantis* (Gower); *Legend of Good Women* (Chaucer): *Legend of Lucrece*
Burrow, John, 110
Byron, Lord, 35

Caesar, Julius, 3, 5, 6, 7, 122
    See also *Confessio Amantis* (Gower); *Fall of Princes* (Lydgate); *Metrical Mirabilia*; *Mirabilia*
Camille, Michael, 161n70
Canterbury Tales (Chaucer), 72
    Clerk's Tale, 90

General Prologue: Pardoner, 99
Knight's Tale, 80, 81; Theseus, 81–82, 95
Man of Law's Tale, 80, 90, 91, 98; Alla, 88, 91, 97; Constance, 80, 86–87, 89, 90–92, 95, 97–98, 99; Emperor, 77, 86–87, 88, 89, 91, 97, 98; Maurice, 98–99; Senator, 88, 91, 97, 98
Monk's Tale, 80, 126, 127; Caesar, 80, 87–88, 91; Nero, 80, 87, 89
Pardoner's Tale, 18, 19, 90; Bailly, Harry, 90
Parson's Tale, 15
Physician's Tale, 68, 80, 81, 90, 94, 95; Apius, 86, 87, 88, 89, 91, 93, 94; Livy, 81; *Roman de la Rose* and, 86, 90, 94; Virginia, 80, 81, 86, 87, 89, 90–91, 92–95, 96, 98, 102; Virginius, 80, 88, 93, 95
Second Nun's Tale, 1, 60, 80, 81, 82, 89, 91, 92, 95–97, 165n7; Almachius, 86, 89, 92, 95–96, 97, 98; Cecilia, 80, 86, 87, 89, 91, 92, 95–97, 98, 99; Maximus, 89; Roman locales, 81; Tiburce, 89, 95, 96'; Urban, 89, 91, 95, 96, 97; Valerian, 89, 95, 96
Sir Thopas, 20
See also Chaucer, Geoffrey
Capgrave, John, 3, 13, 16, 28
Capitol or Capitoline Hill, 5, 156–57n28
    See also *Fall of Princes* (Lydgate); *Metrical Mirabilia*; *Mirabilia Urbis Romae*
Chambers, R. W., 109
Chaucer, Geoffrey, 1, 7, 8, 9, 59, 79–99, 101, 102, 104, 119, 122, 123, 143, 145
    Gower and, 9, 79, 81, 82, 83–84, 85–86, 87, 88, 90–91, 93–94, 96, 98, 99
    Non-Roman ancient cities, 80–81, 82
    sources: Ovid and, 1, 82–83, 90, 101 (see also *House of Fame*; *Legend of Lucrece*); Trevet, *Chronicles*, and, 86, 98, 165n24; Virgil and, 82–83
    themes: Christian women, triumph of, 95–98; Pagan women, tragedy of, 93–95; Roman men, negative view of, 79, 81–89, 98–99; Roman women, positive view of, 79–80, 82, 90–93
    See also *Book of the Duchess*; *Canterbury Tales*; *Consolation of Philosophy*, trans. of; *House of Fame*; *Legend of Good Women*; *Troilus and Criseyde*
Christie, Neil, 149–50n17, 150n20
Churches. See Roman Churches; *Stacions of Rome*
Cicero, 36
    See also *Fall of Princes* (Lydgate)
Circus Maximus, 38–39, 40
City of God (Augustine), 41
    See also *Fall of Princes* (Lydgate)
Clement VI, Pope, 152n36
Confessio Amantis (Gower), 1, 7, 8, 59–78, 174–75n49
    Chaucer and, 9, 79, 81, 82, 83–84, 85–86, 87, 88, 90–91, 93–94, 96, 98, 99
    CHARACTERS
    Amans, 59, 61, 63, 67, 68
    Antonius, emperor, 65, 162n22
    Anubus, 61–62
    Apius, 69–70, 72, 73, 74
    Aristotle, 63, 64
    Aruns, 69, 71, 84, 86
    Boniface VIII, 77–78
    Brutus, 71, 72–73
    Caesar, Julius, 66–67, 74, 79, 126
    Caligula, 72
    Carmidotirus, 162n15
    Constance, 76–77, 80 86, 91, 98
    Constantine, 30, 65, 74–77, 102
    Fabricius, Gaius, 65
    Genius, 59, 61, 63, 64, 65–66, 67, 68–69, 70, 74
    Lucius, 162n18
    Lucretia, 8, 9, 68–74, 84, 86, 88, 89, 93, 94, 96, 138, 141, 176n75
    Maximin, 65
    Mundus, 61–63, 64, 69, 73, 77
    Nero, 72, 87
    Paulina, 61–63, 64, 70, 73
    Phyrinus, 163n23
    Pompey the Great, 66
    Priests of Isis, 61–63
    Scipio, 65
    Tarquins, 8, 69–74, 84, 90, 94
    Tiberius, 61–62, 64
    Tiberius Constantin, 77, 78
    Trajan, 65
    Valentinian, 69

Confessio Amantis (*continued*)
CHARACTERS (*continued*)
    Virgil, 60
    Virginia, 60, 68, 69–71, 73, 74, 91, 162n13
    Virginius, 69–72, 73, 88, 134
SOURCES
    Higden, Ralph, Polychronicon, 162n19, 162n21
    Latini, Brunetto, 63
    Legenda aurea (Jacobus de Voragine), 163n34
    Livy, 163n24
    Ovid, 101; *Fasti*, 73, 84, 163n24
THEMES
    Christian Rome, 74–78
    Donation of Constantine, 31, 77–78
    Kingly virtues, 63–74, 75, 112; Chastity, 66, 68–73, 75; Justice, 64–65, 66, 69, 71, 75; Largess, 63, 66–67, 69, 75, 76; Pity, 63, 65–66, 69, 71, 75; Truth, 63, 64, 67, 69, 75
    Policy, 63, 64, 66, 67, 68, 69, 71, 75
    Roman civic self-correction, 72–74
    Roman civic virtue as vice, 70–72
    Roman tales, list of, 162n12
    Roman triumph, 67–68, 74, 124
    Rome as civic model, 8, 64, 66, 78, 79, 121
    Troy, 59, 61
Coghill, Nevill, 116–17
Colosseum, 4, 6, 27, 157n29, 161n72
    See also *Metrical Mirabilia*; *Mirabilia Urbis Romae*
Comerford, Michael, 151nn27–28
Consolation of Philosophy, trans. of (Chaucer), 164n3
Constance, 7
    See also *Confessio Amantis* (Gower); *Man of Law's Tale* (Chaucer)
Constantine, Emperor, 5, 6, 16–17, 20
    donation of, 31, 76, 130–31
    See also *Confessio Amantis* (Gower); *Fall of Princes* (Lydgate); *Stacions of Rome*
Cooper, Helen, 164n39, 167n46
Cybele, 38

Dante, 41, 60, 77, 106
De casibus virorum illustrium (Boccaccio). See *Fall of Princes* (Lydgate)

Delany, Shelia, 167n41
Donaldson, E. Talbot, 105
Donaldson, Ian, 176n77
Douglas, Gavin, 2, 82
Doyle, A. I., 158n38
Duffy, Eamon, 13
Dunning, T. P., 109

Edwards, A. S. G., 173nn32–33
Edwards, Robert, 82
Edwards, Catharine, 8

Fahrenbach, William, 148n5
Fall of Princes (Lydgate), 1, 2, 7, 8, 9, 59, 67, 102, 121–45
    Analogues of: *De casibus virorum illustrium* (Boccaccio), 122–23, 124, 126, 130, 141; *Metrical Mirabilia*, 130; *Mirabilia*, 133
    influence on Chaucer, 9, 121, 125, 127, 134, 135, 136, 137, 141, 143; *Legend of Lucrece*, 135–36, 137, 141, 177n79; *Monk's Tale*, 126, 127; *Second Nun's Tale*, 134; *Troilus and Criseyde*, 129, 172n23
    influence on *Confessio Amantis* (Gower), 9, 121, 122, 124, 133, 135, 136, 137, 141, 174n46
    influence on Humphrey, Duke of Gloucester, 122, 127, 130, 135, 136, 141, 143
    influence on Lydgate, *Serpent of Division*, 124, 131, 132
CHARACTERS
    Apius, 134
    Augustus (Octavian), 101, 128; in book 2: 9, 121, 134–41, 142, 143, in book 3: 9, 128, 134, 135, 141–43
    Brutus, 133, 134, 135
    Caesar, Julius, 126, 128, 132
    Cato, 128
    Chaucer, 125–26, 141
    Cicero, 126, 128
    Collatinus, 9, 137–38, 141, 142, 143
    Constantine, 121, 130–31
    Coriolanus, 131–32, 133
    Humphrey, Duke of Gloucester, 125–26
    Julian, 174n47
    Lucretia, 102, 121, 144
    Manlius, Marcus, 124

Mucius Scaevola, 133, 134
Nero, 132, 173n39
Petrarch, 126
Pompey, 132–33
Regulus, Marcus, 132, 173–74n40
Remus, 128, 131, 132
Romulus, 123, 128, 131, 132
Scipios, 132, 133
Seneca, 126, 128
Tarquin, 135, 137, 138, 140
Tarquins, 141
Theodosius, 174n43, 174n47
Trajan, 128
Virgil, 124
Virginia, 102, 133–34
Virginius, 133–34
EPISODES
   Envoy to Rome, 121, 123, 127–30, 131, 134, 139, 140, 141
   Prologue to book 1, 125–27, 135, 136
   Roman triumph, 124
PLACES
   Aventine Hill, 131
   Nero's *Domus aurea*, 123
   Olovitreum, 123
   Romulus's Asylum and palace, 123
   Temple with warning bells, 124
SOURCES
   City of God (Augustine), 9, 122, 128–29, 133, 139–40, 143–44, 174n45
   Declamatio Lucretiae (Coluccio Salutati), 9, 136–39, 141
   Des cas des nobles hommes et femmes (Laurent de Premierfait), 122–24, 125, 127, 128, 132, 133–36, 141–42
   Isidore of Seville, 171n17
   Legenda aurea, 130–31
   Livy, 175n58
   Polychronicon (Higden), 171–72n17
THEMES
   Christian view of Rome, 128–29, 131
   Literary ambition, 125, 136, 14
   Paganism, hostility to, 128–29, 135, 139, 140–41
   tragedie, 126–27
   Tragedies of political division, 131–32
   Tragedies of women, Virginia and Lucretia, 133–43

Tragedy of ancient Rome, 122, 127–30
Translation theory, 125, 134–35, 136
Ferster, Judith, 60
Fichte, Joerg O., 164n3
Flannery, Mary C., 172n26
Frank, Robert Worth, Jr., 166n33
Freud, Sigmund, 36–37
Furnivall, Frederick J., 13
Fyler, John, 82

Galloway, Andrew, 104, 164n2, 167n42, 176n74, 177n81
Geary, Patrick, 15
Gellius, Aulus, 171n15
Geoffrey of Monmouth, *Historia regum Britanniae*, 3
Gesta Romanorum, 3
Giles of Rome, 63
Gloucester. See *Fall of Princes* (Lydgate): Humphrey, Duke of Gloucester
Gower, John. See *Confessio Amantis* (Gower); "In Praise of Peace" (Gower); *Vox Clamantis* (Gower)
Grady, Frank, 109, 163n37, 167n4, 168n6
Graphia Aurea Urbis Romae, 41, 42, 159n46, 160n59
Gray, Douglas, 166n27
Green, Richard Firth, 111
Greenhalgh, Michael, 154n56
Gregorius, Master, 3
Gregorovius, Ferdinand, 155n1
Gregory, the Great, 4, 7
   See also *Piers Plowman* (Langland); *Stacions of Rome*

Hammond, Eleanor Prescott, 171n12
Hansen, Elaine Tuttle, 164n1
Harrowing of Hell. See *Piers Plowman* (Langland)
Harwood, Britton J., 109
Henry IV, 64
Henryson, Robert, *Testament*, 30
Higden, Ralph. See *Polychronicon* (Higden)
Higgins, Iain, 44, 155n4, 158n39, 159n42
Hildebert of Lavardin, 5–6, 35, 40
Hirsh, John C., 164n3, 165n7
Historia regum Britanniae (Geoffrey of Monmouth), 3

INDEX | 195

Hoccleve, Thomas, 2
Holy Land, 17, 19, 59
Hospital of Saint Thomas, 4
House of Fame (Chaucer), 82
    Aeneas, 82–83
    Dido, 82–83, 89, 94
    Ovid's *Heroides* and, 82
Howe, Nicholas, 147n6
Hulbert, J. R., 148n3, 150n25, 151–52n29, 153n41, 153n50, 156n11
Humphrey, Duke of Gloucester. See *Fall of Princes* (Lydgate)

Indulgences. See pardons
Indulgentiae Ecclesiarum Urbis Romae, 14, 18, 20, 21, 22, 23, 24, 25, 26, 28, 33, 113, 151n27
    Manuscripts and texts of, 150–51nn25–27, 153nn41–42, 153nn50–53, 154n59, 154n61, 154n67, 169n34; Cotton Titus A.xix, 26, 153nn41–42, 153n50, 153n53, 154n64, 154n67, 159n47
"In Praise of Peace" (Gower) 75, 164n40

Jacks, Philip, 161n72
Jacobus de Voragine. See *Legenda aurea* (Jacobus de Voragine)
Jerusalem, 18, 24, 28, 50, 150n20
John of Salisbury, 60, 106, 112, 116
Julian of Norwich, 15

Kane, George, 105
Kean, P. M., 166n32
Kempe, Margery, *Book of Margery Kempe*, 3, 4, 21
Kinney, Dale, 7, 36, 156n20
Kolve, V. A., 166n34
Krautheimer, Richard, 7, 147n7

Lanciani, Rodolfo, 149n16
Langland, William. See *Piers Plowman* (Langland)
Last Judgment, 168, 171
Laurent de Premierfait, *Des cas des nobles hommes et femmes*. See *Fall of Princes* (Lydgate)
Lavezzo, Kathy, 147n4

Lebowski, *The Big*, 40
Legenda aurea (Jacobus de Voragine), 103, 150n19, 163n34
    See also *Fall of Princes* (Lydgate); *Piers Plowman* (Langland)
Legend of Good Women (Chaucer), 79, 83
    Legend of Cleopatra, 83; Marc Antony, 83; Augustus (Octavian), 83
    Legend of Dido, 83; Aeneas, 83; Dido, 83, 89, 94
    Legend of Lucrece, 9, 68, 80, 81, 84–86, 90, 92–95, 135, 136; Brutus, 88, 96; Lucretia, 9, 80, 84–86, 88, 89, 90, 91, 92–95, 96, 98, 138, 141, 176n75, 177n79; Ovid, *Fasti*, and, 84–86, 88, 90, 92, 93, 166n39; Tarquin, son of King Tarquin, 9, 84–86, 87, 88, 89, 90, 91; Tarquins, 9, 84, 90, 94
Livy, 94, 135, 166n41
Love, Nicholas, *Mirror*, 21
Lucretia, 7, 8, 122. See also Chaucer, *Legend of Lucrece*; *Confessio Amantis* (Gower); *Fall of Princes* (Lydgate)
Lydgate, John. See *Fall of Princes* (Lydgate)
Lynch, Kathryn L.,166n31

McCall, John P., 164n6
Malory, Thomas, *Morte*, 4
Mandeville's Travels, 23
    See also *Metrical Version of Mandeville's Travels*
Manlius Marcus, 122
    See also *Fall of Princes* (Lydgate)
Mann, Jill, 164n1, 167n49
Map, Walter, 5
Margaret of York, 24
Martin, Priscilla, 167n45
Martinus Polonus, *Chronicon*, 41, 42, 47, 157–58nn34–35, 158n36, 159n45, 160n59
Martyrs. See Roman martyrs and individual saints
Mary, Virgin, 17, 19, 24, 38, 41
Matsuda, Takami, 152n35
Metrical Mirabilia (Rome interpolation in *Metrical Version of Mandeville's Travels*), 1–2, 34, 35, 44, 45–55
    additions and omissions, 44–45

hybrid *Mirabilia* as source of, 41–42, 44, 46, 49–53, 159–60n52, 160n55, 161n65, 161n69
    narrative voice of, 44, 45
    pre-history of Rome, 46
    CHARACTERS
        Aeneas, 46
        Ancient Romans, 47
        Caesar, 44, 48
        Nero, 48
        Romulus and Remus, 46
        Sylvester, 51, 52–53, 54
        Virgil, 47–48
    PLACES AND THINGS
        ancient Roman monuments, 2, 7, 8, 33, 44, 46–48, 59, 144; celebration of the magnificence of, 34, 46–47; fear of the pagan power of, 34, 39, 46
        Capitoline, 46, 47, 48–50, 51, 52, 53
        Christian Churches, 37, 48, 52–53, 54
        Colosseum as Temple of Sun, 46, 47, 48, 50–54, 123–24
        Constantine's palace, 47
        Lateran, 54
        Pagan temples, destruction of, 52–53
        Pagan Idols, 48, 49, 50, 51–52
        Romulus's palace, 48, 50, 159n51
    THEMES
        Christian and pagan conflict, 45–46, 47–48, 52–54
        Paganism, hostility to, 74, 114, 130
Metrical Version of Mandeville's Travels, 34, 44–45, 159n50
    additions to, 44
    marvels, 45
    omissions from, 45
    poet's skill, 44–45
    See also *Metrical Mirabilia*
Meyer-Lee, Robert J., 170n1
Middleton, Anne, 166n38
Miedema, Nine Robijntje, 36, 38, 150n25, 154n56, 155n5
Minnis, Alistair, 60, 110
Mirabilia (Bicester), 13, 23, 34, 35, 42–43, 46
    Aeneas, 43
    pre-history of Rome, 43, 46
    Roman walls and gates, 43, 46–47

Romulus, 43
Virgil, 43, 157n35
Ylia (Rhea Silvia), 43
Mirabilia Urbis Romae, 33–43, 54
    authorship and date of, 34
    sources of, 34
    CHARACTERS
        Agrippa, 38, 40, 47, 104
        Augustus (Octavian), 40–41, 47, 76, 104
        Caesar, 39–40
        Nero, 40
    PLACES AND THINGS
        Capitoline and warning bells, 40, 48–49, 157n29, 160n53, 169n58
        Colosseum, 50, 157n29
        Olovitreum, 39, 123, 160n64
        Romulus's palace and statue, 39, 48
        Marcellus, theater, 36
        Tullianum, 36
    TEXTS
        English versions of. See *Metrical Mirabilia*; *Mirabilia* (Bicester)
        fourth version (*Quarta Classis*), 41–42, 161n71; Colosseum as Temple of the Sun, 6, 42, 46, 50–51, 157n29
        hybrid manuscripts of, 35, 42, 157n30, 159n47; Cotton Titus, A.xix, 159n47, 160n56; Harley 562, 43, 157n31, 158n35, 159n47; Harley 2321, 42, 46–47, 48, 49, 50, 51, 52, 53, 54, 157n31, 157n34, 158n36, 159n46, 159n51, 159–60n52, 160n54, 160n58, 160n61, 161nn67–69
        Hybrid *Mirabilia*, 34–35, 41–42, 43, 44, 46, 49–53, 159n44, 159n47, 159–60n52, 160nn54–55, 161n69
        Latin textual tradition of, 34, 41–42 (see also *Graphia* and Martinus Polonus)
        modern texts of, 155n6
        third version (*Tertia Classis*), 41–42, 46, 47, 169n37; Capitoline Hill and warning bells variant, 42, 46, 47, 48–50, 156–57n28, 157n34, 160nn54–55, 160n5
    THEMES
        Ancient Monuments, celebration of, 35–40, 42, 46–47, 48–49, 101, 121, 123–24, 144
        ancient Romans, celebration of, 40–41, 47, 59, 104, 114, 119, 133

Mirabilia (*continued*)
THEMES (*continued*)
    Christian and pagan dual heritage of Rome, 37–41, 45–46, 47, 53–54, 94, 130
    time, binary sense of, 37–38
    Virgil, 46–47
Love, Nicholas, *Mirror*, 21
Mortimer, Nigel, 121, 127, 135, 137, 170n1, 171n8, 172n28, 174n43, 176nn69–70, 176–77n77, 177n81
Moseley, C. W. R. D., 158n39, 159n42
Mucius Scaevola. See *Fall of Princes* (Lydgate)
Mundus. See *Confessio Amantis* (Gower)

Nero, Emperor, 7, 160n62
    See also *Canterbury Tales* (Chaucer): Monk's Tale; *Confessio Amantis* (Gower); *Fall of Princes* (Lydgate); *Metrical Mirabilia*; *Mirabilia Urbis Romae*
Nichols, Francis, ed., 155n4
Nicholson, Peter, 163n38
Nolan, Maura, 63, 121–22, 131, 141, 162n11, 162n19, 162n21, 170n5, 170–71n8, 173n35, 174–75n49, 175n65, 177n82
Norton-Smith, John, 170n5

Octavian, 147n3
Octavian (Emperor). See Augustus
Osborne, John, 38
Ovid, 94
    See also *Confessio Amantis* (Gower); *Legend of Good Women* (Chaucer): *Legend of Lucrece*

Paschal I, Pope, 150n18, 167n47
Palazzo, Robert P., 150n21
Pantheon, 27, 28, 35, 38, 40, 49, 52, 104, 130, 157n28, 160nn54–55
Pardons (Indulgences), 18–20, 154n58. See also *Piers Plowman* (Langland); Roman pardons; *Stacions of Rome*
Parks, George B., 150n25
Patterson, Lee, 81
Paulina. See *Confessio Amantis* (Gower)
Pearl, 50

Pearsall, Derek, 127, 135, 141–42, 143, 163n35, 168n11, 170n3, 172n20, 173n32, 173n37, 177n84
Peck, Russell, 60, 62, 163n24
Percival, Florence, 165n20, 166n31
Petrarch, Francesco, 5, 6. See also *Fall of Princes* (Lydgate)
Piers Plowman (Langland), 1, 7, 8, 13, 15, 32, 52, 59, 94, 100–120, 122, 123
    C-text of, 102, 105, 112, 114, 168n7, 168n11, 170n39
    Chaucer and Gower and, 101, 102, 104, 112, 119
CHARACTERS
    Abraham, 104
    Caesar, 101
    Christ, 118–20
    Gregory the Great, 101–20
    Haukyn, 102
    Holy Church, 101, 117–18
    Imaginatif, 102, 110–11, 117
    Peace, 119
    Piers the Plowman, 103, 117
    Reason, 100
    Rechelesnesse, 105, 112, 168n7, 168n11
    Samaritan, 101, 104, 118
    Scripture, 103
    Sloth, 100
    Trajan, 1, 100–120
    Trajan and widow, 106, 107, 108, 111, 112, 168n18, 169n37
EPISODES
    Four Daughters of God, 119
    Harrowing of Hell, 103, 118–19
    Passus 18; B-text, 118–20
SOURCES
    Legenda Aurea (Jacobus de Voragine) and, 102, 106–8, 110, 111, 114
    Possible sources, 171n14
THEMES AND TERMS
    Ancient world barely mentioned, 101
    clergie, 107, 108, 112, 114, 115
    Commandments, 104, 115–16
    Dowel, 100, 113
    Justice, 103, 111, 115, 117, 118–19 (see also *leautee* [below]; Truth [below])

leautee, 103, 104, 107, 112–13, 114, 115 (see also Justice [above]; Truth [below])
Love, 103–4, 107–8, 111–16, 117–20 (see also Mercy [below])
Mercy (grace), 103, 110, 113, 115, 116, 117–19 (see also Love [above])
Pardons, hostility to, 100–101, 113–14, 116, 119
"Semi-Pelagianism," 109–10
Truth, 100, 101, 103–4, 108, 111–20 (see also Justice [above]; leautee [above])
Pompey the Great. See *Confessio Amantis* (Gower); *Fall of Princes* (Lydgate)
Porter, Elizabeth, 62
Powell, Susan, 157n31
Purgatory, 19, 29, 45, 108, 113, 152n30, 152n35, 154nn63–64

Quadragene, 151n27

Regifugium, 165n23
Regulus, Marcus, 122
  See also *Fall of Princes* (Lydgate)
Relics. See *Stacions of Rome*
Remus. See *Fall of Princes* (Lydgate); *Metrical Mirabilia*; *Stacions of Rome*
Richard II, 64
Richardson, Lawrence, Jr., 155n1
Robinson, P. R., 153n44
Roman churches
  Lateran, 3, 37, 39, 51, 52, 74, 130, 154n61
  Saint Peter's, 4, 16–17, 34, 39, 76, 106, 113, 130, 152n34
  S. Lorenzo fuori le mura, 150n19
  S. Paolo, 76
  See also *Stacions of Rome*
Roman martyrs, 4, 16–17, 19, 26, 27, 28, 30, 31, 33, 39, 60, 82, 101
Roman monuments, 2, 5, 27
  See also Capitoline; Colosseum; *Metrical Mirabilia*; *Mirabilia Urbis Romae*; Pantheon
Roman pardons, 18–20, 24, 31, 37, 52, 54, 99, 100–101
  See also *Stacions of Rome*
Roman relics, 154n56
  See also *Stacions of Rome*

Roman triumph. See *Confessio Amantis* (Gower); *Fall of Princes* (Lydgate)
Rome interpolation in *Metrical Version of Mandeville's Travels*. See *Metrical Mirabilia*
Rome's relation to England, 1, 3–4, 6
Romulus. See *Fall of Princes* (Lydgate); *Metrical Mirabilia*; *Mirabilia Urbis Romae*; *Stacions of Rome*
Rudy, Kathryn M., 24
Runacres, Charles, 68

Saints
  Agnes, 5, 16, 17
  Augustine (see *City of God* (Augustine))
  Cecilia, 7, 17 (see also *Second Nun's Tale* (Chaucer))
  Gregory the Great (see Gregory
  Lawrence, 4, 5, 16, 17, 48
  Martin of Tours, 16
  Paul, 5, 7, 16–17, 18, 30, 38, 76
  Peter, 4, 5, 6, 7, 16–17, 30, 38, 76
  Sebastian, 157n29, 160n64
  Stephen, 17
  Sylvester (*see* Sylvester)
  See also *Stations of Rome*
Salter, Elizabeth, 104
Salutati, Colluccio, 9
  See also *Fall of Princes* (Lydgate)
Saunders, Corinne J., 176n76
Scanlon, Larry, 122, 164n44, 172n21, 172n24, 175nn54–55
Scattergood, John, 157nn33–34, 158n37
Schildgen, Brenda Dean, 166n28, 167n51
Schirmer, Walter F., 170nn7–8, 171–72n17, 173n34
Schism, Great, 4, 13
Schmidt, A. V. C., 105, 112, 168n11
Scipios, 122.
  See also *Confessio Amantis* (Gower); *Fall of Princes* (Lydgate)
Secretum Secretorum, 63
Seven Sages of Rome, 147n3
Seymour, M. C., 158nn38–40, 159n44, 160n55, 161n75
Shaffern, Robert W., 151n28, 152nn30–32, 152n34, 154n60, 154n62

Shakespeare, William, 144
Simpson, James, 60, 82, 83, 110, 122, 162n20, 163n26
Spearing, A. C., 105
Spenser, Edmund, 144
Stacions of Rome, 1–2, 13–32, 34, 42, 43, 44, 54, 55, 59, 60, 75, 144
 Bicester *Stations*, 43
 Indulgentiae and, 14, 18, 20, 21–22, 23, 24, 25, 26, 113, 153nn41–42, 153n51, 154n59, 154n61
 major Roman churches: Lateran, 17–18, 24, 29, 31, 39, 54, 74, 150n21; St. Peter's, 17, 24–25, 28; S. Croce, 17, 21, 25; S. Lorenzo fuori le mura, 29; S. Maria Maggiore, 17, 150n21, 151n27, 169n35; S. Sebastiano, 19, 24, 26, 29
 manuscripts of, 14, 23, 148–49nn5–9
 minor Roman churches: S. Andrea, 29, 113; S. Adriano, 28; S. Anastasio, 25; S Bartolomeo, 17; S. Clemente, 28; SS. Cosma e Damiano, 28; S. Giovanni a Porta Latina, 25, 154n63; S. Maria in palma (*Domine quo vadis*), 22, 23; S. Maria Nova, 28; S. Maria Rochel, 20, 27; S. Maria Rotunda, 29; S Maria Sancta Coeli, 29; S. Matteo, 25; S. Paolo, 24–25; S. Peitro in Carcere, 27; S. Pietro in Vincoli, 25–26, 29, 37; S. Prassede, 28; S Pudenziana, 19–20, 28, 29, 154n55, 169n35; S. Vito e Modesto, 25; SS Apostoli, 17, 29
 Roman churches, 2, 8, 14, 16–18, 20, 24–25, 27–28, 54 (see also *Stacions of Rome*: major Roman churches [above]; *Stacions of Rome*: minor Roman churches
 Saints, 94; Bartholomew, 17, Catherine, 28; Gregory, 20, 27, 113, 153n39; James, 17; Jerome, 17, 151n27; Lawrence, 26; Paul, 116, 153–54n55; Peter, 22–23, 25–26, 153–54n55; Philip, 17; Stephen, 26; Sylvester, 20, 27, 30–31, 74, 153n39; Thomas a Becket, 17
 Style of, 14, 20–23, 26–27
 Versions of, 14, 33, 148n5, 148–49n8, 149n9, 153n54, 154n63–64

CHARACTERS
 Constantine, 23, 27, 30–31, 59, 74–75, 76, 121, 130, 164n40
 Romulus and Remus, 16
 Simplicius, Pope, 28
THEMES
 Imagined pilgrimage and, 15, 23–27
 Paganism, hostility to, 39, 114
 Pardon, 2, 13, 14–15, 19–20, 27–32, 54, 55, 76, 99, 113, 114, 116, 118, 119, 140, 144, 154n70
 Relics, 2, 7, 8, 13, 14, 15–18, 19, 20, 21–23, 25–29, 39, 55, 95–96, 144, 150n21; Veronica, 17, 28
 Rome as source of mercy, 2, 8, 13, 14–15, 21, 29–32, 100
Stationes, Latin, 148n2
Stanbury, Sarah, 1–2, 23, 28
Steiner, Emily, 110
Strohm, Paul, 72, 122
Summit, Jennifer, 38, 155n4, 161n73
Sumption, Jonathan, 24, 149n11, 149n17, 152n34
Swanson, R. N., 19, 20, 24, 151n28, 152n30, 152n35, 153n45, 154n58
Sylvester, Saint and Pope, 5, 6
 See also *Confessio Amantis* (Gower); *Metrical Mirabilia*; *Stacions of Rome*
Sylvester, Louise, 176n75
Syon Abbey, 151–52n29, 157n31

Tarquin, son of king Tarquin, 8
 See also *Confessio Amantis* (Gower): Aruns (character); *Fall of Princes* (Lydgate); *Legend of Good Women* (Chaucer): *Legend of Lucrece*
Tarquins (father and son). See *Confessio Amantis* (Gower); *Fall of Princes* (Lydgate); *Legend of Good Women* (Chaucer): *Legend of Lucrece*
Tatlock, J. S. P., 147n4
Testament (Henryson), 30
Thacker, Alan, 149n15
Tinti, Francesca, 4
Tower of London, 3, 44, 48
Trajan, emperor, 7, 122
 See also *Confessio Amantis* (Gower); *Piers Plowman* (Langland)

Treasury of merit, 19
Trevisa, John, *Polychronicon*, 110, 119
Triumph. See *Confessio Amantis* (Gower);
   Fall of Princes (Lydgate)
Troilus and Criseyde (Chaucer), 54, 80, 81,
   90, 99, 129
   Criseyde, 81–82
   Hector, 82, 165–66n25
   Paganism, hostility to, 54
   Troilus, 82
Troy, 1, 43, 46, 49–50, 54, 59, 61
   See also Chaucer, Geoffrey: Non-Roman
      ancient cities

Unigenitus, 152n36
Urban, Pope. See *Canterbury Tales* (Chaucer):
   Second's Nun's Tale
Urlichs, Carl, 41–42
Usk, Adam, 5, 6

Vatican, 4, 16–17, 23, 39
Virgil, 5, 101, 159n45

   See also Chaucer; *Fall of Princes* (Lydgate);
      Metrical Mirabilia; *Mirabilia* (Bicester)
Virginia, 122
   See also *Confessio Amantis* (Gower); *Fall*
      of Princes (Lydgate); *Canterbury Tales*
      (Chaucer): *Physician's Tale*
Virginius. See *Canterbury Tales* (Chaucer):
   Physician's Tale; *Confessio Amantis*
   (Gower); *Fall of Princes* (Lydgate)
Vox Clamantis (Gower), 60, 64

Wallace, David, 72
Watson, Nicholas, 31
Wetherbee, Winthrop, 60–61
Whatley, Gordon, 105–6
Wickham, Chris, 7
Winstead, Karen, 95
Wittig, Joseph S., 168n7

Yeats, W. B., 70

Zarins, Kim, 161n7

www.ingramcontent.com/pod-product-compliance
Lightning Source LLC
Chambersburg PA
CBHW021947290426
44108CB00012B/984